The Internet and National Elections

A comparative study of web campaigning

Edited by Randolph Kluver,
Nicholas W. Jankowski,
Kirsten A. Foot, and
Steven M. Schneider

Routledge
Taylor & Francis Group

LONDON AND NEW YORK

First published 2007
by Routledge
2 Park Square, Milton Park, Abingdon, Oxon OX14 4RN

Simultaneously published in the USA and Canada
by Routledge
270 Madison Ave, New York, NY 10016

Routledge is an imprint of the Taylor & Francis Group, an informa business

Typeset in Garamond by Wearset Ltd, Boldon, Tyne and Wear
Printed and bound in Great Britain by TJI Digital, Padstow, Cornwall

British Library Cataloguing in Publication Data
A catalogue record for this book is available from the British Library

Library of Congress Cataloging in Publication Data
A catalog record has been requested for this book

ISBN10: 0-415-41736-8 (hbk)
ISBN10: 0-203-01753-6 (ebk)

ISBN13: 978-0-415-41736-5 (hbk)
ISBN13: 978-0-203-01753-1 (ebk)

Contents

Illustrations

Contributors

Pieter Aquilia is Associate Professor of Media and Design at the University of New South Wales Singapore campus. She is the co-author of *The Media in Singapore and the Region*, co-editor of *International Television Drama*, and a number of publications on television in Australasia.

Tom Carlson is research director at Åbo Akademi University, Finland. A political scientist, he is interested in political communication and has published in various journals, including *Press/Politics*, *European Journal of Communication*, and the *Journal of Political Marketing*.

Endre Dányi is a research fellow at the Center for Media and Communication Studies at the Central European University, and scholar-in-residence at the London-based Stanhope Centre for Communications Policy Research. His research focuses on political uses of various communication technologies; recent publications include "Xerox Project: Photocopy Machines as a Metaphor for an Open Society," *The Information Society*.

Meghan Dougherty is a doctoral candidate in Communication at the University of Washington and a researcher for WebArchivist.org. Her work is focused on understanding the dynamics of knowledge production in mediated environments, and particularly the use of digital media in the research, preservation, representation, and interpretation of cultural heritage.

Kirsten A. Foot is Associate Professor of Communication at the University of Washington. Her research focuses on the reciprocal relationship between information/communication technologies and society. As co-director of the WebArchivist.org research group, she is developing new techniques for studying social and political action on the web. With Steven M. Schneider, she has recently published *Web Campaigning*.

Martin Gregor is in the Faculty of Social Sciences, Charles University, in the Czech Republic. He works mainly in the field of public economics, with recent contributions in the *Review of Political Economy* and *Journal of European Integration*.

Carlo Hagemann is Associate Professor of Communication at the Radboud University Nijmegen. His research interests include political communication, computer-mediated communication, and content analysis.

Shahiraa Sahul Hameed was formerly Research Associate at the Singapore Internet Research Centre, Nanyang Technological University, Singapore, where she conducted this research. She currently works at the Singapore Corporation for Rehabilitative Enterprises (SCORE) where she works with the aim of helping ex-offenders reintegrate into society.

Anna Galácz is a PhD student at the Eötvös Loránd University in Budapest, researcher at the Center for Information Society and Network Research (ITHAKA), and project coordinator of the Hungarian section of the World Internet Project. Her research focuses on the effects of new media on political behavior and institutions.

Nicholas W. Jankowski is Associate Professor at Radboud University and Visiting Fellow at the Virtual Knowledge Studio in the Netherlands. He has been involved in the study of new media and research methodology since the mid-1970s, and is the initiator and co-editor of the journal *New Media & Society*.

Hyo Kim is Assistant Professor at Ajou University in South Korea. His interests include communication technologies, organizational communication, and mediated communication. His work has appeared in *Science Communication* and *Annals of Telecommunications*.

Randolph Kluver is Director of the Institute for Pacific Asia and Research Professor in the Department of Communication at Texas A&M University. His work focuses on communication, new media, and politics in Asia. He is the co-editor of *Asia.com: Asia Encounters the Internet*.

Kate A. Mirandilla is a doctoral student in public relations at the University of South Australia, majoring in organizational crisis management and previously was an assistant professor in communication research and mass communication. Her research interests are in public relations, organizational communication, e-governance, and the new media.

Tanja Oblak is Assistant Professor at the Department for Media and Communication Studies, University of Ljubljana, Slovenia. Her research interests include the social and democratic implications of new technologies, comparison of traditional and online media, communication culture within electronic public sphere, online social interactions, and uses of interactive online media.

Han Woo Park is Assistant Professor at YeungNam University in South Korea. His research on the use of new digital technologies in extending social networks has contributed to development of a new research field, "Hyperlink Network Analysis," and his research has appeared in several international journals, including *New Media & Society* and the *Journal of Computer-Mediated Communication.*

Steven M. Schneider is Professor of Political Science at the State University of New York Institute of Technology. He is also the co-director of WebArchivist.org and co-editor of PoliticalWeb.info. His research focuses on the use of the internet for political action. With Kirsten A. Foot, he has recently published *Web Campaigning.*.

Kavitha Shetty is an independent writer, researcher, and editor based in Singapore. She holds a Masters in Mass Communication from Bowling Green State University, Ohio. She has worked as a journalist in India and her research interests include Indian politics, children and online media, and culture and communication in India.

Kim Strandberg is a doctoral student at the Åbo Akademi University, Finland. His research focuses on different aspects of political life on the internet, particularly the ways that political parties and candidates use the web.

Shyam Tekwani is Assistant Professor at Nanyang Technological University, Singapore. He has nearly two decades of experience as a reporter and photojournalist. His works have appeared in publications such as the *New York Times Magazine, Time, Newsweek, Le Figaro, Geo, and Der Spiegel.* His current work focuses on the use of the media, particularly new media technologies, by terrorist groups in their violent campaigns.

Leslie M. Tkach-Kawasaki is a PhD candidate at the University of Tsukuba, Japan. Her PhD focuses on how Japanese political parties and candidates are utilizing the web during election campaign periods.

Renée van Os is a PhD candidate in the Department of Communication at Radboud University in Nijmegen, the Netherlands. Her PhD project focuses on the potential of the internet for enhancing the European democratic process and contributing to a European public sphere.

Gerrit Voerman is Director of the Documentation Centre on Dutch Political Parties of the University of Groningen, the Netherlands. He is editor of the Yearbook of the Documentation Centre and has published frequently on Dutch political parties and the use of information and communication technologies by political parties.

Janelle Ward is a PhD candidate at the Amsterdam School of Communication Research at the University of Amsterdam. Her research interests include young people and political youth websites. She has recently published in the *Harvard International Journal of Press/Politics* and *Information Polity.*

Michael Xenos is an assistant professor in the Department of Communication Arts at the University of Wisconsin-Madison. His research focuses on how the context and content of political communication influences the quality of democratic deliberation, public opinion, and civic engagement.

Katja Željan is a freelance journalist and a post-graduate student of at the University of Ljubljana, Slovenia. Her research interests include the internet in politics.

Preface

As the internet has become more deeply embedded in the daily lives of innumerable people around the world, an increasing number of scholars have been asking significant questions as to the implications for the less technical, perhaps more important, aspects of social life, such as the quality of life, the nature of relationships, and the way in which political power is gained, lost, or transformed. From around the world, scholars have seen in the internet either a new hope for humanizing and democratizing politics, or they have imagined yet another tool for governments to tighten their grip on political power; or perhaps they have seen something between liberation and oppression. Many of these efforts, however, have involved the dynamic interplay of technology and democracy from within the fairly narrow confines of one or, at the most, two nations.

This volume is an attempt to take a much broader, more global look at the way in which political practice is embodied online, in a variety of national and cultural contexts. Our key purpose was to explore how politics was being played out on the internet around the world, and so we set about to secure the funding, and the people, to help us answer that question.

This project arose out of spontaneous conversations at the Association of Internet Researchers conference in Maastricht, the Netherlands, in 2002, among those who later became the editors of this volume; see further elaboration on this encounter in Chapter 1. The project itself then took on larger and larger dimensions until it encompassed much more than we originally envisioned. At one point, researchers from some 22 nations were involved in the project, but a variety of personal and professional obligations and other circumstances prevented contributions from all of these researchers and their teams to this volume. We wish to acknowledge those who participated with us in earlier stages of the project, including Mattio Miani (Italy), Wang Tai-li (Taiwan), Mazni Haji Buyong (Malaysia), Carlos Cunha (Portugal), Fabienne Greffet (France), Wainer Lusoli (U.K.), Patrick Brereton and Farrel Corcoran (Ireland), Simon Delakorda (Slovenia), and Raphael Kies (Luxembourg). Each of these scholars also worked with a research team within that nation, and we would like to acknowledge the contributions that each member of each team made. We particularly want to note the deep commitment to the project of Parichart Sthapitanonda, who continued to work with her research team on the project despite personal loss.

In March 2004, the Singapore Internet Research Centre hosted a methodology workshop with funding from the Asia-Europe Foundation through the ASEF/Alliance grant program. At this meeting, we were able to develop and refine a methodology that all the national teams would use. The editors would like to thank the Asia-Europe Foundation, as well as the staff and students at Nanyang Technological University, particularly Shahiraa Sahul Hameed, Carol Soon, and Chen Yang, for their help in organizing that meeting.

Funding for this project has also been critical to its success. We appreciate the contribution of Nanyang Technological University's School of Communication and Information through Research Grant # RCC 4/2002/SCS, support from the Oxford Internet Institute in the form of a visiting fellowship for Nicholas W. Jankowski, a grant from the University of Washington Royalty Research Fund, and additional funding from the University of Washington College of Arts and Sciences.

The preparation of this volume has been a daunting experience, and we would be greatly remiss if we did not acknowledge all of those who played a role in helping us to gather the reports, essays, chapters, and data sets, and compile them in a meaningful way, including Julian Ng and Shahiraa Sahul Hameed. In addition, we have greatly benefited from the editorial assistance of Nancy Bixler, Adrienne Massanari, Katherine Cantrell, and Carmen Suen. Web-based software enabling the distributed data collection and coordination necessary for this project was provided via *pro bono* licenses for all project participants by Webarchivist.org. We owe an enormous debt for the technical and analytical skills and user support provided by Meghan Dougherty and Mike Xenos, who made contributions to the internet and Elections Project and to this volume that are not fully reflected in their co-author status.

At Taylor and Francis, we are grateful for the assistance and encouragement of Harriet Brinton and Heidi Bagtazo who allowed us the time to finish the book in a proper way and within the parameters that we envisioned.

Finally, we would like to thank our families, whose vacations and other plans were often interrupted, and who brought strength and stability into our lives during the three years of this project.

Randolph Kluver, Kirsten A. Foot, Nicholas W. Jankowski, and
Steven M. Schneider

Part I

Conceptualizing and designing the project

1 Introducing the Internet and Elections Project

Nicholas W. Jankowski, Randolph Kluver, Kirsten A. Foot, and Steven M. Schneider

Since the development of the internet, large sectors of the public – scholars, politicians, journalists, activists – have debated the relation between this "network of networks" and political life. That debate has not abated in the short, two-decade history of the internet, but the original questions have been refined and the accumulated evidence has led to more nuanced understanding. This book reflects the concerted contribution to that debate by a group of social scientists who collaborated in an international comparative empirical research initiative, entitled the Internet and Elections Project. The participants in that initiative pooled their investigative resources to study one facet of the internet and political life: how a wide range of political actors in diverse countries around the world engaged the web during national elections in 2004–2005. This book represents findings from 14 case studies of the web in national elections, and an overarching comparative analysis. This chapter sets the stage of the project: its inception and organization, and its theoretical concerns. By way of introduction to the individual contributions, the organizing principles of the book are outlined and salient findings from the chapters highlighted.

Conception of the Internet and Elections Project

This project developed out of a conference panel of the Association of Internet Researchers (AoIR) in Maastricht, the Netherlands in October 2002. Then, the four coordinators of what subsequently became known as the Internet and Elections Project, contributed to a panel of papers and, at the conclusion of that panel, went to a Maastricht internet café, where Steve Schneider and Kirsten Foot demonstrated a database and analytical tools they had developed to study the appropriation of web technologies in U.S. elections. The data essentially were codes indicating the structure and content of websites that political parties and candidates had prepared during the 2002 U.S. election. Zeros and ones on a computer screen are not often grounds for elation, but that feeling came when we saw how Foot and Schneider's innovations enabled large-scale collaborative research, and could be employed in an international investigation of political websites during elections. The café conversation concluded with a collective toast and resolution to work together in "internationalizing" the conceptual and methodological framework of web sphere analysis. That framework has been elaborated in detail elsewhere (Schneider and Foot 2005; Foot and Schneider 2006). The approach employed in this project is explained in Chapter 2, but basically it consists of examining the features of websites as inscriptions of political actions on the part of site producers, enabling or constraining political actions by site visitors. In the case of websites produced during and related to election campaigns, the sites may conform to conventional political objectives: informing an electorate and getting out the vote. It can, of course, be much more complex and sophisticated, and the analytical procedures and tools that Schneider and Foot had developed provided a way to explore these issues on a global scale in a comparative framework.

In addition to Foot and Schneider, Randy Kluver and Nicholas Jankowski also committed to this comparative project. Kluver was then Executive Director of the Singapore Internet Research Center and he imagined involvement of a wide range of Asian scholars in such an investigation. He had also been engaged for some time in work related to understanding political culture (e.g. Kluver 1997, 2004, 2005; Kluver and Banerjee 2005) and saw such a project as an opportunity to explore that concept within a comparative framework. Jankowski was particularly enthusiastic about both the broad and detailed methodological issues related to internet-based data collection and analysis. Jankowski has been involved in the examination of social science research methodology (e.g. Jensen and Jankowski 1991) and with the transformation of the manner in which research is being conducted in an internet environment (Jankowski 2007). Like Schneider, he also has had a long-standing interest in the concept of the "public sphere" and how it may be manifested in internet environments (Schneider 1996, 1997; Jankowski and van Selm 2000).

With the AoIR conference panel and subsequent internet café demonstration serving as point of commencement, the four of us – Foot, Schneider, Kluver, and Jankowski – began to assemble a team of 30 researchers from 22 countries to examine national-level elections during the 2004–2005 election cycle. We chose to focus on elections held during this limited period, as we knew a more longitudinal study would encounter problems with regard to technological development and degree of diffusion. As it was, we encountered a wide variety of challenges associated with conducting cross-national comparative research, as will be seen in the following chapters. However, we believed that by looking across national contexts during a period in which elections were held around the world, we would gain a greater sense of the diversity of ways in which various types of political actors employ web technologies with regard to elections in a wide variety of contexts.

In Europe, researchers focused on the elections held in 11 countries for the European Parliament, including Finland, the Netherlands, Slovenia, the Czech Republic, the United Kingdom, Ireland, Hungary, Portugal, Italy,

France, and Luxembourg. In Asia and Australasia, the national presidential and parliamentary elections in ten countries were studied: Australia, Malaysia, India, Indonesia, Japan, South Korea, Philippines, Thailand, Taiwan, and Sri Lanka. In North America, the U.S. congressional elections held in November 2004 were the object of attention. With involvement of research teams in these countries, the overall project came to include nations at different levels of technological diffusion, economic power, and styles of democratic governance. As mentioned in the preface to this volume, personal situations resulted in a number of country-based case studies not being completed and represented in this book as individual chapters. Data were, however, collected on the features of websites from the sample of political actors for some of these countries (France, Italy, Luxembourg, Portugal, Thailand, and Taiwan) and these data are included in the overall comparative analysis presented in Chapter 17.

Theoretical considerations

Although the authors of each of the following chapters provide a theoretical basis for their own work, we want to highlight here the three main considerations guiding the overall inquiry. The first addresses how the web may enable increased political presence and engagement for less powerful political actors, particularly during periods of election campaigns. The second relates to how features of political culture may mediate use of the web during elections. Finally, the third consideration important to this study is known as "online structure" and involves examination of structural and contextual conditions within which political action transpires. We are concerned, specifically, with features on the websites of political actors related to information provision, discussion, and forms of political action.

Regarding the first consideration, the *web as a tool for the less politically engaged*, flows from a long-standing claim that the internet has the potential to provide political space to a wide range of segments of society, including individual citizens, interest groups, social movements, political parties, candidates, the press, and governmental bodies. That potential has been the basis of much debate. The "cyber-optimists" in the debate stress that the web provides opportunities for deliberation and direct decision making for a large sector of the public (e.g. Rheingold 1993; Rash 1997). "Cyber-pessimists" contend that the internet reinforces, or even strengthens, political forces already dominant in society. Margolis and Resnick (2000: 14) are advocates of this latter position and suggest that "political life on the Net is ... mostly an extension of political life off the Net". This position is often referred to as the normalization thesis; see the discussion in Chapter 3 for further elaboration.

In contrast, Norris (2001: 233–239) suggests a middle ground between the optimists and pessimists, an area she attributes to "cyber-skeptics". Norris makes three observations regarding this position. First, political institutions are relatively conservative in adopting new communication technologies; second, the internet may be better at supporting the already active than in mobilizing the disengaged; and finally, employment of the internet may favorably serve the interests of less powerful players than established political institutions. This last point suggests possible transformation of the political arena when "transnational advocacy networks and alternative social movements . . . have adapted the resources of new technologies to communicate, organize, and mobilize global coalitions around issues" (Norris 2001: 238–239). In a comparative study of party websites in Europe and the U.S., Norris (2003: 43) observes that European political sites contain more bottom-up elements than their American counterparts. She speculates that "the development of party websites will generate egalitarian patterns of party competition and more opportunities for citizen participation in party politics". This idea can be considered a specialized case of the so-called equalization thesis; see, once again, Chapter 3 for elaboration (see also Lusoli 2005; Chadwick 2006).

These positions are well summarized by Ward, Gibson, and Lusoli who conclude from their own investigations of elections that the internet "will make a modest positive contribution to participation and mobilization" (Ward *et al.* 2003: 667). In a comparative study, Gibson *et al.* find similarities between political campaign websites in the U.K. and U.S. In both countries, political parties fail to incorporate fully possibilities offered by the internet in their campaigns. These researchers suggest that web campaigning, at least in these two countries, may be entering a life cycle of conventional and conservative features: "cyberspace is clearly not jolting traditional political actors into radically different styles of message delivery, nor is it leading to a more egalitarian world of political communication" (Gibson *et al.* 2003: 66–67).

Regarding *political culture*, this concept may be described as the symbolic environment of political practice, shaped by political institutions, historical experiences, and philosophical and religious traditions (Kluver 2005; Martin and Stronach 1992). This broad description includes the assumptions, expectations, mythologies, and mechanisms of political practice within a country and addresses the ways values and attitudes influence political behavior. All too often, research on the political use of the web overlooks political culture, which may constrain use of the technology. Norris (2001), for example, seems to disregard the role of cultural issues in her analysis of the internet in global politics when suggesting that electronic infrastructure may be the primary predictor of internet deployment in political campaigns. In the studies presented in the following chapters a number of contextual and regulatory aspects relevant to the election campaigns in the respective countries are examined, such as geographic location, economic prosperity, internet penetration, voter registration, and campaign restrictions. In Chapter 17, which provides a comparison across the country-based studies, specific features of political culture are incorporated into the analysis.

Regarding the theoretical concept *online structure*, Schneider and Foot

(2002) suggest that the structure of an online environment may be related to ensuing political action. Building on previous studies that examine such structure with regard to social movements (e.g. Klandermans *et al.* 1998; McAdam *et al.* 1996; Cohen and Rogers 1995; Oldenburg 1989, 2001), Foot and Schneider (2002, 2006) argue that the potential for social change may be related to the online structure of a *web sphere*, constituted by the features of websites produced by various types of actors, which can provide web users with opportunities to associate and act.

In the context of electoral web spheres, online structures may facilitate engagement in the election process through three interrelated activities: provision of election-related information, opportunity for discussion and debate, and opportunity for undertaking election-related political action. This formulation of political engagement, based on a typology developed by Tsagarousianou (1999), suggests that obtaining information, engaging in deliberation, and participating in decision making are the constituent components of (digital) democracy. Leaving aside criticisms of this typology regarding the temporal order and interrelationship of these components (e.g. Jankowski and van Selm 2000: 151), it nevertheless provides guidance in understanding the relation between online structure and political engagement. Each of the chapters addresses in some manner these components and in Chapter 17 a more refined extension of this typology is presented and used for a comparative analysis of the online structures of the websites developed during elections in 19 countries.

Organization of the book

The book consists of 18 chapters, which are organized into five parts. Part I consists of two chapters, including this introduction, which elaborate the parameters of the Internet and Elections Project. Chapter 2, prepared by Meghan Dougherty and Kirsten A. Foot, explains the research design of the project. One of the anchor pins of the project involved employment of a common sampling procedure and coding instrument for examining the web spheres of 19 different countries. Dougherty and Foot provide a general overview of the procedures employed to investigate the online structures that emerged within each national electoral web sphere, and to enable comparative analysis across these web spheres.

Contributors to this volume were encouraged to draw on other kinds of relevant data along with the web-based observational data collected under the auspices of the project in their chapters, and to focus their analyses on the aspects of the internet–politics relationship which they considered most interesting or important to the electoral context they studied. Case studies of individual national electoral web spheres are presented in Parts II–IV, organized by the themes of political actors as web producers, reaching diverse constituencies via the web, and political culture and the deployment of information technology.

Part II: political actors as web producers

Part II consists of five chapters that focus on one or more types of political actors in the elections investigated in Finland, the Netherlands, Slovenia, the Czech Republic, and the United States. The chapters in this section examine how different political actors – such as political parties, candidates, citizens, and media institutions – used the web to increase their organizational effectiveness and outreach during the electoral campaigns investigated. Each of the chapters focuses on website elements and actors in the respective electoral web spheres; some of the chapters supplement these data with findings from survey research and interviews.

Chapter 3, prepared by Tom Carlson and Kim Strandberg, focuses on the 2004 European Parliament election in Finland. One of the interesting aspects regarding Finland is that it is among the most wired countries in Europe. And, in contrast to some other European countries, the Finnish electoral system emphasizes campaigning around individual candidates. The authors combined an analysis of features on candidate websites with data from a representative sample of Finnish voters. Questions addressed by the authors include: to what extent did voters say they received important information from candidate websites; what kind of voters stressed the importance of the candidate sites as information sources? The authors find, among other things, that in 2004 traditional media outlets were regarded as more important in guiding the electoral choices of voters. They also note that particularly young voters found candidate and candidate selector sites valuable in coming to a voting decision.

Chapter 4, by Renée van Os, Gerrit Voerman, and Nicholas W. Jankowski, addresses the European Parliament election in the Netherlands. By 2004, use of the web in campaigns had become relatively commonplace and most political parties had developed special websites for their party leaders, along with party-oriented sites. One of the objectives of this chapter is to explore how two prominent campaign strategies, personalization and professionalization, were employed by Dutch political parties during the 2004 election. Findings were drawn from a feature analysis of party and candidate websites and interviews with representatives from political parties. It appears that the primary function of the websites for political parties was provision of information, which could be supplied with more control and to a greater degree than through traditional mass media. Also, information provision seemed more important than establishment of personal relationships between candidates and voters, and interactive features on sites were seldom initiated because of the additional costs and monitoring involved.

Chapter 5 considers the 2004 European Parliament (EP) election in Slovenia, a new European Union (EU) Member State. The authors, Tanja Oblak and Katja Željan, note that considerable progress has been made during the last years to increase general access and use of the internet by the general population. Slovenia is, in fact, one of the more advanced countries among the new EU Member States with regard to implementation of information technology; the percentage of experienced internet users surpasses the average for the EU overall. There is uncertainty, however, whether advances in connectivity are paralleled by a comparable increase in public discourse in Slovene civil society. The authors explore this issue, and ask how the web is used by four groups of political actors – government, political parties, special interest groups, and citizens – regarding dissemination of political information and supporting political action during the 2004 EP election campaign. Most of these sites provided considerable information-oriented features, but the more interactive features were much less common. Political parties, in particular, seemed reticent to provide interactive features and almost none offered opportunity to express support for candidates. The authors suggest that a legalist model of democracy as practiced in Slovenia does not encourage an active citizenry during election campaigns.

Chapter 6 presents findings from another new EU Member State, the Czech Republic. The author, Martin Gregor, argues that e-campaigns may provide a signaling function, in that they provide clues regarding the values and technological sophistication of the party, even though no direct electoral benefit seems evident from the websites constructed for this election. Employing the feature analysis developed for the overall Internet and Elections Project, Gregor demonstrates that few political actors in this election employed the available facilities for information provision and engagement. Political parties were the most proactive producers of websites and some also provided templates for their candidates. Nevertheless, candidates rarely prepared their own sites and some of these candidate sites provided little to no material about election issues. This limited attention to the EP election was partly related to the widely shared feeling that this election was not particularly important for either the candidates or the electorate.

Chapter 7, by Kirsten A. Foot, Steven M. Schneider, and Meghan Dougherty, analyzes the 2004 Congressional elections in the United States, where use of the web has become a common element in campaign strategies. Nearly twice as many internet users sought political information online in 2004 relative to the election in 2000, some four million internet users made political contributions online, and the web proved to be a successful tool for fundraising by parties, politicians, and interest groups. In their chapter, the authors seek to determine what other online structures for political action were provided to election-related website visitors, and what those structures indicate about the web practices of U.S. political actors in 2004. The analysis focuses on four theoretically derived web practices: informing, involving, connecting, and mobilizing. As web producers were more likely to provide opportunities for site visitors to become informed and involved than they were to provide opportunities for connecting and mobilizing, it seems that producers tend to under-utilize the affordances provided by web technologies for enabling multi-actor engagement.

Part III: reaching diverse constituencies via the web

This section consists of four chapters examining the way in which constituencies are created and maintained via the web in the Philippines, Sri Lanka, India, and the U.K. and Ireland. These chapters explore an important issue: the creation and appeal to political identity. One of the most prominent prophecies about the internet has been its ability to transcend time and space in order to create constituencies and achieve a critical political mass. The chapters in this section highlight the efforts of political actors to reach diverse constituencies, such as expatriates and overseas voters, who are often beyond the reach of traditional campaign practices, or seemingly irrelevant to the actual election. These chapters collectively address political identity, as defined through web-based campaigning, and the use of diverse technologies to attract different audiences.

Chapter 8, prepared by Kate A. Mirandilla, examines utilization of the web during the 2004 election in the Philippines. Information and communication technologies have in the past played a crucial role in this country, as in 2001 when blogs, news groups, and mobile phone messaging contributed to the overthrow of the president. This study seeks to add to the anecdotal evidence concerning the role of the internet in Philippine politics and systematically examine uses of the web in the 2004 national election. Mirandilla shows that very few political stakeholders, in fact, utilized the web during the campaign. Although candidates and parties maintained sites more often than other stakeholders, as might be expected, these political actors actually maintained a very limited web presence: only about a third of the senatorial candidates and three of the 11 parties had sites, which mainly consisted of basic information-oriented features. Moreover, candidate sites generally focused on the individuals rather than election issues, reflecting the general personalization of elections prevalent in the Philippines, and the reification of the two-tiered nature of Philippine politics. Mirandilla concludes that incorporation of the web into Philippine elections is presently limited to a small minority of political actors providing little more than basic informational content, limiting its role as a democratizing agent in that country.

Chapter 9, prepared by Shyam Tekwani and Randolph Kluver, presents findings from the 2004 national election held in Sri Lanka. In this developing country the internet is used by only a small portion of the population; primarily consisting of students, governmental officials, and business persons. For the vast majority of citizens, the internet is irrelevant during elections. Still, the web was incorporated into the 2004 campaign by a wide range of political actors, including the insurgent Tamil Tigers. It is this apparent paradox that the authors address in the chapter. They argue that election-related websites are an attempt by political actors to reach an international audience, rather than a local one. This objective is reflected in the use of English on most sites and the limited presence of information and engagement features related to the election. At the same time, these sites exhibit characteristics of Sri Lankan political culture in which ethnic identity is prominent. Most striking is the employment of graphic symbols and images, traditionally common in other forms of electoral communication in Sri Lanka.

Chapter 10, prepared by Janelle Ward, examines data from the 2004 European Parliament elections held in Ireland and the U.K., and focuses on the websites prepared by youth organizations and divisions of parties established for young voters. Although young people are often politically disengaged in Western democracies, many believe that the internet has the potential to reverse such indifference. Based on quantitative and qualitative content analysis, Ward examines possibilities for online electoral participation available to youth in the context of the 2004 EP election campaign. In a comparison of features related to campaign issue positions, these were entirely absent on the sites of youth organizations and present on nearly three-quarters of the political party sites. Overall, sites for both groups of actors provided many information and engagement features, suggesting that the groundwork is present for adapting these features to future election campaigns.

Chapter 11 presents an analysis of websites related to the 2004 national election in India. Shyam Tekwani and Kavitha Shetty note that this election represented the first major election in India since the nation had been transformed into a global technology power. Many believed that the internet would play a major role in this election, perhaps even to the extent of becoming a determinant factor in the eventual outcome. Through analysis of a sample of election-related websites, the authors found only limited deployment of information and engagement features on these sites. Further, most sites were in English, which suggests that the sites were mainly intended for the relatively small English-language urban, educated elite in the country and not the majority of voters who live in rural areas, where the election was eventually decided. The authors conclude that the internet had little to offer Indian political parties and candidates but, given the increase in young voters, together with increasing internet connectivity and use, they predict that the web is likely to play an increasingly important role in future elections.

Part IV: political culture and the diffusion of technologies

This section is aimed at exploring the role of political culture and context – including regulation, technological diffusion, and assumptions regarding politics – on the deployment of the internet during political campaigns, through an analysis of the elections in six countries: Australia, Hungary, India, Indonesia, Japan, and South Korea. These chapters examine how the political traditions and norms of each country impact deployment of the internet and other forms of information technology for political campaigning conducted by different political actors. These chapters also explore the impact of technological diffusion on political culture and how such diffusion may slowly change the political culture of a country.

Chapter 12 examines how the web was employed during the 2004 federal election in Australia. In the past, web use in this country has been characterized as top-down, mainly for information provision with limited possibilities for engagement and interactivity. These earlier observations are considered in the light of this more recent election by Maria Pieter Aquilia. She found that political sites were as likely to incorporate information provision as engagement features. The feature analysis was complemented with a close examination of three prominent sites involved in the 2004 election regarding a political party, press agency, and a citizen site. Aquilia found that these sites contributed to a substantial arena for public discourse and demonstrated the potential for supporting civic engagement. She concludes that these sites illustrate the possibilities for political minority groups and promotion of alternative viewpoints during election campaigns.

Chapter 13 considers the use of the web in another new EU Member State, Hungary, during the 2004 European Parliament election. Based on an analysis of site features and interviews with persons associated with press sites, authors Endre Dányi and Anna Galácz observe that the sites represents an arena in which the *strategies* of powerful political players clash with the *tactics* of the less powerful. The authors conclude that the traditional conception of actors using the technologies is inadequate; what is needed is appreciation of the ways in which technologies and the lives of people are intertwined.

Chapter 14, prepared by Shahiraa Sahul Hameed, addresses the 2004 national election in Indonesia. Although Indonesia is considered a democratic nation, the actual practice of this political form is relatively unstable due to the widely disparate understanding of democracy between the elite and general population. The 2004 election in Indonesia represented, however, a degree of change in that both citizens and politicians debated issues such as the role of Islam in the nation's political culture and the effectiveness of the post-Suharto regime. The election also marked the first time that Indonesians were voting directly for the nation's president and the first time that the internet had a formal role in a national-level election in the country. One of the most prominent results of the study was the lack of engagement features found on the websites examined. The lack of these and other features, together with the popularity of face-to-face campaigning in Indonesia, may be a reflection of the collectivist nature of Indonesian society.

Chapter 15 focuses on the role of the internet in Japanese elections and explores the role of political regulation on the impact of the internet. Leslie M. Tkach-Kawasaki argues that the traditional campaign roles and regulations, two mutually supporting aspects of a nation's political culture, contributed to shaping the Japanese political web sphere – and political actors' use of the web – during the 2004 Upper House election campaign period.

The approach to the campaign use of the internet in Japan is distinctive because it is one of the few nations to apply regulations to online campaigning.

Chapter 16, by Hyo Kim and Han Woo Park, examines the way in which the internet was deployed in one of the most active democracies, as well as one of the most technologically advanced countries, in the world. The authors argue that the vibrant political clashes of 2003 and 2004, and the unprecedented presidential impeachment during that period, intensified political competition and the appeal for moral righteousness by political parties. The authors found that the internet was a major means for organizing and disseminating information, as well as a powerful political channel for participatory politics.

Part V: comparisons and conclusions

In this section, we integrate and compare the data collected in all of the countries included in the Internet and Elections Project. Chapter 17, prepared by the book editors together with Michael Xenos, incorporates data from 19 of the national web spheres included in the project and explores patterns in the production of election-related sites. Four key practices are operationalized – informing, involving, connecting, and mobilizing – and these are compared to a range of indices related to human, technological and political development, and political culture and genre effects related to the producer types. One of the more salient results of the regression analyses conducted is that political actors are more likely to produce sites similar to those produced by their counterparts in other countries than to those produced by other types of actors within their own country. This suggests that the type of political actor producing a site may be a stronger determinant in the features employed on a site than the other conditions examined – human, technological, and political development. At the same time, though, measures of political culture suggest that this component also influences web production practices.

Chapter 18, prepared by the book editors, provides an overall reflective treatment of the findings emerging from the Internet and Elections Project, and suggests areas for further study and considerations in designing cross-national comparative research. Although this chapter is far from the final word on how the internet is transforming, reinforcing, or otherwise interacting with political practice around the world, the authors suggest important lessons emerging from the project with regard to the interrelation between information technology, political practice, and political culture.

References

Chadwick, A. (2006) *Internet Politics: States, Citizens, and New Communication Technologies*. New York: Oxford University Press.

Cohen, J. and Rogers, J. (1995) *Associations and Democracy*. New York: Verso.

Foot, K.A. and Schneider, S.M. (2002) "Online action in Campaign 2000: An exploratory analysis of the U.S. political Web sphere", *Journal of Broadcasting & Electronic Media*, 46: 222–244.

Foot, K.A. and Schneider, S.M. (2006) *Web Campaigning*. Cambridge, MA: MIT Press.

Gibson, R.K., Margolis, M., Resnick, D., and Ward, S.J. (2003) "Election campaigning on the WWW in the USA and UK: a comparative analysis", *Party Politics*, 9, 1: 47–75.

Jankowski, N. (2007) "Exploring e-science: an introduction", *Journal of Computer-Mediated Communication*, 12, 1.

Jankowski, N.W. and van Selm, M. (2000) "The promise and the practice of public debate", in K.L. Hacker and J. van Dijk (eds), *Digital Democracy: Issues of Theory and Practice*, pp. 149–165. London: Sage.

Jensen, K.B. and Jankowski, N.W. (eds) (1991) *A Handbook of Qualitative Methodologies for Mass Communication Research*. London: Routledge.

Klandermans, B., Kriesi, H., and Tarrow, S. (1998) *From Structure to Action: Comparing Social Movement Research Across Cultures*. Greenwich, CT: JAI Press.

Kluver, R. (1997) "Political identity and national myth: toward an intercultural understanding of political legitimacy", in A. Gonzales and D. Tanno (eds), *Politics, Culture, and Communication: International and Intercultural Communication Annual*, pp. 48–75. Newbury Park, CA: Sage.

Kluver, R. (2004) "Political culture and information technology in the 2001 Singapore general election", *Political Communication*, 21: 435–458.

Kluver, R. (2005) "Political culture in online politics", in M. Consalvo and M. Allen (eds), *Internet Research Annual, Volume 2*. Newbury Park, CA: Sage.

Kluver, R and Banerjee, I. (2005) "Political culture, regulation, and democratization: the internet in nine Asian nations", *Information, Communication, and Society*, 8, 1: 1–17.

Lusoli, W. (2005) "The internet and the European Parliament elections: theoretical perspectives, empirical investigations and proposals for research", *Information Polity*, 19: 153–163.

Martin, C.H. and Stronach, B. (1992) *Politics East and West: A Comparison of Japanese and British Political Culture*. Armonk, NY: M.E. Sharpe.

McAdam, D., McCarthy, J.D., and Mayer, N.Z. (eds) (1996) *Comparative Perspectives on Social Movements: Political Opportunities, Mobilizing Structures, and Cultural Framings*. New York: Cambridge University Press.

Margolis, M. and Resnick, D. (2000) *Politics as Usual: The Cyberspace Revolution*, London: Sage.

Norris, P. (2001) *Digital Divide? Civic Engagement, Information Poverty and the Internet Worldwide*. Cambridge: Cambridge University Press.

Norris, P. (2003) "Preaching to the converted: pluralism, participation and party web sites", *Party Politics*, 9, 1: 21–45.

Oldenburg, R. (1989) *The Great Good Place: Cafes, Coffee Shops, Community Centers, Beauty Parlors, General Stores, Bars, Hangouts, and How They Get You Through the Day*. New York: Paragon House.

Oldenburg, R. (2001) *Celebrating the Third Place: Inspiring Stories about the "Great Good Places" at the Heart of our Communities*. New York: Marlowe & Co.

Rash, W. (1997) *Politics on the Nets: Wiring the Political Process*. New York: W.H. Freeman and Co.

Rheingold, H. (1993) *The Virtual Community: Homesteading on the Electronic Frontier.* New York: Harper.

Schneider, S. (1996) "A case study of abortion conversation on the Internet", *Social Science Computer Review*, 14, 4: 373–393.

Schneider, S. (1997) "Expanding the public sphere through computer-mediated communication: political discussion about abortion in a Usenet Newsgroup", PhD dissertation, MIT. Available: <http://www.sunyit.edu/~steve/> (accessed 12 September 2006).

Schneider, S. and Foot, K. (2002) "Online structure for political action: exploring presidential campaign Web sites from the 2000 American election", *Javnost – The Public*, 9, 2: 43–60.

Schneider, S.M. and Foot, K. (2005) "Web sphere analysis: an approach to studying online action", in C. Hine (ed.), *Virtual Methods: Issues in Social Research on the Internet*, pp. 157–170. Oxford: Berg Publishers.

Tsagarousianou, R. (1999) "Electronic democracy: rhetoric and reality", *Communications: The European Journal of Communication Research*, 24, 2: 189–208.

Ward, S., Gibson, R., and Lusoli, W. (2003) "Online participation and mobilisation in Britain: Hype, hope and reality", *Parliamentary Affairs*, 56, 652–668.

2 The Internet and Elections Project research design

Meghan Dougherty and Kirsten A. Foot

The Internet and Elections Project employed the concept of political culture including the assumptions, values, beliefs, and institutional context in which political activity occurs within the political sphere of a nation (Kluver 2005). Project coordinators trained participating researchers in the conceptual and operational definitions of political culture. The coordinators asked participants to draw upon political culture in providing an explanatory mechanism in areas such as regulation of political speech, the assumptions concerning the appropriate use and role of political media, and the unique assumptions and values regarding politics in each country. These insights could then be used to inform the analysis of feature variance across spheres, should any emerge. However, "political culture" is not easily reduced to a set of factors that will surface consistently across many different nations. As a result, the Internet and Elections Project attempted to demonstrate the role of political culture in the deployment of the internet, with a full awareness of the difficulties of making generalizable claims.

Participants in the project investigating the web in national and international elections in 2004 and 2005 generated both case specific and comparative data about online structures for political action in electoral web spheres across a diverse array of political cultures. A web sphere is a set of dynamically defined digital resources, often connected by hyperlinks, spanning multiple websites relevant to a central event, concept, or theme and bounded temporally (Foot and Schneider 2002; Schneider and Foot 2005). Online structure has been defined as an electronic space, comprised of various features, links, and texts, which provides users opportunities to associate and act (Schneider and Foot 2002). In an electoral context, online structures may facilitate political action focused on engagement in the election process through information seeking, associating and discussing electoral issues with others, and promoting a party, candidate, or issue (Schneider and Foot 2002). An electoral web sphere is a dynamic array of web materials created by political actors who are likely to participate in the electoral process within a particular political culture.

Participants in the Internet and Elections Project generated data using software and protocols developed and supported by Webarchivist.org; these data were the basis for both case-specific and comparative analyses. Websites comprising each case, or each electoral web sphere, were identified as systematically and comprehensively as possible. The websites participants identified populated a project database with URLs for future annotation. Project coordinators used the database to draw samples for systematic coding. Websites corresponding with sampled URLs were coded in accordance with a protocol shared by all participants in the project to generate structured observations that could be compared across web spheres. Coders were encouraged to create a set of "field notes" from unstructured observations about particular sites and the electoral web sphere in general in order to document phenomena of particular interest or significance to online structure and political action within the electoral web sphere. Field notes about each web sphere provided important contextual data for interpreting the coding data in light of the political culture of each web sphere.

Training

Project coordinators trained lead researchers during a three-day training workshop in March 2004, and a one-day workshop in April 2004. Training included instruction on how to identify websites, how to use the Webarchivist software, how to interpret operational definitions used in the primary coding frame, and also included suggestions on how to develop a set of open-ended observations regarding online structure and political action. After a demonstration of coding procedures, participants coded a sample of five English-language websites. Some participants subsequently enlisted the help of additional coders. Participants trained additional coders using the same coding materials demonstrated in the original training workshop.

Identification

Systematic identification of sites within each electoral web sphere took place 30 to 45 days before the election; however, participants were encouraged to continue ongoing identification of election-related sites until their case election day. To facilitate consistency in the identification of sites across web spheres, participants used a shared "sleuthing guide." The guide provided detailed advice for the identification of sites produced by different political actor types involved in elections in various nations.

Twelve web producer types were identified as relevant to elections in the different political contexts covered by the Internet and Election Project. These types were: candidates, political parties, press, governments, non-governmental organizations, labor unions, citizens, educational organizations, political professionals, religious organizations, and web portals. These 12 producer types were derived from Schneider and Foot's studies of online action in U.S. elections and the post-9/11 web (Foot and Schneider 2002; Schneider and Foot 2003). The sleuthing guide also provided search strategies in the form of sample internet search queries that could be customized to reflect the political culture of each case web sphere.

Researchers were asked to run identical search queries relevant to the election in two internet search engines (Google and a second search engine of their choice), and follow the first 50 links from the search results page to identify resources within the web sphere. Websites produced by political actors with a role in the election were identified as part of the electoral web sphere even if they did not have election-related content at the time of identification. The rationale for this was that such websites could be significant in structuring online action – or the lack thereof – within an electoral web sphere even if those actors have not (yet) produced web materials relevant to the election at the time of identification. Participants included websites as part of their nation's electoral web sphere based on the expectation that the political actors responsible for the sites included would participate in the electoral process in some way. The lack of online election content by certain political actors in some political cultures is commented on in other chapters in this volume.

Once a site was identified, project participants followed links appearing on the site to sleuth out other sites by the same producer or other political actors to discover additional elements of the electoral web sphere. Participants identified as many sites as possible for each producer type (see Table 2.1). Participants entered the homepage URL for each site in the shared project database and generated metadata about the site and its producer.

At the beginning of the Internet and Elections Project, participants submitted estimates of the electoral web spheres, including the types of political actors they expected to produce election-related web materials, the number of actors within each type for a particular sphere, and the number of sites produced by each actor. These estimates varied widely across the spheres to be studied. Project coordinators used these estimates to develop a sampling frame prototype, stratified by producer type (see Table 2.2). The aim of the sampling design was to assure inclusion of a mix of website producer types within the sample of sites to be coded for each electoral web sphere; the prototypical sampling frame was not representative of the number of election-related sites produced within any individual sphere.

Four weeks prior to the election, coordinators drew a sample of 100 sites from the sites identified in each sphere after modifying the sampling frame as needed for each sphere. When the number of sites identified within each category was fewer than the rubric required, the remaining empty slots in each producer type category were filled by sites by other prominent producer types. When the total number of sites identified was fewer than 100, all sites identified were included in the sample. Coordinators adjusted the sampling frame for each sphere to represent the multiplicity of producers present in a multi-actor sphere, not to be representative of the proportion of actors identified in the web spheres.

Table 2.1 Number of sites identified by producer type

Producer type	Web sphere																				
	AUS	CSK	EUP	FIN	FRA	HUN	IDN	Pr IND	IRE	ITA	JPN	KOR	LUX	NL	PHL	PRT	SVN	THA	U.K.	U.S.	Total
Business	7	7	2	1	8	3	7	4	5	19	0	0	0	13	13	3	3	7	2	2	106
Candidate	17	21	0	122	30	11	12	7	7	71	188	441	8	74	29	4	1	7	80	752	1882
Citizen	25	17	9	1	27	2	17	4	3	6	5	4	0	14	34	3	3	6	33	26	239
Educational	9	8	2	1	2	3	3	1	13	11	3	8	1	4	1	1	3	1	4	8	87
Government	5	11	31	9	43	42	11	35	39	35	60	94	2	37	33	3	67	31	94	65	747
Labor Union	10	12	3	8	18	3	0	0	6	4	29	4	5	30	0	0	0	0	75	4	211
NGO	15	18	63	20	50	10	15	9	18	20	35	208	6	35	36	4	12	5	124	34	737
Party	37	31	34	17	75	14	34	27	17	27	17	10	9	48	5	17	21	8	97	155	700
Political professional	5	5	13	0	19	7	0	1	29	8	3	23	0	19	5	0	3	1	1	3	145
Portal	6	6	9	5	5	4	20	8	2	8	8	16	0	13	28	0	17	2	7	3	167
Press	11	31	20	10	30	21	60	11	21	13	12	130	12	30	71	19	30	38	72	43	685
Religious	7	0	1	0	1	0	2	0	4	17	0	22	0	0	2	0	3	0	8	1	68
Other	0	0	1	0	9	3	0	0	0	1	0	0	0	2	1	1	0	0	0	1	19
Total	154	167	188	194	317	123	181	107	164	240	360	960	43	319	258	55	163	106	597	1097	5793

Table 2.2 Number of sites sampled by producer type: prototype sampling frame

Producer type strata	Sites sampled
Candidate	30
Press	10
Party	20
Government	10
NGO/Labor Union	10
Other*	20

Note
* Other category includes Citizen, Educational, Political Professional, Portal, and Religious.

Coding

Participants in the project did not attempt to comprehensively catalog all elements of election-oriented websites. A set of 24 measures were employed in coding the sampled sites in each sphere, based on the core objective to study online structure. The coding frame was originally developed and tested for both conceptual and operational validity by Foot and Schneider in their study of candidate sites in the U.S. elections in 2002.[1] The measures and operational definitions can be found in the Appendix to this book. The project coordinators adapted this coding frame so that it would be applicable to sites produced by a broad range of political actors in different cultural contexts. The coding frame included measures for the presence or absence of particular types of information and other features. Most coding measures pertained to the presence of an item and employed a set of four response options: (1) Yes, present on a page produced by this site producer; (2) Yes, but present on a page produced by a different site producer; (3) No; and (4) Not clear. Coders were instructed to examine the first and second levels of pages linked from the front page for evidence of the item, then to follow links to access the item itself. European participants developed a secondary coding frame with additional items that was employed in coding sites across all of the European Union (EU) web spheres. The coding of the sample of identified websites took place during a period of two weeks ending three days prior to the election, using the Webarchivist Coder, a web-based system for distributed, collaborative coding of web objects.

The cultural differences in campaign periods between spheres made it impossible to specify one common time frame for coding that would capture the most active campaigning periods for every sphere included in the study. Formal campaign periods of the countries included in the Internet and Elections Project vary drastically. Each country included in the project has differing regulations on publicly funded campaign advertising, which impacts the time in which candidates choose to campaign. For example, Japan's formal campaign period is only 12 days for the Lower House and 17 days for the Upper House. This formal campaign period ends prior to the election. Campaigning activities between the close of the formal campaign period and the election are limited. During this time, candidates are not permitted to approach voters, and although it is not formally addressed in campaign laws, many candidates remove their campaign websites from the web; others maintain their campaign sites, but do not update the content during the restricted period. Australia's campaign period lasts from the time the official election writ is issued until the close of polls. The U.S. has an expanded campaign period that has no official start; candidates who may choose to run in an upcoming election begin issuing campaign-like messages through a variety of media, sometimes years before an election will take place. The two-week period ending shortly before the election date in each country included in the project enabled coders to view sites over a period of time of high and low campaign activity and provided some consistency for case comparison.

In addition to coding the five training sites, all participants were required to code a set of ten archived English-language sites as a means of measuring agreement among coders. Coordinators evaluated inter-rater reliability according to the percent of agreement among coders, based on two important characteristics of the data. First, the primary concern in systematic coding was with either the presence or absence of certain types of features and information and thus did not incorporate continuous variables. Neuendorf (2002) notes that percent agreement is particularly appropriate in instances "wherein each pair of coded measures is either a hit or a miss" (p. 149). Second, the distribution of our measures is skewed. Fewer than half the sites sampled for reliability testing offered half of our 24 measures. Such distribution forces lower reliability calculations of agreement beyond chance even when coding is reasonably reliable (Potter and Levine-Donnerstein 1999).

Percent agreement was calculated between each individual coder in the project and a set of master codes agreed upon by the four project coordinators. Percent agreement was also calculated between the coders within each sphere, relative only to the coders working within each sphere. The four response options were collapsed into three responses (Yes, No, and Not Clear). To take into account the unreliable display of archived websites, disagreements between coders that involved a Not Clear response were not counted as disagreements. Coordinators assumed that a Not Clear response was due to technical archival display difficulties and not to misunderstanding among coders. Agreement within coding spheres ranged from 50 percent to 100 percent by item. Average agreement among coders for all items within each sphere ranged from 81.2 percent to 98.4 percent. The average percent agreement score over all spheres on all items was 86.9 percent.

In additional to calculating the reliability of coders, coordinators calculated Cronbach's alpha to assess the reliability of the theoretically derived information and engagement scales used to assess feature data. Cronbach's alpha assesses the extent to which a set of test items can be treated as measuring a single latent variable. Using Cronbach's alpha typically leads to three problems.

The first problem is that alpha is dependent not only on the magnitude of the correlations among items, but also on the number of items in the scale. A scale can be made to look more "homogeneous" simply by doubling the number of items, even though the average correlation remains the same. This leads directly to the second problem. If we have two scales, which each measure a distinct construct and combine them to form one long scale, alpha would probably be high, although the merged scale is obviously tapping two different attributes. The third relates to situations when alpha is high; this may suggest a high level of item redundancy, that is, a number of items asking the same question in slightly different ways (Streiner and Norman 1989: 64–65).

The scales employed in the Internet and Elections Project included a large number of items (approximately 13 items for each construct); this may yield slightly higher alpha scores. However, there is strong theoretical support to include these items together in engagement and information constructs, and prior testing of the measures adds support for their usefulness (Foot and Schneider 2002; Schneider and Foot 2004). The theoretical basis for developing these constructs in the manner used in this study suggests an exploratory examination into information and engagement as latent attributes of web structure. The exploratory nature affords some leniency to this reliability measure.

The widely accepted range for Cronbach's alpha scores includes scores of 0.7 and higher in the social sciences. However, exploratory data is afforded a more lenient range from 0.6 and higher (Santos 1999). There are no references to the ideal number of items to include in a scale. Our engagement construct produced a range from 0.212 to 0.753, with 13 of the 21 web spheres scoring 0.5 or higher. Eight web spheres scored 0.6 or higher. Our information construct produced a range from 0.1 to 0.854 with 17 of 21 web spheres scoring 0.5 or higher. Ten web spheres scored 0.6 and higher. Data reported in this study reflect 0.6 as an acceptable alpha score (see Table 2.3).

Researchers participating in the project represented many languages but shared English as a common language. Based on this shared language, the initial training workshop was held in English. Training offered by lead researchers to additional coders enlisted after the original workshop was held in other languages. The coding instrument, code books, sample training sites, and sites used to calculate inter-rater reliability remained in English. Coders were encouraged to contact the project coordinators and technical support team with functional and operational questions during the coding process. Coders contacted the support team via e-mail and instant messaging services for quick resolution. All the English-language training documents, including instrument manuals, operational definition code books, and pro-

Table 2.3 Construct reliability by web sphere: Cronbach's alpha score

Web sphere	Engagement score (items included)	Information score (items included)
AUS	0.639 (11)	0.603 (13)
CSK	0.588 (10)	0.677 (13)
EUP	0.639 (11)	0.706 (13)
FIN	0.301 (9)	0.654 (11)
FRA	0.585 (11)	0.52 (13)
HUN	0.407 (9)	0.648 (13)
IND	0.249 (10)	0.481 (13)
IDN Pa	0.456 (8)	0.111 (10)
IDN Pr	0.61 (10)	0.725 (13)
IRE	0.377 (9)	0.563 (13)
ITA	0.639 (10)	0.529 (12)
JPN	0.25 (10)	0.322 (13)
KOR	0.719 (11)	0.745 (13)
LUX	0.51 (8)	0.76 (13)
NL	0.547 (10)	0.606 (13)
PHL	0.555 (11)	0.517 (13)
PRT	0.691 (11)	0.854 (13)
SVN	0.601 (11)	0.642 (13)
SR	0.212 (10)	0.493 (13)
THA	0.402 (9)	0.238 (12)
U.K.	0.753 (11)	0.552 (13)
U.S.	0.592 (11)	0.577 (13)

duction schedule were available to coders at all times through the project website.

Annotation

In regular, repeated observations, participants noted phenomena of particular interest or significance to their web sphere. Participants' knowledge of the political culture of their respective spheres guided their annotations and informed their observations of significant or noteworthy features. Participants made these observations throughout the election period, during the identification process, and during the coding process. Participants created notes and memos about online structure and political action by observing web artifacts and significant or interesting features and political activity in each web sphere. Participants used their knowledge of the political culture of the sphere under investigation to structure their annotations and inform them of significant or noteworthy features. Annotation, like identification, was a process that continued throughout the study period. Participants recorded their notes in text documents, in the Webarchivist Resource Identifier, and in the Webarchivist Resource Coder. Qualitative annotations, or field notes, were created to document sphere-specific phenomena. They were used to interpret coding data within each sphere. Structuring these observations could have excluded important political cultural data; however, leaving them unstructured resulted in unevenness in the qualitative data that could be used to interpret structured observations across spheres.

Discussion of affordances and constraints

The scope of the Internet and Elections Project, encompassing 22 national and international elections, and the short time available for launching the project and training participants before election campaigns began in several participating countries, posed many challenges. For example, the Sri Lankan election took place within a week after the initial training workshop, necessitating an adaptation of the identification and sampling strategies. The complexity of cross-cultural research influenced the project's planning and data collection processes in several ways. In order to ensure comparability of data sets and results concerning the role of the web in elections, project coordinators requested that all participants employ the web sphere as a shared unit of analysis that encompassed heterogeneous web objects produced by a range of political actors. Adherence to a common set of guidelines for site identification and shared coding procedures was necessary for comparability. However, although the common coding frame took into account a diverse array of online structures across spheres, there were interesting phenomena in each web sphere that were not captured by the codes. The research design attempted to address these challenges by soliciting both structured observations for comparative analyses and open-ended annotations for contextual, in-depth, and more nuanced data.

The nature of the EU Parliament election made it particularly difficult to bound the participating national electoral web spheres. Participants examining European national electoral web spheres and EU Parliament electoral web spheres found that not all political actors were equally active through the campaign periods, nor were they equally active in the EU Parliament elections and the national elections. For example, several candidate sites in the U.K. posted an announcement reading, "To comply with rules, this site has to be frozen 30 days before the elections. For updated information, please go to..." Since candidates could not update their official sites toward the end of the campaign period, some provided alternative sites for updated information. Project participants examining sites in the EU Parliament web sphere suggested that the presence of alternative national sites might speak to the candidates' perception of the relevance of national elections and the importance of European elections. Several EU researchers discuss the strategies they developed in response to these challenges elsewhere in this volume.

The decision to include websites produced by election-relevant actors that did not contain election-related content at the time of identification involved trade-offs regarding the coding and open-ended annotation data. In order to generate comparative data, the sites constituting an electoral web sphere had to be defined in a way that was sustainable across political cultures, and a cross-national typology of election-related political actors was easier to generate than a typology of election-related topics would have been. In some spheres, the absence of election content on particular sites had political significance, and identification of these sites at approximately four weeks before the election gave researchers the opportunity to observe whether the political actors producing the sites added election-related content at a later date. However, some coding measures were irrelevant for sites that lacked election-related content and ended up in the coding sample.

A strategy of identifying sites based on the presence of election-related content would have posed several difficulties as well, including the following: (1) operationalizing topics as "election-related" cross-culturally, (2) determining the amount of election-related content necessary for a site to be to included in the electoral web sphere, and (3) excluding sites that may have election content at some other point in time leading up to the election. Basing the inclusion criteria on the site producer's role in the electoral context, despite the presence or absence of electoral content at the moment of identification time, enabled analyses of political culture and online structure that would not have been possible with a content-based criterion for inclusion. In sum, the research design for web sphere analysis employed in the Internet and Election Project provided a framework for investigating the online structure for political action, as potentiated and mediated by structural elements of websites (Schneider and Foot 2005).

Note

1 Available online: politicalweb.info/e2002.html.

References

Foot, K.A. and Schneider, S.M. (2002) "Online action in Campaign 2000: an exploratory analysis of the U.S. political Web sphere," *Journal of Broadcasting & Electronic Media*, 46: 222–244.

Kluver, R. (2005) "Political culture in online politics," in M. Consalvo and M. Allen (eds), *Internet Research Annual, Volume 2*, pp. 75–84. Newbury Park, CA: Sage.

Neuendorf, K.A. (2002) *The Content Analysis Guidebook*, Thousand Oaks, CA: Sage.

Potter, W.J. and Levine-Donnerstein, D. (1999) "Rethinking validity and reliability in content analysis," *Journal of Applied Communication Research*, 27: 258–284.

Santos, J.R.A. (1999) "Cronbach's Alpha: a tool for assessing the reliability of scales," *Journal of Extensions*, 37. Available online: www.joe.org/joe/1999april/tt3.html (accessed 8 April 2006).

Schneider, S.M. and Foot, K.A. (2002) "Online structure for political action: exploring presidential Web sites from the 2000 American election," *Javnost (The Public)*, 9: 43–60.

Schneider, S.M. and Foot, K.A. (2003) "Crisis communication and new media: the Web after September 11," in P.N. Howard and S. Jones (eds), *Society Online: The Internet in Context*. London: Sage.

Schneider, S.M. and Foot, K.A. (2004) "The Web as an object of study," *New Media & Society*, 6: 114–122.

Schneider, S.M. and Foot, K.A. (2005) "Web sphere analysis: an approach to studying online action," in C. Hine (ed.), *Virtual Methods: Issues in Social Research on the Internet*. Oxford: Berg.

Streiner, D.L. and Norman, G.R. (1989) *Health Measurement Scales: A Practical Guide to their Development and Use*. New York: Oxford University Press.

Part II

Political actors as web producers

3 Finland

The European Parliament election in a candidate-centered electoral system

Tom Carlson and Kim Strandberg

Introduction

In examining electoral web spheres during the 2004 European Parliament (EP) elections, two circumstances make the Finnish case interesting. First, the basic prerequisite for using the web during elections – a high level of internet penetration – was achieved relatively early in Finland. Already in 1999, Scandinavia, including Finland, was the most "wired" area in Europe (Norris 2000). In spring 2004, the highest levels of internet usage by individuals in the EU were recorded in Sweden (82 percent), Denmark (76 percent) and Finland (70 percent) (Eurostat 2005). Second, as compared with other European countries, the Finnish electoral system is strongly oriented towards individual political candidates (CVCE 2004). In both national and EP elections, Finnish voters do not cast ballots according to lists of candidates but for unranked individual candidates representing parties or electoral alliances. This system leads to candidate-driven campaigning. Thus, Finnish candidates invest in personal campaigns and usually have their own support groups that organize campaigning activities, raise money, and generate publicity. This candidate-centered model of campaigning makes Finland a case apart in EP elections.

Given these aspects, it is not surprising that 28 percent of the Finnish candidates had independent websites as early as the 1996 EP elections (Isotalus 1998). Since candidate-centered systems, as Gibson (2004) suggests, result in individualized cyber-campaigning spurring innovations and dynamic development in web use, the early adoption of the web in Finnish EP campaigns makes the Finnish case especially interesting. Candidates, as well as other actors, were probably "learning the ropes" in the 1996 campaign; we might expect their use of the web during the 2004 EP elections to have undergone considerable change.

In determining the Finnish electoral web sphere during the 2004 EP elections, we identified 196 websites produced by ten actor groups (Carlson and Strandberg 2005). As expected, electoral candidates were the most significant actors in this web sphere. Of the 196 websites identified, 63 percent were candidate sites. Since the Finnish 1996 EP election, the percentage of candidates having websites has nearly doubled: in the 2004 campaign, 123 of the 227 nominated candidates (54 percent) had their own websites. Moreover, in comparing the web presence of the candidates in nine EU countries in the 2004 elections (Carlson and Strandberg 2005), we found that the percentage of candidates online was considerably higher in Finland than in the other EU Member States (Czech Republic: 8 percent; France: 2 percent; Hungary: 4 percent; Ireland: 16 percent; Luxembourg: 0 percent; Netherlands: 27 percent; Slovenia: 1 percent; United Kingdom: 11 percent).

The candidate-centered system was reflected on the web in another way, too. In scanning news media sites for inclusion in the Finnish electoral web sphere, we noted that so-called candidate selectors were frequently present on the sites of the major news media organizations (Carlson and Strandberg 2005). A candidate selector is a web-based tool that compares the site visiting voter's answers to a set of topical questions with those given by the candidates. The selectors then suggest to the voters a selection of candidates who are most likely to have similar opinions on political issues. In recent Finnish elections, these tests have become very popular (Moring and Mykkänen 2005). The selectors also attracted a substantial public during the 2004 EP campaign.[1] Moreover, the candidates were very responsive when providing answers to the questionnaires that made up the main selectors; the answer rates ranged from 77 to 87 percent.

With these developments as a backdrop, this chapter focuses on two web features that could possibly mobilize Finnish voters. Primarily, we concentrate on the websites of candidates. First, we examine the supply side. What kind of candidates launched websites? What opportunities for political information and voter engagement were provided online? What characterizes candidates that excelled in providing information and engagement features? Second, we focus on the demand side: how did voters respond to candidate sites? As to the second significant web feature, the candidate selectors, we focus on the demand side. Two questions regarding the demand side are posed. To what extent did voters believe that they received important information from candidate websites and the candidate selectors with regard to voting preferences? Which voters stressed the importance of these web features as sources of information?

Theoretical underpinnings

Inasmuch as the internet has the potential to offer a more affordable and manageable campaign ground for smaller political actors, as for fringe party candidates, scholars have argued that the internet may balance the inter-actor strengths on the electoral arena (e.g. Davis 1999). This scenario is often referred to as the *equalization* of electoral competition online (e.g. Margolis *et al.* 2003). However, some scholars have argued that there is no reason to expect major overhauls of electoral competition due to the use of the web (e.g. Gibson *et al.* 2003). Major parties, and candidates fielded by these parties, are still better off than their smaller counterparts at making their websites known to voters as they are more likely to make the news and have more money to spend on traditional campaigning (Margolis *et al.* 2003). Both of these factors are useful in raising voter interest and know-ledge of their websites. In addition, even if web campaigning currently requires comparably little investment, there is no guarantee that the costs will remain low. Over time, the costly expertise of full-time web designers and managers could probably become an essential element of the successful online campaigns (Gibson *et al.* 2003). Hence, this no-change scenario – "politics as usual" – is usually referred to as the *normalization* of online poli-tics (Margolis and Resnick 2000).

As for theories about online electoral competition, scholars have sug-gested the internet as a cause for both major and minor changes in citizens' political activity. First, the internet is claimed to activate increasing numbers of citizens politically. Accordingly, this line of thought has been labeled the *mobilization* theory (Norris 1999). A central argument is that online political activity differs on several important aspects from traditional political activity and might thus help to activate new types of citizens, those that are typically inactive or less active in "offline" politics. Political activity online is easily accessible and relatively low cost. Finally, when compared to traditional forms of political activity, internet activity has the potential to offer opportunities for interactivity that are desired by citizens (Norris 1999). Indeed, these advantageous features could raise the participation rate among those citizens who perceive traditional political activity as excessively time consuming, demanding, and unsatisfying.

However, many scholars have been skeptical about the mobilizing effects of the internet (Davis 1999; Norris 1999, 2001). One important distinction between the internet, as it was commonly used in 2004, and traditional mass media is that the former requires the user to seek political information actively whereas, for instance, television exposes the passive viewer to polit-ical information. Thus, only the politically interested citizens would search for political web content (Davis 1999; Norris 2001). From this perspective, the internet is a new channel for the politically motivated to do what they have always done. Citizens lacking political interest would also lack the motivation to seek political websites. Another dimension of this *reinforcement* argument is based on the unequal access to the internet by the population, which follows certain socio-economic patterns. Evidence suggests that the typical political internet user is a young, highly educated male with a relat-ively high income (Norris 2001). According to Bimber (1999), the demo-graphic characteristics of online politically active citizens resemble those of citizens already engaged in offline politics – age being the notable exception.

In the light of the Finnish context, the scenarios of normalization versus equalization and mobilization versus reinforcement generate a number of issues relevant to our analysis. What is the significance of the fact that three major parties dominate the Finnish political stage:[2] did the major party candidates utilize the web better, both in terms of quantity and quality, than the candidates representing minor and fringe parties? The fact that Finnish campaigning is deregulated and cost intensive – candidates can purchase as much advertising time as they want on commercial television channels – would give minor and fringe candidates, with fewer financial resources, a good rationale to go online. Moreover, the fact that the Finnish candidates rely on support groups that are relatively independent of the parties may level the online playing field for the candidates representing minor and fringe parties. On the demand side, then, what is the significance of long-term high levels of internet penetration in Finland; does the reinforcement argument still hold? Or did the candidate sites and the candidate selectors of the news media in the 2004 elections, due to a less skewed socioeconomic distribution of internet access, attract and mobilize a new and varied strata of voters?

Research design

The identification of candidate websites within the Finnish electoral web sphere was done between mid-April and mid-May 2004. Primarily, in locating these sites, exhaustive candidate listings published on the parties' websites were used. We found that 123 of the 227 nominated candidates had their own websites. In content-analyzing the candidates' websites, we used a random sample of 62 sites. The coding of the sites, which took place during a period of two weeks ending three days prior to the election, followed the coding frame constructed for the Internet and Election Project, noting the presence or absence of site features. As indicated in the research questions, we theoretically assume that two broad practices are central in the candidates' web campaigns: online, the sites, on the one hand, provide information and, on the other hand, contribute to the political engagement of site visitors (cf. Schneider and Foot 2006). These practices, we suggest, are associated with particular site features. For this reason, ten of the coded features are termed "information features": biography, endorsements, issue positions, speeches, calendar/list of events, comparison of issue positions, information about campaign process, information about voting process, images, audio/video files. Moreover, we distinguish ten "engagement features": contact producer, join/become a member, get e-mail, donate, contribute to forum, engage in offline distribution, send links, provide public support statement, download e-paraphernalia, and sign up to volunteer.

In examining the demand side, we analyzed survey data from the research project "Changes in Finnish TV Election Campaigns" led by Professor Tom Moring at the University of Helsinki. Within this project, *Gallup Finland* has conducted a series of panel surveys since 1992 measuring voter behavior and preferences just before and immediately after the elections. The survey conducted after the 2004 Finnish EP elections, which we use here, comprised 1362 respondents. The respondents are demographically representative of people living in Finland but with one exception: all respondents have internet access from their homes. This is because *Gallup Finland*, in order to facilitate electronic participation in the panel, has equipped those respondents that lacked internet access with home computers. However, given the high internet penetration in Finland, a majority of the respondents already had household access to the internet. For the purpose of this chapter, this situation, which, to some extent, exaggerates the use of internet, can be considered more of an asset than a problem. This unique sample portrays, as Moring and Mykkänen (2005) have emphasized, an ideal population that makes it possible to explore how a representative sample of voters act when they have internet access from their homes. Moreover, given the high Finnish internet penetration, the panel's representativity with respect to internet use is not a critical issue. This is especially true for the younger age groups that are today predominantly regular internet users.

Findings

Candidates' web campaigning

Initially, we turn our attention to the proportion of candidates having a website according to four variables related to candidate characteristics.[3] We find these variables intriguing within the theoretical framework of this chapter. First, we pay attention to the role of the size of the candidate's party by examining the web presence of candidates representing major, minor, and fringe parties.[4] Second, we examine whether incumbent candidates were more likely than challenger candidates to have websites. It has been argued that incumbency could be advantageous since sitting politicians generally have greater access to governmental resources to assist with website development and maintenance (Gibson and McAllister 2003). On the other hand, Kamarck (2002: 87) notes that challengers may "feel that they have to try harder and thus become more likely to adopt new technologies." Third, we look at the distribution of male and female candidates having websites. Gibson and Römmele (2003: 7) have noted that the great keenness of female candidates to use the new medium, observed by other research, "offers something of a challenge to the 'politics as usual' thesis." Finally, we examine the propensity to go online of different age cohorts of candidates. At least in Finnish elections, young candidates tend to have less financial and organizational resources for mounting expensive offline campaigns; thus they have a good rationale to go online. Moreover, as young people generally show greater familiarity with and interest in the internet, young candidates should be more likely than older candidates to launch websites (Gibson and McAllister 2003). Table 3.1 presents our findings.

Table 3.1 shows that candidates representing fringe parties had websites to a considerably lower degree than the major and minor party candidates. Almost all candidates running for major parties campaigned online. A

Table 3.1 The online propensity of different kinds of candidates

Sub-groups of the candidates		Total number of candidates	Number of candidates having a website	Share of candidates having a website
Party size	Major	60	58	97%
	Minor	75	59	79%
	Fringe	92	11	12%
Incumbency	Incumbent (MEP or MP)	24	24	1.00*
	Challenger	203	104	51%
Gender	Male	141	73	52%
	Female	86	55	64%
Age	18–24	22	14	0.6*
	25–34	27	19	0.7*
	35–49	75	46	61%
	50–	96	49	51%

Note
* The size of the total *n* is considered too small to warrant percentage representation; the reported figure is a ratio (the number of candidates having a website divided by the total number of candidates).

surprisingly large share of minor party candidates maintained websites. Incumbency mattered, too. Whereas all incumbent candidates were online, just over half of all challengers opted for web campaigning. Concerning gender, the new technology was not a predominantly male concern. Quite the opposite was the case: the female candidates set up websites to a higher degree than did the male candidates. Finally, we note that more than half of all the candidates in the four age groups ran sites. However, taken together, the two youngest groups were more engaged in web campaigning that the two older groups (67 percent and 56 percent online respectively).

In order to test the independent influences of the variables related to candidate characteristics on having a website, we ran a logistic regression model. The model is presented elsewhere (Carlson and Strandberg 2005: 197). The incumbency variable was not included in the model; it did not meet the requirements of sampling adequacy. As was expected, the model showed that representing a major party was the most significant predictor for being online. Running for a minor party had a significant impact, too. In addition, the model revealed an independent age effect; the youngest candidates (aged 18 to 24) were more likely to go online than older candidates. Finally, when age and party size was accounted for, gender was not a significant predictor for having a website.

Once online, what kind of information features and engagement opportunities were commonly prevalent on the candidate sites? Concerning information, the sites frequently provided biographies (95 percent of the sites), issue positions (63 percent), calendars (79 percent) and images (98 percent). These features are, except for calendars, "brochure-ware," that is, standard features of traditional campaign brochures (Kamarck 2002). It is noteworthy that few sites provided endorsements (5 percent) or comparisons of issue positions (2 percent). Moreover, beyond offering the possibility to contact the site producer (84 percent), engagement opportunities in general were infrequently provided.[5]

Were there, nevertheless, a significant minority of sites that provided a wider variety of information and engagement opportunities? To explore this question, a two-step cluster analysis of the sampled candidate sites was carried out in order to classify the sites into homogeneous sub-groups according to the extent to which they provided various information and engagement features.[6] In building the cluster model, two variables were used: (a) an additive information index assigning one point for the presence of each of the ten "information features" on a site; (b) an additive engagement index assigning one point for the presence of each of the ten "engagement features." The automatic clustering algorithm identified three clusters; see Table 3.2.

First, looking at the mean scores on the two indexes, Table 3.2 shows that the candidates provided, on average, fewer than two engagement features, and slightly more than four information features. Second, Table 3.2 reveals significant differences between the groups of sites. The most important finding is that sites in the third cluster provide more information features and more engagement opportunities than sites in the other clusters. The question that now arises is whether the candidates whose sites belong to cluster III differ systematically from the other candidates regarding background characteristics. Table 3.3 answers this question using the earlier presented variables related to candidate characteristics. Given the small number of cases, we opted for 2×2 cross-tabulations.

Table 3.2 Three clusters of candidate websites: mean index scores

Clusters	N	%	Information index (0–10)	Engagement index (0–10)
Cluster I	16	26	2.88	1.31
Cluster II	30	48	4.17	1.20
Cluster III	16	26	5.13	3.06
Combined	62	100	4.08	1.71

Notes
ANOVA: the clusters differ significantly on both the information index ($p < 0.001$) and the engagement index ($p < 0.001$). Pair-wise *post hoc* Bonferroni tests: Cluster I and II, cluster II and III and cluster I and III differ significantly on the information index ($p = 0.000$ in each comparison). As to the engagement index, cluster I and III and cluster II and III differ significantly ($p < 0.001$ in both comparisons).

Table 3.3 Characteristics of candidates with websites belonging to the clusters

Characteristics		Cluster I and II		Cluster III	
		n	Ratio	n	Ratio
Gender	Male	24	0.5	11	0.7
	Female	22	0.5	5	0.3
	Total	46		16	
Age	18–34 years	13	0.3	1	0.1
	35+ years	33	0.7	15	0.9
	Total	46		16	
Candidate's party	Major party	20	0.4	9	0.6
	Minor/fringe party	26	0.6	7	0.4
	Total	46		16	
Incumbency	Incumbent (MEP or MP)	9	0.2	5	0.3
	Challenger	37	0.8	11	0.7
	Total	46		16	

The contingency tables compiled in Table 3.3 revealed no statistically significant differences between the clusters at the 5 percent level (Fisher's exact test). Nonetheless, bearing in mind that being young was a significant predictor of candidates' online presence, we find it interesting to note that the ratio of young candidates – those one would have expected to be more web savvy – is lower in the third cluster than in the other clusters. This difference is almost statistically significant ($p = 0.06$). In general, with due caution because of the small number of cases, the findings in Table 3.3 tentatively point in the direction of the normalization hypothesis: websites of candidates belonging to a major party and being male are more common in the third cluster of sites.

Impact on voters

How, then, did the Finnish voters respond to the candidate websites in the election campaign? Moreover, were the candidate selectors, which provided the voters with a possibility to compare the issue positions of the candidates, important to the electorate? In the aforementioned survey, respondents were asked to estimate the extent to which different sources provided information that contributed to their voting decision.[7] Relatively few voters said that they obtained "very much" or "quite much" information to support their voting decision from candidate sites (9 percent) or candidate selectors (14 percent).[8] A larger share stressed the importance of information in the newspapers (26 percent) and in television news and current affairs programs (28 percent).

What, then, characterizes voters that attached great importance to web sources? The regression models presented in Table 3.4 address this question. The six predictors used in the models are demographic characteristics commonly associated with political behavior: gender, education, age, income, class, and urbanity (see Norris 2003). The two models show a similar pattern. First, gender, class (white-collar position), and income proved insignificant in both models. Second, among the voters estimating that they obtained very much information to support the voting decision from candidates' sites and candidate selectors, there is a significant bias towards younger voters (18–34 years), those that are better educated and those living in urban milieus. Notably, the youngest voters (18–24 years) are most likely to stress the importance of the two web sources.

Table 3.4 Voters who estimated receiving important information from candidate websites and candidate selectors: logistic regression models

	Candidate sites[a]			Candidate selectors[b]		
	B	SE	Exp(B)	B	SE	Exp(B)
Gender	0.346	0.275	1.413	−0.097	0.227	0.908
Basic education	0.919*	0.320	2.507	0.819**	0.257	2.267
Age						
18–24	2.743**	0.471	15.532	2.317**	0.432	10.148
25–34	1.250**	0.390	3.490	1.576**	0.332	4.835
35–49	0.612	0.393	1.845	1.135**	0.320	3.112
Income (€)						
20,001–35,000	0.126	0.385	1.134	−0.295	0.340	0.745
35,001–50,000	−0.214	0.404	0.807	−0.163	0.334	0.850
>50,000	−0.388	0.424	0.678	−0.095	0.339	0.910
Class	0.025	0.378	1.026	0.109	0.291	1.115
Urbanity	1.938*	0.737	6.947	1.076*	0.414	2.934
Constant	−5.533			−4.118		

Notes
a Nagelkerke $R^2 = 0.224$; % correct = 91.4; $n = 811$.
b Nagelkerke $R^2 = 0.196$; % correct = 86.9; $n = 809$.
* $p < 0.01$.
** $p \leq 0.001$.

The dependent variable in the two models is a dichotomy that represents answers to the question of whether respondents estimated that they obtained "very much" or "quite much" information to support their voting decisions from the source in question: 1 = yes; 0 = no. Predictors – gender: male (1), female (0); basic education: general upper secondary education (1), not general upper secondary education (0); age: reference category (0) = 50 years or older; income: reference category (0) = less than €20,001; class: white collar (1), not white collar (0); urbanity (using the *Statistics Finland*'s established classification): lives in urban or semi-urban municipality (1), lives in a rural municipality (0).

Table 3.5 Importance attributed to information sources by age groups

Source	Age groups			
	18–24 years	*25–34 years*	*35–49 years*	*50–69 years*
Candidates' websites	38%	17%	7%	4%
n	48	175	285	405
Candidate selectors	43%	25%	15%	5%
n	49	174	285	403
Television news/current affairs programs	31%	33%	22%	29%
n	52	178	289	409
Newspapers	27%	23%	23%	30%
n	52	178	289	409

Notes
The percentages are of respondents that estimated that they obtained "very much" or "quite much" information to support their voting decisions from the source in question.

Table 3.4 suggests that young voters in particular found online candidate information valuable in making up their voting decisions. Table 3.5 more closely examines to what extent different age groups estimated that they received important information to support the voting decision from candidates' sites and candidate selectors. In order to observe whether the young voters attached more importance to the new media sources than to conventional sources in this respect, two traditional media are included in the table.

Table 3.5 confirms the central results of the regression analysis. Thus, the share that attaches much importance to the online information is considerably larger in the young voter cohorts than in the older age groups. Strikingly, the percentage of voters within the youngest age group (ages 18 to 24) that believe they obtained very much information from the web sources is larger than the share that emphasizes the value of information found in traditional media sources.

Conclusions

To return to the theoretical framework and questions elaborated earlier, what conclusions can be drawn? Regarding the candidates' online presence in the EP election, the web did not level the playing field for fringe party candidates. Whereas only 12 percent of the fringe party candidates campaigned online, 97 percent of the major party candidates had websites. Moreover, in predicting the candidates' web presence, a logistic regression model revealed a strong independent effect for representing a major party.

Obviously, these findings support the normalization thesis. One reason for this, beyond the usual explanations for the normalization thesis, could be the Finnish EP election itself, where only 14 seats were contested and where the entire country served as a single voting district. Certainly, many of the 227 candidates, particularly candidates fielded by fringe parties, knew from the start that they did not stand a chance to win a seat in this election and, thus, campaigned half-heartedly. Another finding, that only half of all challenger candidates ran websites whereas every incumbent candidate did so, adds some support to the normalization thesis, too. Apparently, challengers had a more difficult time putting together the resources needed for establishing websites. In addition, among the challengers there were, of course, many non-competitive candidates that did not take pains with web campaigning.

Some findings concerning the propensity to go online, nevertheless, are inconsistent with the normalization thesis. First, a strikingly large majority (79 percent) of the minor candidates campaigned online. In addition, representing a minor party was a significant factor in predicting whether the candidates had websites. Second, the logistic regression showed that young candidates (ages 18–24), who in Finland often struggle in offline campaigns due to lack of resources, are more likely to adopt web campaigning than their older counterparts. Finally, although the share of female candidates campaigning on the web was higher than the share of male candidates doing the same (64 percent and 52 percent respectively), the logistic regression revealed that gender itself had no independent effect on having a website. Hence, internet campaigning was not "a man's world."

Examination of information and engagement provision features on the candidate sites suggests that, in general, most sites resembled traditional brochures rather than new interactive, innovative campaign outlets. Apparently, many candidates still viewed the web as a second-order medium and merely followed the current fashion of going online. Indeed, a survey conducted by *Suomen Lehdistö*, a periodical of the Finnish Newspapers Association, showed that one-third of the EP candidates deemed the web as being an unimportant tool in their campaigns, but they nonetheless launched sites because, in their words, "it was a must" (Kuikka 2004). Thus, in a situation where the candidates are still relatively uncertain of how efficient this new communication tool is, they tend to imitate their counterparts' moves and thus maintain an image of professionalism and being modern; what is done online is apparently regarded as less important than simply being online.

Nonetheless, some findings concerning the information and engagement features merit attention. First, the high prevalence of issue positions on the candidates' websites is remarkable considering that Finnish candidates usually stress image characteristics rather than positions on issues in offline political advertising (e.g. Carlson 2001). Second, the cluster analysis showed that a reasonably large minority of the candidate sites (26 percent) provided a wide range of information and, particularly, engagement features. Then again, considering this finding in the light of the normalization versus equalization debate, the notion of "politics as usual" is not challenged: The candidates launching these sites were not primarily running for minor or fringe parties, nor were they primarily young or female.

Regarding the demand side, then, our data provides some limited support for the mobilization thesis, especially for younger and less traditionally active voters. First, though, it should be stressed that relatively few voters indicated that they obtained very much information to support their voting decisions from the candidate sites. The percentage of voters attaching importance to the candidate selectors was somewhat higher. For the Finnish voters in general, websites and the candidate selectors were not nearly as important sources for political information as traditional news media, particularly newspapers and television. However, looking beyond the general picture, three interesting trends emerge. First, young Finnish voters seemed to place greater importance on the candidate sites and the candidate selectors found in the news media when deciding how to vote than they did on newspapers or television. Second, not only young voters but voters of middle age attached importance to the selectors. Third, the analysis does not confirm that having a high income, being employed in a white-collar position, or being male are associated with stressing the importance of political websites. Thus, demographically, the political web users did not fully resemble the citizens known to be politically active offline (Bimber 1999; Norris 2001). Theoretically, these findings are intriguing as they may, in time, lend support to the mobilization thesis.

Acknowledgments

This chapter is based on an article published in *Information Polity* (Carlson and Strandberg 2005). We wish to thank Toril Aalberg, Nicholas Jankowski, Wainer Lusoli, Steven Schneider, and the two anonymous reviewers of *Information Polity* for commenting on different versions of this text. The data on the Finnish voters was kindly provided to us by Professor Tom Moring, University of Helsinki; we are solely responsible for any shortcomings in the results and conclusions reported here.

Notes

1 For instance, the selector provided by the state-owned Finnish Broadcasting Company, YLE, attracted approximately 60,000 different visitors during the last week of the campaign. All in all, the selector was visited by more than 100,000 different citizens during the period 1–13 June 2004 and by more than 80,000 in May 2004 (figures provided by researcher Eija Moisala at YLE's Audience Research unit). About four million Finns were eligible to vote in the 2004 EP elections.
2 The Finnish party system is relatively fragmented. The core consists of three parties that capture the majority of the votes (60–70 percent) in national

parliamentary elections. Besides these major parties, there is a group of minor parties as well as numerous fringe parties.

3 As the entire country served as a single voting district, constituency character-istics (e.g. level of urbanity and internet penetration) is not considered here.

4 The classification is based on a categorization by Norris (2003): "Major parties" are those with more than 20 percent of all seats in the national parliament; "minor parties" are those with more than 3 percent but less than 20 percent of the seats; "fringe parties" are those that lack at least 3 percent of the elected members of the parliament.

5 The prevalence of all observed information and engagement features is reported elsewhere (Carlson and Strandberg 2005).

6 Clustering criterion: the Akaike information criterion; cluster distance measure: log-likelihood.

7 Hence, the analysis can only shed light on the role of information provided on the web to the voters; we cannot examine in what ways candidate sites engaged voters. Then again, the content analysis suggests that candidates in general pro-vided more information features than engagement opportunities.

8 Only the 928 respondents that reported voting in the election were asked to estimate the information value of different sources. This explains the uneven age distribution in Table 3.5: there was a low youth voter turnout in the election.

References

Bimber, B.A. (1999) "The Internet and citizen communication with government: does the medium matter?," *Political Communication*, 16, 4: 409–428.

Carlson, T. (2001) "Gender and political advertising across cultures: a comparison of male and female political advertising in Finland and the US," *European Journal of Communication*, 16, 2: 131–154.

Carlson, T. and Strandberg, K. (2005) "The European parliament election on the Web: Finnish actor strategies and voter responses," *Information Polity*, 10, 3–4: 189–204.

CVCE (Centre Virtuel de la Connaissance sur l'Europe) (2004) "The electoral systems in the member states of the European Union applicable to European elections of June 2004." Available online: www.ena.lu/?doc= 21022&lang=2 (accessed 28 March 2005).

Davis, R. (1999) *The Web of Politics: The Internet's Impact on the American Political System*. New York: Oxford University Press.

Eurostat. (2005) "Internet usage by individuals and enterprises 2004," *Statistics in Focus: Industry, Trade & Services*, 18/2005. Luxembourg: Office for Official Publica-tions of the European Communities.

Gibson, R.K. (2004) "Web campaigning from a global perspective," *Asia Pacific Review* 11, 1: 95–126.

Gibson, R.K. and McAllister, I. (2003) "Does cyber campaigning win votes? Online communication in the 2001 Australian election," paper presented at the annual conference of the American Political Science Association, Philadelphia, PA, August.

Gibson, R.K., Margolis, M., Resnick, D., and Ward, S.J. (2003) "Election cam-paigning on the www in the USA and UK: a comparative analysis," *Party Politics*, 9, 1: 47–75.

Gibson, R.K. and Römmele, A. (2003) "Regional web campaigning in the 2002

German federal election," paper presented at the annual conference of the American Political Science Association, Philadelphia, PA, August.

Isotalus, P. (1998) "Euroehdokkaat kotisivuillaan," in P. Isotalus (ed.), *Kaveri vai peluri: poliitikko mediassa*, pp. 153–171. Jyväskylä: Atena.

Kamarck, E.C. (2002) "Political campaigning on the internet: business as usual?," in E.C. Kamarck and J.S. Nye Jr (eds), *Governance.com: Democracy in the Information Age*, pp. 81–103. Washington, DC: Brookings Institution Press.

Kuikka, T. (2004) "EU-parlamenttiin pyritään sanomalehtien ja Internetin kautta," *Suomen Lehdistö*, 74, 5: 6–8.

Margolis, M. and Resnick, D. (2000) *Politics as Usual: The Cyberspace "Revolution."* Thousand Oaks, CA: Sage.

Margolis, M., Resnick D., and Levy, J. (2003) "Major parties dominate, minor parties struggle: U.S. elections and the Internet," in R.K. Gibson, P.G. Nixon, and S.J. Ward (eds), *Political Parties and the Internet: Net Gain?*, pp. 53–69. London: Routledge.

Moring, T. and Mykkänen, J. (2005) "Voter choice and political mediation: net-based candidate selectors in Finnish elections," paper presented at the annual conference of the International Communication Association, New York, NY, May.

Norris, P. (1999) "Who surfs? New technology, old voters and virtual democracy," in E.C. Kamarck and J.S. Nye Jr (eds), *Democracy.com? Governance in a Networked World*, pp. 71–98. Hollis, NH: Hollis Publishing.

Norris, P. (2000) "The Internet in Europe: a new north–south divide?," *Harvard International Journal of Press Politics*, 5, 1: 1–12.

Norris, P. (2001) *Digital Divide? Civic Engagement, Information Poverty and the Internet Worldwide*. Cambridge: Cambridge University Press.

Norris, P. (2003) "Preaching to the converted? Pluralism, participation and party websites," *Party Politics*, 9, 1: 21–45.

Schneider, S.M. and Foot, K.A. (2006) "Web campaigning by U.S. presidential primary candidates in 2000 and 2004," in A.P. Williams and J.C. Tedesco (eds), *The Internet Election: Perspectives on the Web in Campaign 2004*, pp. 21–36. Lanham, MD: Rowman & Littlefield.

4 The Netherlands

Party and candidate websites during the 2004 European Parliament election campaign

Renée van Os, Carlo Hagemann, Gerrit Voerman, and Nicholas W. Jankowski

Introduction

In election campaigns held in the Netherlands since the 1960s and before the "Age of the Internet," television served as the primary campaigning vehicle for political parties and candidates. Inasmuch as television programming involves news personalities "whom viewers can see, like and trust," scholars believe this medium has stimulated the rise of personality-centered politics (Gunther and Mughan 2000: 21). By increasingly focusing on politicians and reducing political content to short video clips and sound bites, television has been criticized for contributing to the simplification of politics (Pels 2003). The emergence of the internet, however, has fostered hopes for a new type of politics based on abundant information, rational deliberation, and active participation (Rash 1997; Selnow 1998). Campaign activities on the web, it was argued, would be able to address the substantive issues of elections to a greater degree than has been possible on television. Various authors address aspects of this expectation and the related transformation in political campaign strategies in the Netherlands (see, for example, Kleinnijenhuis *et al.* 1998; Tops *et al.* 2000). During Dutch national election campaigns in 1998, 2002, and 2003, this transformation seemed well underway. Most political parties had developed special websites for party leaders, along with party-oriented sites. In addition, many candidates constructed their own websites (Voerman 2000; Voerman and Boogers 2005).

Taking these changes into account, election campaign scholars in both Western Europe and North America have addressed four types of transformation in political communication: increased personalization and professionalization of campaigns, greater awareness of competitive pressures, and increased importance of communication via the media (Blumler and Kavanagh 1999; Bowler and Farell 1992). As early as the mid-1970s, Agranoff (1976) remarked that these features reflect a new style of campaigning. Today, political parties in the Netherlands increasingly incorporate this new style into their campaign strategies.

In this chapter, we focus on the first two transformations noted above. First, we consider the *professionalization* of the 2004 European Parliament election campaign of Dutch political parties and candidates, and examine the role the web played within the overall campaign strategy. Second, we investigate the *personalization* of the election campaign, defined by Bowler and Farell as "campaign communication focused on the candidate rather than the party" (Bowler and Farell 1992: 3). Findings are culled from two sources of data: a content analysis of party and candidate websites related to the 2004 EP election campaign, and interviews with party representatives from five of the political parties involved in this campaign. The general question addressed in this chapter is: *what strategies – in terms of professionalization and personalization – did Dutch political parties and candidates employ during the 2004 EP election campaign, and how did these political actors incorporate the web into these strategies?*

Professionalization and personalization of election campaigns

Political parties are generally considered central actors in representative democracies. Throughout the western world – and most certainly in the Netherlands – the societal embedding of political parties is eroding. Partially as a consequence of a wider process of individualization in past decades, traditional loyalties to collective and civic organizations (for example, political parties, churches, labor unions) have decreased. In understanding this phenomenon, Putnam refers to the "decline of social capital" (Putnam 1995: 67). Symptoms of the crisis facing parties include: declining membership; declining participation of party members (for example, volunteering during election campaigns); declining party identification; the rise of protest parties; and increasingly lower turn-out at elections (Mair and Van Biezen 2001; Voerman 2004). At the same time, parties can no longer count on support from friendly media. "Media logic" has replaced a "partisan logic" – rather than favoring certain parties, media now tend to pursue their own interests in political reporting (Gulati *et al.* 2004). To an increasing extent, in the Netherlands as elsewhere, the media rather than political parties set the political agenda (Blumler and Kavanagh 1999). Moreover, the fragmented media landscape increases the difficulty for parties to reach undecided voters.

As their social and electoral environment becomes more unpredictable and complicated, parties are inclined to professionalize their organizational structures and activities, in particular the organization and conduct of election campaigns. This has involved changes on the part of parties in several respects. First, within campaign communication, there is a move towards strategic thinking and formulation of clear, central campaign messages for target groups (Farell and Webb 2000). In order to mobilize (new) voters, parties direct campaign messages not only in an undifferentiated manner at the entire electorate, but also narrowcast messages to specific audiences. The larger parties in the Netherlands started to systematize and professionalize their electoral market segmentation approaches during the 1990s. This included the growing use of electoral research and marketing techniques (through, for example, opinion polls and focus groups), incorporation of new information and communication technologies, and the increasing reliance on external professional consultants such as spin doctors, opinion pollsters, market researchers, and fund raisers (Adriaansen and Van Praag 2005; Farrell *et al.* 2001; Kolodny and Dulio 2003; Kriesi 2004; Van Praag and Penseel 1998). As a result, campaigns have become more capital intensive. Also, the internal organization of parties has changed. Because of the stronger need of national coordination and control of the election campaign, a more centralized, managerial structure has developed as compared to the former, predominantly amateur party organizations (Mancini 1999). Consultants and other specialists are becoming more influential in directing electoral campaigns, and their influence sometimes matches that of the party leaders.

Engaging citizens in party communication and providing them with information are thus central characteristics of professionalization of the campaign, and it is argued that the internet can help parties in achieving these objectives. First, with its capacity to make essentially unlimited quantities of information available very rapidly and inexpensively, the internet is becoming an important source of information for voters (Ward *et al.* 2003). This is particularly the case for the already committed voters – researchers suggest that communication via the internet is mainly directed at such audiences (Bimber and Davis 2003). Both parties and voters recognize this potential of websites. Research among users of party websites during the 2002 and 2003 parliamentary election campaign in the Netherlands reported that about 80 percent of the respondents visited political sites primarily to obtain campaign-related information. These voters searched mainly for information on party policies (nearly 50 percent); considerably fewer voters (10 percent) searched for information about candidates (Voerman and Boogers 2005). Bimber and Davis found that for the U.S. presidential campaign in 2000, visitors to candidate websites believed that their knowledge of the campaign increased. Attitudes regarding the candidates improved, and there was a correlation between perceived knowledge gain and this more positive attitude (Bimber and Davis 2003).

The second characteristic of the professionalization of campaigns is the use of party websites to obtain information regarding voters' perceptions, thereby engaging them in the campaign. This is considered essential in terms of political marketing. Scholars note the high potential provided by the interactive qualities of the internet, which can become "a primary tool in providing the direct link in communicating citizen preferences to politicians" (Ward *et al.* 2003: 16). By seeking feedback through online opinion polls and surveys, and offering opportunities to discuss policy issues with politicians or other party members and/or voters (through interactive forums, online discussion groups, etc.), party leadership can be informed on a continuous basis. Moreover, parties can use the internet for resource mobilization, recruiting campaign volunteers, and soliciting financial donations.

At the same time, election campaigns are becoming more personalized. The growing importance of media presentation, especially on television, and the increasing volatility of voters, has increased the importance of candidates in the electoral process – not only in presidential but also in parliamentary systems (King 2002; Ohr and Oscarsson, forthcoming 2008). Meanwhile, political parties in this process are transforming into facilitators rather than principle actors. Some parties presently function as centers for communicating party leaders' positions and perspectives (Mancini 1999). This emphasis on the politician and their personality has consequences regarding the content of the campaign, "with image and style increasingly pushing policies and substance aside" (Farrell and Webb 2000: 122). The "personalization of politics" also entails a growing electoral relevance of the individual characteristics and qualities of politicians, including information about their private lives (Pels 2003).

This trend towards stronger candidate-centered campaigns is evident in the Netherlands. For example, during the 2002 and 2003 Dutch parliamentary elections nearly all party leaders had personal websites, which focused entirely on themselves. The format of these sites had much in common, including presentation of publications by party leaders, media reports about them, speeches they had given, campaign agendas, and media ads in which they had been featured. Some party leaders included a personal touch by providing biographical information in text, images, and sound (Voerman and Boogers 2005) and by maintaining a weblog. These trends in the increasing professionalization and personalization of campaigns constitute the theoretical backdrop for our investigation of Dutch political parties and candidates during the 2004 EP election.

Research design

This study is organized around the two central concepts *professionalization* and *personalization* of the campaign. We examined two sources of data: a content analysis of party and candidate websites conducted prior to the 2004 EP election in June 2004, and interviews held with party representatives from five of the parties involved in the campaign. The content analysis followed the guidelines developed for the Internet and Elections Project.[1] These guidelines involved gathering the addresses of sites prepared by a wide range of political actors that were expected to be involved in the 2004 EP election campaign. We consulted several sites during a two-month period prior to the election: search engines, politically oriented portals, and other depositories of website addresses. Stratified samples ($n = 100$) were drawn from the identified sites within five actor categories: candidates, political parties, governmental sites, NGOs and labor unions, and other actors. In addition to the above sampling procedure, all other identified party and candidate sites were included in the study; three party sites were coded after the election from the archive of political websites of the Documentation Centre for Dutch Political Parties (DCDPP).[2]

In this chapter, we only report on the party ($n = 22$) and candidate ($n = 51$) sites. These sites were coded for the presence of 32 features, including candidate endorsements, comparison of candidate platforms, speeches, audio and video files, contact information, recruitment of volunteers, voter registration, online newsletters, discussion forums, and provision of promotional materials such as banners and screensavers. After the election, an additional analysis was conducted on 48 of the 51 candidate sites archived by the DCDPP with regard to features related to "personalization" of the campaign.

We then constructed indexes for two clusters of features: *information provision* and *citizen engagement*.[3] These indexes are considered indicators of the sophistication of websites and the professionalization of the online campaign. Two characteristics of parties were included in the analysis: party orientation, and party size (determined by the number of seats won in the most recent elections for both the Dutch and European Parliaments).[4] Four characteristics of candidates were included: political position, size and orientation of the party with which the candidate is affiliated, and the gender of the candidate.[5] Since all parties and candidates with websites were included in the analysis, statistical procedures such as analysis of variance (ANOVA) were unsuitable and not presented.

We conducted face-to-face interviews with the communication managers of five Dutch political parties: Christian Democratic Party (*Christen Democratisch Appèl*, CDA), Social Democratic Party (*Partij van de Arbeid*, PvdA), Liberal Party (*Volkspartij Voor Vrijheid en Democratie*, VVD), Green Party (*GroenLinks*), and Social Liberal Party (*Democraten '66*, D66) in the six-week period preceding the EP election. The main goal of the interviews was to obtain information on how political parties were professionalizing their campaign activities and how they dealt with trends towards personalization of political campaigns. Specifically, our objective was to explore the role the internet played in these strategies. The interviews were semi-structured and topics were presented in general terms, inviting respondents to elaborate. For this study, interview transcripts were examined with regard to comments on the concepts professionalization and personalization. Aspects related to professionalization discussed during the interviews included strategic thinking about communicating political issues, target groups, employment of external consultants, and centralization. Aspects related to personalization discussed during the interviews included the maintenance of sites, and personalization of the campaign, as reflected on sites.

Results

In this section, we compare the presence of features on Dutch candidate and party sites in the 2004 EP election campaign. Comparison of these features is organized along two characteristics considered indicators for the level of sophistication of the sites and the professionalization of the online campaign: campaign information and opportunities for civic engagement they provided.

As Table 4.1 shows, all parties participating in the 2004 EP election maintained websites. In addition, some parties had produced specific campaign-oriented websites. Also noted in Table 4.1 is an overview of the percentage of candidates having produced personal campaign sites from the total number of candidates officially participating in the 2004 EP election ($n = 276$). Almost a fifth (18 percent) of the candidates produced personal campaign sites.

Professionalization of the campaign

Table 4.2 details the nine information-related features present on party and candidate websites. Mean scores for the index *information provision* has been calculated for party and candidate sites. Variation is evident between party and candidate sites. Of the maximum score of seven, party sites scored 3.68 ($n = 22$), compared to 3.18 ($n = 51$) for candidate sites. Party sites provided more diverse types of information.

Features involving comparison of positions on campaign issues (COMPARE) and provision of information on the campaign (INFOC) were essentially absent. Comparison of party and candidate positions on issues is not common in Dutch political culture, which continues to reflect aspects of a consensus democracy (Van Praag 1992). Dutch political parties have traditionally maintained respectful relations; negative campaigning, such as engaging in personal attacks on candidates, remains unusual in Dutch elections.

Features on which most party and candidate sites scored relatively high are provision of biographical information (BIO), maintaining a calendar of campaign events (CALENDAR) and provision of lists of campaign issues (ISSUE). Party sites included, slightly more frequently than candidate sites, calendars of events (CALENDAR) (0.86 vs 0.69) and issue lists (ISSUE) (1.00 vs 0.84). There was considerable difference in the proportion of sites with audio or video files (AV). While half of the party sites offered these files, less than a fifth of the candidate sites offered audio and video.

The mean scores on the information provision index were compared to the two independent variables for political parties – party size as measured by number of seats in the national and European Parliament, and party orientation. New parties in the 2004 EP election scored relatively low on the information provision index: 3.11, in comparison to 4.50 for parties with

Table 4.1 Dutch parties and candidates with websites during the 2004 EP election*

Party	Number of sites produced by party	Party orientation	Party size	Number of candidates on list (n = 276)*	Candidates with websites (%)
CDA	3	Center	Major	30	50
PvdA	2	Left	Major	18	22
VVD	1	Right	Major	30	57
GroenLinks	1	Left	Mid-range	17	24
CU-SGP**	3	Right	Minor	20	15
D66	1	Center	Mid-range	14	43
SP	1	Left	Minor	29	0
Democratisch Europa	1	N.C.***	New	8	0
Leefbaar Europa	1	N.C.	New	7	0
Partij v/h Noorden	1	N.C.	New	30	0
Nieuw Rechts	1	Right	New	25	4
Europa Transparant	1	N.C.	New	20	0
LPF	2	Right	New	7	14
Partij voor de Dieren	1	N.C.	New	19	0
Respect Nu	1	N.C.	New	2	0
Total	22			276	18

Notes
* The numbers of candidates per party is based on the official list of parties and candidates distributed by the Dutch government prior to the 2004 EP election.
** CU-SGP: combination of parties *Christen Unie* (CU) and *Staatkundig Gereformeerde Partij* (SGP).
*** N.C. = not classifiable.

Table 4.2 Information features on websites of EP candidates and parties – proportion scores

Features present on site	Candidate* (n = 51)	Party (n = 22)	total (n = 73)
AV	0.18	0.50	0.27
BIO	0.92	0.86	0.90
CALENDAR	0.69	0.86	0.74
COMPARE	0.00	0.00	0.00
ENDOR	0.22	0.14	0.19
INFOC	0.02	0.00	0.01
INFOV	0.04	0.23	0.10
ISSUE	0.84	1.00	0.89
SPEECH	0.29	0.09	0.23

Notes
* Proportion of scores for candidate and party sites.

Abbreviations and descriptions of site features
AV: audio or video files.
BIO: biography/history of party/candidate.
CALENDAR: a calendar/list of events with election-related events.
COMPARE: comparison of issue positions of candidates/parties.
ENDOR: endorsements for a candidate/party.
INFOC: information about the electoral campaign process.
INFOV: information about the voting/registration process.
ISSUE: list of issue positions held by party/candidate site.
SPEECH: speech by candidate or party representative.

mid-range indicators of party size (see Table 4.3). In terms of party orientation, right-wing parties scored lower than did left-wing parties on this index (3.33 vs 4.40).

For candidates, information provision index means were compared on four independent variables: political position, size and orientation of the party to which the candidate was affiliated, and gender of the candidate. Sites for those candidates affiliated with minor parties scored higher on the index (4.00) than mid-range party candidates (3.46) and major party candidates (3.00) did. This relation suggests that the smaller the party with which a candidate is affiliated, the more sophisticated the candidate's site is in terms of information provision. No similar pattern was found for orientation of the party with which candidates were affiliated.

Another indicator of site sophistication is how much opportunity for civic engagement they provide. Table 4.4 provides an overview of the presence of 11 engagement-related features on party and candidate websites. These data indicate a high score for both party and candidate sites offering contact information (CONTACT: 0.90). Other engagement-related features were present much less frequently, especially on the candidate sites. For example, the possibility for site visitors to post statements supporting the political

Table 4.3 Information provision and citizen engagement; mean index scores for party and candidate websites

	Information provision (mean index scores)	Citizen engagement (mean index scores)
Parties		
Party size (*n* = 22)		
Major party	3.83	5.17
Mid-range party	4.50	7.00
Minor party	4.00	5.33
New party in EP 2004	3.11	5.11
Party orientation (*n* = 22)		
Left-wing party	4.40	7.20
Center party	3.75	4.25
Right-wing party	3.33	5.00
Not classifiable	3.50	5.75
Candidates		
Political position of candidate (*n* = 36)		
MEP	3.47	1.94
Elected political position	3.38	2.63
Appointed political position	2.73	2.00
Party size, affl. candidate (*n* = 51)		
Major party	3.00	2.23
Mid-range party	3.46	2.38
Minor party	4.00	3.33
New party in 2004 EP	–	–
Party orientation, affl. candidate (*n* = 51)		
Left wing	3.15	2.15
Center	2.95	2.57
Right wing	3.67	1.89
Not classifiable	3.16	2.28
Sex (*n* = 51)		
Male	3.19	2.23
Female	3.50	2.50

actor (PUBSUP) was low on both candidate and party sites. This is unsurprising, as this action is uncommon in Dutch political culture. As for the other five engagement-related features, party sites scored much higher on the features DONATE, FORUM, GETMAIL, JOIN and OFFDIST than did candidate sites. For example, party sites often contained a forum or other communication space (FORUM) more frequently than did candidate sites: 0.68 compared to 0.20. Party sites score much higher on the feature JOIN (the possibility to become members of the site organization) than did candidate sites: 0.86 versus 0.16. In Dutch elections, candidates still campaign mainly within the structures provided by political parties. Candidates do not recruit party members, nor do they generally motivate citizens to join

Table 4.4 Engagement features on websites of EP candidates and parties – proportion scores

Features present on site	Candidate* (n = 51)	Party (n = 22)	Total (n = 73)
CONTACT	0.88	0.95	0.90
DONATE	0.04	0.59	0.21
EPARA	0.20	0.36	0.25
FORUM	0.20	0.68	0.34
GETMAIL	0.33	0.55	0.40
JOIN	0.16	0.86	0.37
OFFDIST	0.18	0.64	0.32
PUBSUP	0.08	0.18	0.11
REGIS	0.00	0.00	0.00
SENDLINKS	0.24	0.23	0.23
VOLUNTEER	0.04	0.45	0.16

Notes
*Proportion of scores for candidate and party sites.

Abbreviations and descriptions of site features
CONTACT: information provided on site for contacting party or candidate.
DONATE: donations are encouraged or enabled through site.
EPARA: e-paraphernalia available on the site (e.g. banners, posters, screensavers).
FORUM: possibility to participate in online forum or other communication space.
GETMAIL: possibility to sign up to receive e-mail from party/candidate.
JOIN: opportunity for visitors to join, or become member of party.
OFFDIST: site encourages offline distribution of election-related materials.
PUBSUP: site encourages/enables visitors to make a public statement supporting a political actor.
REGIS: site enables visitors to register to participate in election.
SENDLINKS: site enables a visitor to send a link from this site to a friend.
VOLUNTEER: site encourages visitors to volunteer for the electoral camping.

their own campaigns; such affairs are coordinated at the level of the political parties. As a result, the score for the feature VOLUNT was low for candidates (0.04) as compared to parties (0.45).

Variation between party and candidate sites regarding citizen engagement in the campaign becomes particularly prominent when the means of the scores for the index *citizen engagement* are calculated. Party sites scored 5.50 (*n* = 22), compared to 2.33 (*n* = 51) for candidate sites. In other words, party sites provided more opportunity for citizens to become engaged in the campaign. For parties, means on the index *citizen engagement* were compared to the party size and orientation variables. Medium-sized parties scored relatively high on the index as compared to larger parties (7.00 vs 5.17). Similarly, left-wing parties scored relatively higher on the index than right-wing parties did (7.20 vs 5.00); see Table 4.3.

For candidates, means on the index citizen engagement were compared on four independent variables: political position, size and orientation of the party with which the candidate is affiliated, and sex of the candidate. As indicated in Table 4.3, there are variations between the candidates. Female candidates scored slightly higher on the index than did male candidates (2.50 vs 2.23). Candidates affiliated with minor parties also scored relatively high (3.33 vs 2.23 for major party candidates), a pattern that corresponds to the information provision index discussed earlier. Also, elected politicians scored higher than the other categories of political positions (2.63 vs 1.94 for MEPs). Finally, right-wing candidates, who scored the highest on the information provision index, scored lowest on the index for citizen engagement (1.89 vs 2.57 for mid-range parties).

Findings from the interviews with party representatives reinforced the above observations regarding the centrality of information provision on party and candidate websites. Although small differences existed between the ways in which the parties communicated with the electorate, all parties viewed information provision as their primary concern. Parties saw informing the public as an important persuasive technique, especially when they communicated with the electorate using the internet. The party representatives emphasized that, since websites have the possibility to give an almost unlimited amount of space for information, they are a potentially important source of information for the visitors. The communication manager of the Christian Democratic Party (CDA) considered this to be in line with the behavior of voters visiting websites. He believed citizens are primarily interested in political positions; party candidates are only of secondary concern. However, party representatives seemed aware of the limitations of the information function of websites. For example, they acknowledged the risk of "information overload," which could result in losing visitors' attention.

In contrast to the perceived crucial role of information provision, party representatives considered site interactivity in election campaigns of less importance. The CDA, for example, was reticent about including such features on its website for two reasons. First, implementation of interactive features such as discussion forums is very demanding of party staff. Second, a discussion forum is interesting only if it provides additional value for site visitors. Other parties shared these reservations, although some implemented limited interactive features. For the Social Liberal Party, D66, site interaction was viewed as mainly valuable for intra-party opinion formation. However, on the most basic level, every party experienced the effects of interaction via the internet. More than ever before, candidates receive e-mail correspondence from voters. This new channel of direct communication is valuable for information provision, but also for receiving political signals from constituents.

Personalization of the campaign

In this section, we report on various indicators of personalization. As we already mentioned, almost a fifth (18 percent) of the total number of candidates produced personal campaign sites (see Table 4.1). Considerable variation existed, however, between the candidates from different political parties: candidates of the parties already residing in the European Parliament since 1999 or earlier (the first seven parties in Table 4.1) more frequently produced personal campaign sites than candidates affiliated with political newcomers at the European level. Nearly a third (31 percent) of the candidates affiliated with the established parties produced personal sites.

When looking at the first category in more detail, candidates of the mainstream, right-of-center parties – CDA (50 percent), D66 (43 percent), and VVD (57 percent) – more frequently produced personal campaign sites than candidates affiliated with the mainstream left-wing parties; PvdA (22 percent) and the Green Party (*GroenLinks*) (24 percent). Candidates affiliated with the smaller party, CU-SGP (15 percent), scored lower. Candidates affiliated with the new, minor Eurocentric parties such as *Democratisch Europa*, *Nieuw Rechts*, and *Europa Transparant* produced no personal campaign sites. For most other parties, as we noted earlier, at least the party leader or main party representative had a personal campaign site. An important exception to this trend was the Socialist Party (SP). SP, being relatively influential in Dutch national politics, provided extensive information about its candidates on the party website.

Differences found between the established parties regarding candidates having personal campaign sites, may have been related to ideological issues. Left-wing parties such as PvdA, *GroenLinks* and SP, which traditionally have a stronger collective party identity, probably had more reservations supporting high levels of personalized campaigns. This is in direct contrast to other parties that were more oriented towards principles emphasizing individuality, such as VVD and D66.

Comments made by a representative of the Social Democratic Party (PvdA) suggest a general reluctance in supporting individual candidate campaign sites: "we have an instruction manual on how to maintain a website, but it is purely technical. If candidates call us for support, we will give them that, but we do not maintain websites for them." In contrast, the liberal party VVD developed a standardized template in accordance with the party's house style that candidates could adapt as they wished for their own campaign sites. This way the party could retain uniformity in party communication and, at the same time, candidates could campaign on a more individual basis. All other parties expressed the intention to strive for uniformity in campaign communication; some parties mentioned this as the reason for hesitating to decentralize party communication. As expressed by the representative of the Green Party (*GroenLinks*), "experiences from the past – a 'jungle' of different sites – led us to centralize the party website. Visitors experience this new situation as more quiescent." Moreover, the Green Party representative did not see the benefit of different sites for their candidates. She considered this is a waste of effort since most people go the main party site and not to the site of individual candidates.

Table 4.5 Personalization of candidate websites per party – proportion scores

Party*	Personal bio**	Political weblog	Personal weblog	Personal photo
CDA (14)	0.21	0.29	0.00	0.07
PvdA (4)	0.25	0.25	0.00	0.00
VVD (17)	0.41	0.47	0.18	0.35
GroenLinks (3)	0.00	0.33	0.33	0.33
CU-SGP (3)	0.33	0.33	0.33	0.33
D66 (6)	0.17	0.33	0.17	0.17
LPF (1)	1.00	1.00	1.00	0.00
Total (48)	0.31	0.38	0.15	0.23

Notes
* Number of candidates with website per party noted in parentheses.
** Proportion of scores for candidate sites (DCDPP Archive).

Table 4.5 summarizes analysis conducted after the election on 48 candidate sites included in the Documentation Centre for Dutch Political Parties (DCDPP) internet archive of the 2004 EP election. Four features, suggesting the personalized nature of candidate websites, were coded as being present or absent: (1) a life history or biography, (2) a weblog with political content, (3) a weblog with personal content, and (4) personal photographs. It appears that Dutch candidates in the 2004 EP election did not score particularly high;y with regard to personalization of the campaign. About a third of the candidates' sites provided some sort of personal information: 0.31 of the candidates offered biographies on their sites; 0.38 provided weblogs with only political content; 0.15 offered weblogs with personal content in addition to political content; and 0.23 provided personal photographs. Candidates from the Liberal Party (VVD) scored relatively highly on all three features in comparison to candidates from CDA, PvdA, and *GroenLinks*.

Summary and conclusions

In this chapter, we were concerned with the following general question: *What strategies did Dutch political parties and candidates employ during the 2004 EP election campaign, and how did these political actors incorporate the web into these strategies?* The findings presented focus on the theoretical concepts *professionalization* and *personalization* of campaign strategies, using two sources: a content analysis of party and candidate websites, and interviews with party representatives from five of the political parties involved in the 2004 EP election campaign.

In terms of campaign professionalization, candidate sites provided relatively more information-related features in comparison to opportunities for citizens to become engaged in the campaign. Party sites scored higher on both indicators of professionalization. Most party representatives mentioned providing information on party websites as an important concern, more so than promotion of citizen engagement (through, for example, hosting discussion forums on the sites). Almost all sites, however, provided a minimum level of citizen engagement offering contact information and the opportunity to join the respective political parties. The observed variation in website content – information provision versus citizen engagement – provided by parties and candidates can be seen as a form of strategic political communication. A "professionalized" campaign for these actors seems to include providing information that can help citizens make a voting decision, but encouraging a minimal level of citizen engagement.

We found some variations between the parties' sites and candidates' sites. Left-wing parties, for example, had more sophisticated sites than right-wing parties did. Parties with a mid-range number of seats in Parliament had the most sophisticated sites, compared to both large and small-size parties. At the candidate level, those affiliated with minor parties had relatively sophisticated sites and scored relatively higher on both the indexes measuring information provision and citizen engagement. Perhaps these candidates were attempting to compensate for the less sophisticated character of their parties' sites. Candidates of the major parties did not seem to apply a similar strategy and scored the lowest on both indexes. A possible explanation for this difference may be that the European Parliament election is usually considered a "second order" electoral event and is less important to both parties and candidates.

In a more general sense, the professionalization of political campaigns extends beyond employment of spin doctors and other campaign advisors. It signals a changing "state of mind" among political parties and involves strategies for reaching target groups and defining electoral as well as policy goals. In the Netherlands, political parties are in the process of gradually transforming previously member-centered associations into more professionalized institutions. This transformation process is in part a result of the decreasing number of active party members. One of the results of this change is the implementation of websites in campaigns. The main objective of these websites is to reach target groups and achieve the electoral goals set through providing information on party activities and policy. Engaging citizens in political discourse on these websites is undeveloped and apparently viewed as less important.

In terms of personalization, nearly a fifth of the candidates officially participating in the 2004 EP election in the Netherlands incorporated personal websites into their campaign strategies. However, there was variation between candidates of the parties who were already members of the European Parliament and those candidates affiliated with political newcomers at the European level. Among the established parties, most representatives at the European level (MEP since 1999 or earlier) maintained personal sites. Across the board, about a third of the candidates affiliated with established parties maintained sites. Examination of nearly all candidate sites revealed that only about a third of the candidates with sites provided some form of personal information about themselves. This suggests a reluctance or at least indifference on the part of a large majority of the candidates to share personal information on the web-based components of their campaign strategies.

Taken together, these findings suggest that the 2004 EP online campaign in the Netherlands did not reflect a high degree of personalization – although compared to previous elections the number of candidate sites is increasing. The campaign in 2004, however, was still primarily party centered. The Dutch political system, which is still largely party based, may partially explain this approach. For a long time intra-party competition was almost non-existent.[6] For example, rallies and television debates during (EP) electoral campaigns are mainly held among party leaders. The political style of Dutch campaigns tends to limit personal information sharing by candidates. Information on the political positions of candidates is generally regarded as more important to voters than information about candidates' personalities and most certainly more important than political discourse involving the public on their websites. The relatively low interest among parties and society as a whole in the European Parliament elections may also contribute to this still-limited degree of personalization of the campaign – in comparison to the trend evident in other countries and in other election campaigns in the Netherlands.

It should be stressed that these indications of a transformation are based on an investigation of parties and candidates during a relatively unimportant electoral event. Other events with more at stake and involving a greater number of political actors may produce different findings. In other words, this study merits replication during other campaigns. Through such replication, it may be possible to ascertain more precisely the nature and extent of professionalization and personalization encompassing Dutch electoral politics.

Notes

1 webarchivist.org.
2 www.archipol.nl.
3 Features are included in the respective indexes where the score in total collection is greater than 1. On the basis of this criterion, three features were excluded: COMPAR, INFOC, REGIS. The index *information provision* (maximum score: seven) was constructed by summing the following features: AUDVID, BIO, CALEN, ENDOR, INFOV, ISSPOS, SPEECH. The index *citizen engagement* (maximum score: ten) was constructed by summing the following features: CONTACT, DONATE, EPARA, FORUM, GETMAIL, JOIN, OFFDIST, PUBSUP, SLINKS, VOLUNT.
4 Independent variables for parties:

   ORIENT Political orientation of party (left, center, right, not classifiable).
   SIZE   Size of party, based on percentage of votes received by party in NL election 2003/EP 1999 election (collapsed into four categories: major (>15 percent), mid-range (5–15 percent), minor (<5 percent), and new party in EP 2004 election).

As concerns SIZE: comparing the categories of election results for the two elections noted, almost no differences were found; only one party (D66) was placed in different categories for the two elections; in this case, the results for the EP 1999 election were given priority (mid-range category).

5 Independent variables for candidates:

POST   Indication of political position (MEP, other elected position, appointed political position)

SEX   Sex of candidate (male/female)

ORIENT   Political orientation of the party the candidate is affiliated with

SIZE   Size of the party the candidate is affiliated with

6 This situation may change in the near future inasmuch as most parties have recently adopted new procedures for selecting party leaders and candidates.

References

Adriaansen, M. and Van Praag, P. (2005) "Hoe systematisch zijn partijen op zoek naar hun kiezers? Politieke doelgroepmarketing bij de verkiezingen van 2002," *Jaarboek 2004 Documentatiecentrum Nederlandse Politieke Partijen*. Groningen: Universiteitsdrukkerij.

Agranoff, R. (1976; 2nd edn) *The New Style in Election Campaigns*. Boston: Halbrook Press.

Bimber, B. and Davis, R. (2003) *Campaigning Online*. Oxford: Oxford University Press.

Blumler, J.G. and Kavanagh, D. (1999) "The third age of political communication: Influences and features," *Political Communication*, 16, 3: 209–230.

Bowler, S. and Farell, D. (1992) "The study of election campaigning," in S. Bowler and D. Farell, (eds), *Electoral Strategies and Political Marketing*. London: Macmillan.

Farell, D. and Webb, P. (2000) "Political parties as campaign organizations," in R.J. Dalton and M.P. Wattenberg (eds), *Parties without Partisans. Political Changes in Advanced Industrial Democracies*, pp. 102–128. Oxford: Oxford University Press.

Farrell, D., Kolodny, R., and Medvic, S. (2001) "Parties and campaign professionals in a digital age. Political consultants in the United States and their counterparts overseas," *The Harvard International Journal of Press/Politics*, 6, 4: 11–30.

Gulati, G.J., Just, M.R., and Crigler, A.N. (2004) "News coverage of political campaigns," in L.L. Kaid (ed.), *Handbook of Political Communication Research*, pp. 237–256. Mahwah, NJ: Lawrence Erlbaum Associates.

Gunther, R. and Mughan, A. (2000) *Democracy and the Media: A Comparative Perspective*. Cambridge: Cambridge University Press.

King, Λ. (2002) "Do leaders' personalities really matter?," in A. King (ed.), *Leaders' Personalities and the Outcomes of Democratic Elections*, pp. 1–43. Oxford: Oxford University Press.

Kleinnijenhuis, J., Oegema, D., De Ridder, J., and Ruigrok, P.C. (1998) *Paarse polarisatie. De slag om de kiezer in de media*. Alphen aan den Rijn: Samson.

Kolodny, R. and Dulio, D.A. (2003) "Political party adaptation in US congressional campaigns," *Party Politics*, 9, 6: 729–746.

Kriesi, H. (2004) "Strategical political communication: mobilizing public opinion in 'audience democracies'," in F. Esser and B. Pfetsch (eds), *Comparing Political Communication: Theories, Cases and Challenges*, pp. 184–212. Cambridge: Cambridge University Press.

Mair, P. and Van Biezen, I. (2001) "Party membership in twenty European democracies 1980–2000," *Party Politics*, 7, 1: 5–21.

Mancini, P. (1999) "New frontiers in political professionalism," *Political Communication*, 16, 3: 231–245.

Ohr, D. and Oscarsson, H. (forthcoming 2008) "Leader traits, leader image and vote choice," in K. Aarts, A. Blais, and H. Schmitt (eds), *Political Leaders and Democratic Elections*, Oxford: Oxford University Press.

Pels, D. (2003) "Aesthetic representation and political style: re-balancing identity and difference in media democracy," in J. Corner and D. Pels (eds), *Media and the Restyling of Politics*, pp. 41–66. London: Sage.

Putnam, R.D. (1995) "Bowling alone: America's declining social capital," *Journal of Democracy*, 6, 1: 65–78.

Rash, W. (1997) *Politics on the Nets: Wiring the Political Process*. New York: W.H. Freeman.

Selnow, G.W. (1998) *Electronic Whistle-Stops: The Impact of the Internet on American Politics*. Westport: Praeger.

Tops, P.W., Voerman, G., and Boogers, M. (2000) "Political websites during the 1998 parliamentary elections in the Netherlands," in J. Hoff, I. Horrocks, and P.W. Tops (eds), *Democratic Governance and New Technology. Technologically Mediated Innovations in Political Practice in Western Europe*, pp. 87–99. London: Routledge.

Van Praag, P. (1992) "The Netherlands: the 1989 campaign," in S. Bowler and D.M. Farell (eds), *Electoral Strategies and Political Marketing*, pp. 144–162. London: MacMillan.

Van Praag, P. and Penseel, S. (1998) "Politieke marketing in de verkiezingscampagne van 1998," *Jaarboek 1998 Documentatiecentrum Nederlandse Politieke Partijen*, pp. 95–120. Groningen: Universiteitsdrukkerij.

Voerman, G. (2000) "Elektronisch folderen: de digitale campagne," in P. Van Praag and K. Brants (eds), *Tussen beeld en inhoud*, pp. 193–213. Amsterdam: Het Spinhuis.

Voerman, G. (2004) "De politieke partij tussen staat en maatschappij," in J.W.M. Engels and M. Nap (eds), *De ontwikkeling en toekomst van de vertegenwoordigende democratie*, vol. 37–60. Rijksuniversiteit Groningen: Deventer.

Voerman, G. and Boogers, M. (2005) "Digtaal informeren en personaliseren: De opkomst van de website als campagne-instrument," in K. Brants and P. Van Praag (eds), *Politiek en media in verwarring: De verkiezingscampagne in het lange jaar 2002*, pp. 195–217. Amsterdam: Het Spinhuis.

Ward, S., Gibson, R., and Nixon, P. (2003) "Parties and the Internet: an overview," in R. Gibson, P. Nixon, and S. Ward (eds), *Political Parties and the Internet: Net Gain?*, pp. 11–38. London: Routledge.

5 Slovenian online campaigning during the 2004 European Parliament election

Struggling between self-promotion and mobilization

Tanja Oblak and Katja Željan

Introduction

More than any other communication media, the internet as a new communication technology holds promise to enhance democracy and change traditional one-way processes of political communication. To some, the political role of this new communication tool is considered a "great transformation" (Grossman 1995: 149) enabling citizens to search for relevant political information, to contact government officials, and to exchange views on political topics; it also stimulates participation in the political arena and facilitates voting. Klein calls the internet "a powerful technology for grassroots democracy," which, "by facilitating discussion and collective action by citizens, strengthens democracy" (quoted in Davis 1999: 20). Moreover, Schwartz (quoted in Davis 1999: 20) refers to the internet as "the most powerful tool for political organizing developed in the past fifty years."

Not everyone takes such an optimistic position about what this communication technology can do to enhance political processes and electoral practices (Bimber 1998; Hill and Hughes 1998; Davis 1999; Kamarck 1999; Jankowski and Van Selm 2000; Wilhelm 2000). The opponents of so-called mobilization theories coinciding with reinforcement theories of new communication technology's political role suggest that the internet – no matter how large the democratic potential – will be mainly used by those already politically interested and motivated and will therefore only reproduce existing political communication and power relations.

If new media like the internet and its prominent web sphere are truly "technologies of freedom" (de Sola Pool 1983), it is valuable to question to what extent they contribute to democratic political culture, political mobilization, and finally, to the notion of active citizenship. From this perspective it seems that the embodying of democratic potentials that modern communication technologies offer very much depends on the way such technologies are used by different political actors and especially by political parties, that is, whether they emphasize participatory aspects or focus on the possibilities for top-down information dissemination and broad monitoring of public opinion (Rommele 2003); whether they stimulate citizen engagement in political communication by so-called "mobilizing structures" (McAdam *et al.* 1996); and, lastly, whether they contribute to what is usually called "deliberative" (Fishkin 1991), "discursive" (Dryzek 2000), "substantive" (Kaldor and Vejvoda 1999), or "strong" (Barber 1984) democracy.

Most of the recent empirical studies that focus on how different election campaigns were attributed to the web sphere discuss the potential novelties and changes in political participation within the American context (Benoit and Benoit 2000; Foot and Schneider 2002; Gibson *et al.* 2002; Stromer-Galley 2004). In this chapter we offer a case study of online election campaign in Slovenia. Looking at the "traditional" media landscape within the Slovenian context, one could argue that election campaigns at the local or national levels are often homogeneous.

The main research concern of this study is to explore which democratic potentials of the internet were employed and which were neglected by the main political actors during the first European Parliament election campaign in Slovenia in 2004. Following the notion that the internet is a special political tool providing many political practices through the web on different levels (Davis and Owen 1998), we provide a comparison between informative, interactive, and mobilizing features of online political communication during the election campaign for the European Parliament. In the conclusion, we reflect on the findings in light of the legalist and pluralist models of digital democracy (Van Dijk 2000). This chapter illustrates how various political actors used the internet for political purposes during this politically new electoral event and considers the kind of political communication and democratic culture favored. In other words, we explore in this chapter whether the internet has realized its potential to turn the politics of representation toward the politics of participation (Sassi 1996).

Before presenting an analysis of the data, we survey what is already known regarding the Slovenian online political sphere. Other studies (Oblak 2000, 2003) support the idea that development, at least in the context of the Slovenian web sphere, has stopped on the second level of the so-called "information ladder" (Bellamy and Raab 1999: 158). Internet-based communication tools are used primarily for accessing public information, whereas more direct elements of participation between political institutions and Slovenian citizens is only being implemented slowly.

As additional context for the analysis, specific characteristics of the 2004 election campaign for European Parliament are presented. When official voting results were announced, it was generally agreed in the media that a "calm, non-haughty, but still active election campaign strategy" (Dravinec 2004: 2) was a key to success in this election. Based on a recently published analysis (Kustec-Lipicer 2005), this election was, at least within the Slovenian context, presented as a preliminary match for parliamentary elections scheduled to be held a few months later. For this reason, the 2004 EP campaign was not limited to EU topics and problems. In contrast, debates and discussions within the campaign were strongly integrated into another venue that for many political actors was more important.

The findings to be presented suggest that the Slovenian web sphere during European Parliament election campaign can best be characterized as an *"underdeveloped" political space, favoring the strongest among the political actors – political parties.* In other words, we consider whether contemporary liberal democracy in Slovenia has succeeded in engaging citizens in the European Parliament elections through the web, or whether the process reflects what Kuzmanić (2002: 123) calls Slovene "partitocracy."

The internet as a political tool: high penetration, great expectation, low interaction

In Slovenia great strides have been made during the past decade to get the population online and introduce citizens to the possibilities of the internet. As Norris (2001) reports, Slovenia belongs to those few smaller European nations, including the Netherlands, Belgium, Switzerland, and Estonia, with above-average internet use. A recent report on information society indicators (SIBIS [Statistical Indicators Benchmarking the Information Society] Project 2003) suggests that Slovenia is the leading country among the "Newly Associated States" of the European Union regarding information society technology developments. Slovenia surpasses many EU Member States in this regard. For example, the percentage of experienced internet users (persons using the internet for more than two years) is above the EU average. According to the SIBIS report, 40 percent of users in Slovenia prefer to complete their income tax returns via the internet; in the EU-15 only 29 percent report doing this.

Although internet penetration is high in Slovenia, this aspect has not resulted in extensive public discourse and engagement between political actors (traditionally considered political authorities) and those excluded from such public discourse in the past. This conclusion emerges from previous studies focusing on the role of the internet in stimulating political mobilization and active citizenship (Franz 2003; Oblak 2000, 2003). According to Lubecka (2000), such technologically supported dialogue between politically powerful actors and ordinary citizens was hardly the case in many countries of the so-called New Europe, including Slovenia. Franz (2003), for example, notes that the internet does not play an important role in the political communication between Slovenian citizens, political parties, and government, while Oblak (2000) points out that wide dissemination of political participation through the internet is hardly evident. Slovenian internet users mostly use the web for writing to media or for publicly expressing their own political opinions, but they rarely use it for writing to politicians or state institutions (Oblak 2000: 126).

The use of the online forms for public and political participation can be explained through users' perceptions of the democratic character of the internet. What kind of attributes do Slovenian internet users give, for instance, to new forms of opinion expression (public forums) and new possibilities for making contacts with political actors or new practices of standard political activities (signing petitions, mobilizing supporters, etc.)? A small-scale study of internet users (Oblak 2000)[1] suggests how some possibilities might positively affect more use of the internet for public participation. Slovenian internet users, those who primarily participate in politics online, positively perceive the potential of the internet. In other words, the users who believe that the internet is much more effective for personal involvement in public discussions, for opinion self-expression, for finding other people with similar opinions, and for knowing what other think about public issues, are using the web more often and more actively for political purposes. However, users perceive that the possibility of making contacts with and getting feedback from political actors, such as members of parliament, of government, or of other political institutions, as the most difficult challenge. In practice, this challenge goes unrealized, and this has a negative impact on users' online political participation.

An earlier analysis of Slovenian governmental websites from 2002 revealed that the majority of ministries have pages on the web in order to transmit information to the population – information, news, or public relations messages – and only a small fraction of the sites are constructed to receive information (Oblak 2003: 102). Even in the informational sense, the pages are rather limited in value: a small number of web pages enable access to records of government meetings; even less access is made available to information on governmental decisions.

One reason the democratic potential of modern technology is not used to its full extent is the almost non-existent political communication among citizens and the state. Although Slovenia faced huge changes in the political decision-making processes in the last decade, Lubecka (2000) explains that "the process of democratization of the whole ex-Communist bloc is hindered by private interests, passivity, lack of experience in self-organization, opportunity for economic activity, and even less experience in self-government, in political activity and in citizenship" (p. 36).

EP elections online: a new communication challenge for Slovenian political actors

How then was the Slovenian online sphere perceived and used by the main political actors, who were struggling in a new political environment formed through the event of the first elections for EP? One characteristic deserving attention is *the potential of interactivity*. Interactivity as a term is usually accompanied with optimistic visions derived from the idea of "hyper-modernity," in which a set of values prevails, like higher individual freedom of choice, greater self-control, and higher political independence.[2] In spite of its frequent use, interactivity it is not easy to define. Interactivity has been considered an implicit feature of computer-mediated communication from the very beginning. For the purposes of this study we circumvent nuances in the concept suggested by various authors (e.g. Rafaeli 1988; Van Dijk 1996; Oblak 2005) and lean on the more general formulation proposed by Dahlgren (1996).

In Dahlgren's opinion (1996: 64), where interactivity is understood in reference to new technical relations between production and reception of mediated contents, the potential for interactivity is especially relevant in the context of its probable effects: the greater chance for interactivity offers the audience free choice in selecting the media content they want and thus limiting the productive power of traditional content providers and its impact on selecting the news. The notion of interactivity also enables new possibilities for a more direct connection between media producers or journalists and their publics. In this sense interactivity plays a significant role as a *stimulating factor for social interaction and integration* that can consequently change the existing power relations. The question remains: to what extent is interaction between different actors through the web taking place online?

Another advantage of computer-mediated communication is its potential for intensifying more interactive, two-way communication flows between citizens, representatives, political actors, and members of civil society movements. However, the selection of such potentials is not generally present in the minds of web producers, nor is it commonly used by web users. The degree of different online interactive tools, like e-mail contacts, chat rooms, or forums, is strongly determined by decisions taken by web producers and also by selected strategies that content providers apply to their web presentations.

Another important factor within online election campaigns is the provision of access to diverse content through the web. Informational diverse content presented from different positions is mainly an indicator of a more heterogeneous political platform, in which citizens have access to different opinions, perspectives, and visions. Foot and Schneider (2002), in their analysis of the American election in year 2000, stressed the importance of independent websites, which represent an important novelty on a structural level of a political system. Among the traditional and already-known political actors emerge new forms for political participation and education about politics, new places for political speech, patterns for mobilization of voters, and new ways for candidate promotions.

Setting the online election agenda in Slovenia

What was happening in the Slovenian online political world when the election campaign for the EP was at its peak? Which political actors determined the structure of the event? Three analytical steps represented a framework

Table 5.1 Identified Slovenian online producers in the election campaign for the European Parliament in 2004

Website producers	Number of identified online sites
State institutions	70
Media	31
Political parties	22
Portals	17
NGOs	12
Educational institutions	3
Political analysts	3
Religious organizations	3
Companies	3
Citizens	3
Candidates	1
Total	168

for data collection about the structure and political activities within the Slovenian online space in the period of the EP election campaign. At the first step we identified the proper websites just one month before the elections.[3] The purpose of this phase was to identify as many websites as possible, which were related to the elections in the EP, and to define a database on their basis. In the second step a systematic sampling of identified web addresses was taking place.[4] With the help of a detailed analysis of conceptual relations between the selected sites, a general sample of 168 websites was identified, of which a final sample of 94 sites was then selected and weighted according to the group of political actors to which a single site belonged.[5] In a final survey, we identified 11 different website producers (see Table 5.1).

The data collected in the identification phase of the project suggest that the Slovenian election web sphere was largely dominated by institutions of public and political authority and mass media. The most visible part in the election campaign was played by state institutions (70 identified pages), followed by the media (with 31 websites), political parties (22 sites), portals (17 sites), and non-governmental organizations (NGOs) (12 sites). Sites producers classified as "other producer types" were minimal and included corporations, citizens, and educational, religious, and professional organizations. And there was just one candidate in this campaign with a personal homepage.

Slovenian EP election campaign

Although Slovenia participated in the European Parliament election for the very first time in 2004, the overall impression about the campaign could best be described as being "silent," "uninteresting," and, most of all, "non-prominent."[6] The campaign for the EP in Slovenia, in which 91 candidates on 13 different lists competed for seven out of 732 seats in the European Parliament, officially started on 14 May 2004, four weeks prior to the election. A very recent study on the Slovenian first election campaign for European Parliament (Kustec-Lipicer 2005) offers findings that merit attention. One part of a broader research project was mainly concerned with the behavior of political parties during the campaign. When discussing the parties' strategies and organizational aspects, some authors revealed that the Slovenian campaign for EP elections should be understood as a part of more "central and local campaigns" (Kustec-Lipicer 2005: 14). This central and local nature of the campaign was intensified by the use of more traditional, conservative forms of making contacts with voters: the most effective practices turned out to be personal, face-to-face gatherings with people and mobilization of the local party's sympathizers (Deželan 2005: 62).

Political actors online: state, parties, media, and NGOs

Media cover during the election campaign could be regarded as a pure and conservative one; it was mostly focused on national policies of Slovene political parties and mainly presented in traditional newspapers and TV programs. Judging from different studies (Kustec-Lipicer 2005; Bačilja and Chan 2004; Zadnikar 2005), most of the Slovenian political parties strategically "deviated" themselves from the potential offered by new communication media like the internet. On the other hand, the traditional media only partially covered the topics that were directly related to parties' political information and strategies of EP elections. What then, was happening online? To what extent was the internet used as a political tool in this first election campaign in Slovenia? Additionally, how well was the internet explored as a medium for disseminating relevant information about the election to different publics?

The internet represents a challenge for common understandings of political participation and communication about politically-relevant information. As Davis and Owen (1998: 113) note, the internet enables four political functions. First, the internet offers easier access to news and political information. Second, the internet enables new ways for making contacts with public officials and citizens. Third, it opens up new places for political discussions. Finally, the web supports new ways for opinion gathering and for analyzing the public climate.

In Table 5.2 we focus on the first political function of the internet and present findings regarding the kind of information content available online by four major online producers in the Slovenian election campaign for the European Parliament. Political parties seem to have the highest proportion of selected information categories. In comparison to other actors, political parties had the most visible position in offering access to candidates'

Table 5.2 Type of online content and information about the election for the EP on selected websites in Slovenia

Online producer	Number of cases	Election content	Election agenda	Information about campaign	Information on voting procedure	Issues positions	Speeches	Issues comparison
State institutions	30	1	0.10	0.63	0.60	0.13	0	0
Political parties	21	1	0.71	0.81	0.19	0.95	0.62	0.19
Media	10	0.90	0.30	1	0.50	0.10	0	0
NGOs	8	1	0.25	0.50	0.75	0.63	0	0

attitudes and to party programs (0.95), followed by detailed information about events related to the election (0.71), and access to candidates speeches (0.62). Political parties thus contributed to more diverse election content and provided election-related information. The role of state websites was in this sense very different: due to their presence online, citizens could mainly access information about the procedure of election campaign (0.63) and the general voting strategy (0.60). Government websites, therefore, played the role of legally regulating the actors responsible for procedural matters.

With regard to information provision, media and NGOs provided a weaker and less convincing image. None of these websites offered comparisons of different views between the candidates. Still, they played an important educational role: NGOs mostly offered access to information about voting procedures (0.75), whereas media covered information about the election campaign. However, it is difficult to conclude that NGOs and media completely recognized their role as mediators between the political elite and citizens.

Interaction and communication dimensions

If we follow Davis and Owen's (1998) understanding of the internet as a political tool, then its next role is to provide new mechanisms for more intensive relationships between politicians and citizens. In this context we might expect the use of the more interactive potentials of the web, especially those aspects that allow discussion and deliberation between citizens. In this section we focus our attention on the evaluation of those communicative practices within online election campaigns that could offer grounds for further interaction between selected political actors and citizens who visit online sites. What interactive possibilities did government, political parties, NGOs, and media provide, and to what extent did they provide them?

Based on data presented in Table 5.3, we can assume that the offer of interactive communication tools was in general quite homogenized. None of the selected web producers is outstanding as an important "debater" with online visitors. In addition, similar to already-mentioned studies, the online campaign for the EP showed that communicative and discussion elements of online space do not have much relevance within the Slovenian public context.

The most present mechanism for interaction was the possibility of contacting the website provider; here, media and political parties have the highest proportion (1 and 0.95), followed by state institutions (0.90), and finally by NGOs' web producers (0.88). Surprisingly low opportunity during the election campaign was realized in simple engagement features, such as getting e-mail from site, information or offline distribution of election material. Along with political parties, NGOs were the major providers of additional public space for discussion: half of NGOs' websites offered forum discussions, and political parties and media websites offered a slightly

Table 5.3 The interactive and communication features on selected websites in Slovenia

Online producer	Number of cases	Contacting producer	Getting e-mail	Forum	Sending link to a friend	Public support statement
State institutions	30	0.90	0.23	0.23	0	0
Political parties	21	0.95	0.24	0.48	0.05	0.05
Media	10	1	0.20	0.30	0.10	0.10
NGOs	8	0.88	0.25	0.50	0.13	0.13

smaller proportion. The most outstanding finding in this respect is the very low proportion of certain interactive features on political parties' websites: out of 21 political parties' websites, almost none offered the opportunity for expressing support for their candidates (0.05). A similarly low proportion of political parties enabled the integrative potential for sending links to other interested voters, which can in the context of computer-mediated communication, function as an important promotion strategy, leading to greater popularity for candidates.

Mobilization and self-promotion aspects of the online campaign

With the spread of the internet and of the online presence of several diverse political groups, common understanding of political activities is widening (Gibson *et al.* 2004; Margolis and Resnick 2000; Oblak 2003). Computer-mediated communication opens up new methods for political activity, like submitting electronic petitions, writing and distributing e-mails, and participating in online opinion polls. Along with these novelties, the ways of identifying people with similar opinions are changing; with the help of the web, new political coalitions and interest groups are forming in order to present their own political preferences and recruit potential advocates. These new mobilization mechanisms and practices change the existing circumstances for collective and individual political action. Therefore, new ways of politics can be formed, stimulated by more horizontal communication patterns.

In this section of our analysis we were interested in determining the extent to which the two most relevant groups of political actors – political parties on the one hand and NGOs on the other – used online space for mobilization of potential voters and supporters during the election campaign for the EP. Have they explored the potential for their own self-promotion? Was it possible to join a certain party or group? Was it possible to distribute propaganda material through the web? Table 5.4 illustrates the findings on these questions.

A relatively large number of websites offered opportunities for joining an organization or political group; such a strategy was most common on the political parties' websites (0.71) and less on NGOs' sites (0.38). A small

Table 5.4 Mobilization and self-promotional strategies on selected websites in Slovenia

Online producer	Number of cases	Joining website	Register producers	Offline distribution to vote	E-paraphernalia of election material	Volunteering	Donations
State institutions	30	0.03	0.13	0	0.17	0	0
Political parties	21	0.71	0	0	0.19	0	0.07
NGOs	8	0.38	0.13	0.13	0.63	0.13	0.25
Media	10	0.20	0	0	0	0	0.08

proportion in this analytical category on state websites (0.03) is expected and normal due to their specific political function. However, a more surprising finding refers to another online image of political parties. Viewed in the light of mobilization, they were very static and almost unworkable. Political parties did not use the online political space for recruiting volunteers, something which might have spread their political preferences outside the web. Even the digital distribution of web content was rare (0.19 proportion of political parties' websites).

Within this context, NGOs made much more use of the internet. Although separate proportion values are still rather low, they point to the conclusion that NGOs showed more interest and therefore had a better understanding of how to involve citizens in an election campaign: five out of eight websites offered digital distribution of promotional material; accepting of donations was enabled on two websites. The fact that media had low proportions in all selected categories reflects an additional point: in the context of election mobilization, the media played the role of being "independent" or at least being a "quiet" informer and did not act as promotional agitators.

Conclusion

The first European Parliament elections campaign in Slovenia was characterized by the elites of political parties contending for seats in the European Parliament and promoting the European Union rather than encouraging a wide public debate on important and common European issues (the economy, agriculture, and foreign policy). In terms of the web sphere overall, information delivery was oriented towards informing and promoting the EP election. It could be said that political parties, government, and mass media – the political actors with the prevalence of information delivery within the web sphere – put more emphasis on democratic election procedures than on democratic issues (opinion formation) in the information part of the election campaign. On the other hand, possibilities for engagement between political actors and Slovene voters on the web were very low. The only exception was the possibility of contacting website producers, which could be considered as the minimum level of engagement. Most engagement features were provided on NGO websites, while some of the lowest scores were found on governmental websites. Such results suggest that the Slovene government and other state institutions were not really interested in discussion and deliberation with Slovene citizens. NGOs showed the greater interest and, therefore, a better understanding of integrating citizens into the election campaign, while political parties were very static and almost unworkable from a mobilization point of view.

In the Slovenian case, it became very obvious that the most influential political actors – political parties and the Slovene government – have not yet adopted all the democratic potentials that the internet offers and are not yet ready to play an important role in challenging new communication processes with the public. It could be argued that the Slovenian election web sphere during this campaign was mainly characterized as a "top-down," one-way, representative style of online political communication, favoring the strongest among the political actors, the political parties. Citizens, NGOs, civil society in general (syndicates, religious organizations, education, and business), and even the mass media played minor roles in the online election campaign process. There were few opportunities for citizens to engage directly in political action via websites during this election. For example, engagement features provided online, such as opportunities to make public support statements, volunteer and give donations, register to vote, or distribute election materials were rarely provided by political actors. Citizens had only slightly better opportunities to join the campaign, receive e-mails, or participate in online forums. This suggests that the websites in the Slovene electoral sphere attached more importance to information distribution than to engagement features.

According to Van Dijk (1996, 2000) this pattern corresponds to the legalist model of information and communication technology (ICT) use, which favors attention to information shortages and reinforcement of the present political system through more effective and efficient ways of information processing and organization. ICT, in this model, is also applied to increase the transparency of the political system (Van Dijk 1996: 47). In general, the legalist model does not favor an active citizenry in terms of enabling deliberative public and political discussions or in strengthening citizens' participation. From this perspective, ICT instruments, such as online discussions among citizens, e-conferences, and e-referendums, are rejected or not trusted. In the case of the 2004 EP election, websites of political actors were used mainly to legitimize and to promote present EU policy.

Contrary to such a legalist model of ICT use, the pluralist model practices more participatory aspects of democracy. By stimulating the technical support of computer-assisted political information or debate systems and through access to interactive communication networks that support the network concept of politics, communication within and among a civil society can consequently be made much stronger (Lukšič and Delakorda 2003: 121). Viewed within the general context of the Slovenian political web sphere, it seems that the inclination of political actors towards more integrative relationships and engagement processes with their selected publics (voters, sympathizers, and civil society members) has still not become the strategic starting point in planning an online presence. This limitation coincides with the primary goal that political actors want to achieve through ICT implementation. The majority of Slovene political actors are still focused more on democratic outputs or procedures instead of the new possibilities of opinion formation. Hence, the internet as a new communication tool is "preferred for information campaigns, civic service and information centres, mass public information systems, registration systems for the government or the public administration and computer-assisted citizen enquires" (Van Dijk 2000: 40).

In order to change this long-lasting institutional perception of new media as services for allocution and registration instead of using them for conversation and consultation, trust in the internet as a conversation media needs to be cultivated. If political actors strongly disregard the potentials for public discussions, conversations, and interactions, then they disregard also all those internet users who are willing and eager to participate actively online in the matters related to political issues. Judging from this case study – the Slovenian online election campaign for EP – some organizations and members of civil society already started to explore such potentials in a more productive way. But for a more general turn towards the pluralist model of online democratic web sphere, additional effort, especially from the institutionalized political actors, is still needed.

Notes

1   The survey "What do cybercitizens do and how do they socialize?" was conducted within a research seminar entitled "Methods for Communication Research" that was held at the Faculty of Social Sciences at the University of Ljubljana. The data gathering was made online from 6–16 May 2000. Only 177 internet users responded to the questionnaire, so we should not generalize these findings to the whole online population. Nevertheless, the statistical regression model we tested was statistically significant, with the explained variance value 0.31.

2   It is therefore not surprising that some dimensions of the term interactivity have direct implications also for our own understanding of those social phenomena that are related to democracy, personal power, or freedom of speech.

3   In the identification phase of the project, we used Google and Najdi.si search engines in order to access all relevant websites containing two sets of keywords: "European elections in Slovenia" and "Elections in European parliament in Slovenia." A total of 168 websites were identified for a purposes of this project, and 94 of them were included in the Slovenian sample of coded sites: 30 governmental sites, 21 political parties sites, ten press sites, and eight non-governmental organization (NGO) sites. Twenty-five sites in a sample were classified as "other political actors," that is, business, citizen, educational, political–professional, and religious sites. The identification phase of the project ran for just four weeks prior to elections. A final sample of websites was computer-generated independently from researchers participating in the project.

4   The Slovenian research team used the computer program WebArchivist Coder in order to explore basic characteristics of election web spheres in Slovenia. A questionnaire with 25 selected characteristics was the basis for analysis of mediated information and intercommunication possibilities during the online European Parliament elections campaign. Ten days after site identification was completed, researchers started with coding, examining their information features (election content, biographies, endorsements, issue positions, speeches, calendars of events, issue comparisons, information about campaigns, information about voting procedures, images, audio-video files, privacy statements, and terms of use agreements) and engagement features (labeled contact, join us,

register to vote, get e-mail from site, donate, take part in a discussion forum, offline distribution of campaign materials, send link to a friend, public support statement, e-paraphernalia, and volunteer).
5   A website producer is the organization or individual responsible for online publication of the website. As such it differs from the web master, who usually takes care of the technical aspects of web presentation.
6   This general impression may be the major reason why voter turnout was particularly low: 28.4 percent of the eligible voters in Slovenia cast ballots on 13 June 2004.

References

Bačlija, I. and Chan Ka-lok, K. (2004) "First time in the European parliament elections: Central and Eastern Europe in the 2004 European parliament elections," *Družboslovne razprave*, 46/47: 109–131.

Barber, B. (1984) *Strong Democracy: Participatory Politics for a New Age*. Berkeley, CA: University of California Press.

Bellamy, C. and Raab, C.D. (1999) "Wiring-up the deck-chairs?," in S. Coleman, J. Taylor, and W. van de Donk (eds), *Parliament in the Age of the Internet*, pp. 156–172. Oxford: Oxford University Press.

Benoit, W.L. and Benoit, P.J. (2000) "The virtual campaign: presidential primary websites in campaign 2000," *American Communication Journal*, 3, 3: 1–22.

Bimber, B. (1998) "The Internet and political transformation: populism, community, and accelerated pluralism," *Polity*, 31, 1: 133–169.

Dahlgren, P. (1996) "Media logic in cyberspace: repositioning journalism and its publics," *Javnost/The Public*, 3, 3: 59–72.

Davis, R. and Owen, D. (1998) *New Media and American Politics*. Oxford: Oxford University Press.

Davis, R. (1999) *The Web of Politics: The Internet's Impact on the American Political System*. Oxford: Oxford University Press.

de Sola Pool, I. (1983) *Forecasting the Telephone: A Retrospective Technology Assessment*. Norwood, NJ: Ablex Publishing.

Deželan, T. (2005) "Z 'evrobusom' po Sloveniji" [Around Slovenia by "eurobus"], in S. Kustec (ed.), *Politološki vidiki volilne kampanje: Analiza volilne kampanje za volitve v Evropski parlament 2004* [Political aspects of election campaign: Analysis of election campaign for European Parliament 2004], pp. 55–57. Ljubljana: FDV.

Dravinec, S. (2004) *Ostali so doma* [They remained at home] *Primorske novice*, 48, 2.

Dryzek, J.S. (2000) *Deliberative Democracy and Beyond*. Oxford: Oxford University Press.

Fishkin, J.S. (1991) *Democracy and Deliberation. New Directions for Democratic Reform*. New Haven, CT: Yale University Press.

Foot, K.A. and Schneider, S.M. (2002) "Online action in campaign 2000: an exploratory analysis of the U.S. political web sphere," *Journal of Broadcasting and Electronic Media*, 46, 2: 222–244.

Franz, D. (2003) *Digitalna demokracija in politična kultura na primeru Slovenije* [Digital democracy and political culture in Slovenia], in A.A. Lukšič and T. Oblak (eds), *S poti v digitalno demokracijo* [From the journey to digital democracy]. Ljubljana: Fakulteta za družbene vede.

Gibson, R.K., Lusoli, W., and Ward, S.J. (2002) "The public response. A survey of citizens' political activity via the Internet." Salford: ESRC Report.

Gibson, R.K., Lusoli, W., Römmele, A., and Ward, S.J. (2004) "Representative democracy and the Internet," in R.K. Gibson, A. Römmele, and S.J. Ward (eds), *Electronic Democracy: Mobilisation, Organisation and Participation via new ICT's*, pp. 1–16. London: Routledge.

Grossman, L. (1995) *The Electronic Republic*. New York: Penguin Books.

Hill, K.A. and Hughes, J.E. (1998) *Cyberpolitics: Citizen Activism in the Age of Internet*. Lanham, MD: Rowman & Littlefield.

Jankowski, N. and Van Selm, M. (2000) "The promise and practice of public debate in cyberspace," in K. Hacker and J. van Dijk (eds), *Digital Democracy: Issues of Theory and Practice*, pp. 149–165. London: Sage.

Kaldor, M. and Vejvoda, I. (1999) *Democratization in Central and Eastern Europe*. London: Continuum.

Kamarck, C.E. (1999) "Campaigning on the Internet in the elections of 1998," in E.C. Kamarck and J.S. Nye (eds), *Democracy.com? Governance in the Networked World*. Middlesex, UK: Hollis Publishing.

Kustec-Lipicer, S. (2005) *Usmeritve v preučevanju politoloških vidikov volilnih kampanj* [Directions in studying political aspects of election campaigns], in S. Kustec (ed.), *Politološki vidiki volilne kampanje: Analiza volilne kampanje za volitve v Evropski parlament 2004* [Political aspects of election campaign: Analysis of election campaign for European Parliament 2004], pp. 2–19. Ljubljana: FDV.

Kuzmanić, T. (2002) "Slovenia: from Yugoslavia to the middle of nowhere?," in M. Kaldor and I. Vejvoda (eds), *Democratization in Central and Eastern Europe*. London, New York: Continuum.

Lubecka, A. (2000) "Contemporary economic, sociocultural, and technological contexts in New Europe," in L. Lengel (ed.), *Culture and Technology in the New Europe*, Stamford, CT: Ablex Publishing Corporation.

Lukšič, A. and Delakorda, S. (2003) "Digital democracy – the case of Slovenia," in F. Trček (ed.), *Community-net in South and East Europe*, pp. 112–146. Ljubljana: FDV.

McAdam, D., McCarthy, J.D., and Zald, M.N. (1996) *Comparative Perspectives on Social Movements: Political Opportunities, Mobilizing Structures and Cultural Framings*. Cambridge: Cambridge University Press.

Margolis, M. and D. Resnick (2000) *Politics as Usual: The Cyberspace Revolution*. London: Sage.

Norris, P. (2001) *Digital Divide: Civic Engagement, Information Poverty, and the Internet Worldwide*. Cambridge: Cambridge University Press.

Oblak, T. (2000) "Elektronska demokracija in nova prizorišča političnega delovanja" [Electronic democracy and new spaces of political actions], in S. Splichal (ed.), *Vregov zbornik – Supplement, Javnost/The Public*, 7: 121–132.

Oblak, T. (2003) *Izzivi E-demokracije* [Challenges of e-democracy]. Ljubljana: Fakulteta za družbene vede.

Oblak, T. (2005) "The lack of interactivity and hyperextuality on Slovenian media online," *Gazette*, 67, 1: 87–106.

Rafaeli, S. (1988) "Interactivity: from new media to communication," in R.P. Hawkins, J.M. Wiemann, and S. Pingree (eds), *Advancing Communication Science*. London: Sage.

Rommele, A. (2003) "Political parties, party communication and new information and communication technologies," *Party Politics*, 9, 1: 7–20.

Sassi, S. (1996) "The network and the fragmentation of the public sphere," *Javnost/The Public*, 3, 1: 25–43.

SIBIS (Statistical Indicators Benchmarking the Information Society) Project. Country Report for Slovenia, 2003. University of Ljubljana: Faculty for Social Sciences.

Stromer-Galley, J. (2004) "Will Internet voting increase turnout? An analysis of voter preference," in P.N. Howard and S. Jones (eds), *Society online: The Internet in context*, pp. 87–102. London: Sage.

Van Dijk, J.A.G.M. (1996) "Models of democracy – behind the design and use of new media in politics," *Javnost/The Public*, 1: 43–56.

Van Dijk, J. (2000) "Models of democracy and concepts of communication," in K. Hacker and J. van Dijk (eds), *Digital Democracy*, pp. 30–53. London: Sage.

Wilhelm, G.A. (2000) *Democracy in the Digital Age: Challenges to Political Life in Cyberspace*. London: Routledge.

Zadnikar, G. (2005) "'Evropski' molk slovenskih medijev" ["European" silence of Slovenian media], in G. Zadnikar (ed.), *Evrovolitve: Spremljanje volilne kampanje za Evropski parlament v slovenskih medijih* [Euroelections: Analysing election campaign for European parliament in Slovenian media], pp. 134–148. Ljubljana: Inštitut za civilizacijo in kulturo.

6 The consequence of e-excellence

Party websites in the Czech campaign for the 2004 European Parliament

Martin Gregor

Introduction

European Parliamentary elections are generally not approached with genuine interest, and the role of online campaigns therein may strike some (not least academics) as even less intriguing. The use of the internet in European electoral campaigns has, in fact, been referred to as "a second-order medium in a second-order election" (Carlson and Strandberg 2005: 201). The Czech campaign leading to the 2004 European elections underscored the lack of engagement: voter turnout of 27.9 percent proved significantly below the European Union average of 48.2 percent, and related web-based campaigning took place here in an environment where experience with such online campaigning was virtually non-existent.

At the same time, the domestic campaign and the results thereof were not unexceptional. Despite seeming irrelevant, Czech website excellence during the European campaign is found to correlate with electoral gains or better-than-expected results. Above average e-presentations were produced by parties that won more seats than predicted, especially when compared with the 2002 Czech general election. Also, the 2004 European elections, the first ever held in the Czech Republic, proved deeply significant for Czech domestic politics: the shockingly low support polled by the Social Democrats, the senior partner in a left-of-center coalition government, deepened a crisis in the government that eventually saw the resignation of the cabinet and of Prime Minister Vladimir Spidla.

One explanation might be that online structures are not as irrelevant as previously thought; rather, they indicate some strategic information. Websites are certainly instrumental in providing direct information and engagement, but what makes them special is that they also signal flexibility, care for marginal voters, and political entrepreneurship. A party that does not market its platform signals that it does not care about political marketing, from which it could be further extrapolated that it does not care about its product. Below, we consider this neglected aspect of electoral campaigning. We argue that while the direct impact of e-campaigns may be yet marginal, a committed web presence still serves as a device signaling quality and commitment. And voters tend to use cheap signaling devices.

In this chapter, we examine the 2004 European Parliament elections in the Czech Republic, and document how certain parties dominated the e-space before the campaign, crowding out individual candidates. Next, we compare parties by activities in the web sphere. In the final part, we examine whether the Czech e-campaign successfully delivered political success, and, if it did, how so. We demonstrate that numbers of effective features on websites are, in fact, correlated with electoral gains, and suggest that such a correlation hardly stems from instrumental use of the websites. For an explanation, we resort to the concept of "political signaling," which has been relatively under-researched in the literature on political communication. Direct tests of the signaling hypothesis are, however, left for future research.

The instrumental and signaling use of websites

The process of "maintaining an image of professionalism and bringing up-to-date communication features" is often regarded as purely symbolic (Weber and Murray 2002: 7). However, in certain cases, symbols may be quite relevant. Not many voters study party websites in depth, but many of them at least visit such sites looking for information; for the U.S. experience, see Rainie *et al.* (2005). A rational voter need not spend too much time per visit to deduce a lot from first-hand impressions. Specifically, by scanning a party website, a voter might discern whether the party is interested in expertise, whether it reaches out to marginal voters, and whether it addresses timely issues in an expedient manner. Each visitor will obtain these impressions (signals), and use them, consciously or not, when casting a vote. Therefore, parties should pay attention to these signals, especially when their production and delivery is so cost-effective.

This argument invokes signaling theory, a well-established component of game theory with asymmetric information (Riley 2001; Mas-Colell *et al.* 2002). Signaling theory argues that people are motivated to signal a particular ability in activities in which they participate. For example, a social sciences degree from a renowned university may have low instrumental use in a business career, but it is valuable as a signal of the student's abilities. A developed ability to solve complex issues is what many companies demand from a prospective employee, and that is why many non-instrumental degrees are sought at prestigious universities.

A compelling website with effective features signals responsiveness and flexibility. Moreover, the use of and association with new technologies typifies post-material political values – deep volunteer involvement, open discussion, shared expertise, and, equally importantly, entertainment. Websites as a means of political communication are the best indicators of a willingness to innovate and of progressiveness. The medium is contemporaneous and highly fluid; features can be easily supplemented, and information can be quickly transmitted. Innovations are neither prohibited by sunk costs nor by lack of capital; in fact, to launch and maintain an attractive, informative, and responsive website costs arguably less than contracting a public-relations agency or employing party speakers with (limited) access to the media. In cyberspace, content updates are quickly and widely proliferated by user-friendly editorial systems of hypertext preprocessors. Therefore, even if the flow of information is unexceptional and engagement opportunities limited, a well-maintained website indicates dedication and professionalism and serves as effective marketing/signaling/symbolic tools with essentially non-instrumental uses.

Research design

As agreed in the terms of the Internet and Elections Project, we studied the Czech 2004 electoral web sphere by means of the WebArchivist Coder, a web-based system for collaborative coding of web objects, constructed by Schneider and Foot (2005). Gathering data with this instrument requires two independent steps, identification and coding. In the first phase, approximately eight weeks prior to the election, sites with potential electoral content had been "sleuthed." Out of approximately 600 hits found by search engines and portals, we identified 166 sites with potential election-relevant content. We classified the websites according to producer types into 12 categories: business, candidate, citizen, educational, government, labor, NGO, party, political, professional, press, and religious websites. Second, four weeks prior to the election, project coordinators drew a sample of 100 sites from the population of sites, which resulted into 95 coded sites (five websites ceased operation, suffered connection problems, or undertook reconstruction).

The sample included 24 party sites, 21 candidate sites, 18 NGO/labor sites, nine government sites, nine press sites, and 14 sites of other producers. In order to check relevance of the sample, we also conducted a follow-up identification in the last stage of the campaign, during which we looked for unidentified sites. We recognized no additional candidate site, but we did recognize three new party sites that were launched after the identification phase. One of those parties – Political Movement of Independent – passed the electoral threshold, so it constitutes an exception which could not be captured in the study due to its delayed emergence. The coding of the sample of identified websites took place during a period of two weeks, ending three days prior to the election. The items coded by the WebArchivist template are described in detail in the Appendix to this volume. Very broadly, they can be classified into informational and engagement features.

For each feature, we calculate the average frequency of use in the entire sample. We also calculate the frequencies of use of each feature for each producer type. Further, we rank our six producer types by the frequencies; we attribute the first position to the most active and the sixth position to the least active producer type. So as to compare parties, we construct indices of web sphere activity for each party. An attending feature adds a value of one to the index, or zero if absent. The first index, *web sphere information development*, WI, counts occurrences of the 13 informational features. Each political party is thus assigned an index value ranging from zero to 13. The second index, *web sphere engagement development*, WE, counts occurrences of engagement features, with value score from zero to ten. The last index, *total web sphere development*, WT, is a sum of the two previous indices, WT = WI + WE, taking integer values from zero to 23.

Last, we measure to what extent the web presence contributes to electoral success. The electoral success is measured by two variables, *2004 electoral result* (E2004) and *2002–2004 electoral gain* (GAIN) both in percentages of votes cast. The latter is the deviation of the 2004 European Parliament electoral result from the 2002 Lower Chamber electoral result. Having denoted the 2002 electoral result as E2002, we thus define the electoral gain as GAIN = E2004 − E2002. We partition the sample of all coded parties in two dimensions. In the first one, we distinguish between *established* parties and *newcomers*. The established parties participated both in 2002 and 2004 elections, and the newcomers are parties that emerged prior to the 2004 election. In the second partitioning, we distinguish between *EP-elected* parties that passed the electoral threshold of 5 percent, and the other, *EP-non-elected* parties.

Electoral campaign

Offline campaign

In 2004, growing dissatisfaction among Czech voters with the center-left coalition government (of the Social Democrats, the Christian Democrats, and the Liberal Democrats) informed the European campaign. Tax-code changes, crisis in the public health sector, and intra-coalition squabbling set the conditions under which more right- and left-wing candidates would outpoll coalition-party candidates in the European ballot.

During the campaign, in fact, a few dark-horse candidates emerged. The Green Party and European Democratic Party ultimately posted gains, both thanks to support from former president Vaclav Havel. A slate of independent candidates – the so-called Political Movement Independent (*Nezavisli*, NEZ) – largely played the Euroskeptic card, taking advantage of the fact that the bulk of the Czech campaign was concerned with attitudes toward the EU (the parties of the governing coalition in the Czech parliament being Euro-optimists; the Communists and conservatives the Euroskeptics), and by taking a distinctively more populist line than the Euroskeptic parties. The case of the NEZ was also notable in that its nominal leader, the former media entrepreneur Vladimir Zelezny (who now heads the Independent

Democrats, a party he founded), had a clear if not dubious personal stake in the campaign – by becoming an MEP, Zelezny would receive parliamentary immunity in the face of domestic investigations into tax evasion and criminal charges of fraud. Zelezny was elected, though the Czech judiciary seeks the lifting of his immunity. (In 2002, the Czech Senate stripped then-Senator Zelezny of his parliamentary immunity at the request of the state prosecutor's office.)

EU decision making drew most of the attention and became the vehicle for both insightful analyses and populist proclamations; loose parliamentary spending and accountability were also hot-button issues. Interestingly, a week before the elections, the Euroskeptic Czech president, Vaclav Klaus (ODS), signed into law a bill setting the gross salaries of Czech MEPs at the relatively low level of approximately €2000 per month (determined as 120 percent of the salary of Czech parliamentarians). Thereby, he reinforced the popular image that the candidates are motivated by attractive salaries rather than professional interests. All of the above may explain why Czech voters, the majority of which are pro-EU, favored a national-interest platform over deeper European integration.

Overall, however, there was little interest in the elections, both on the supply and the demand side. The site of the prominent newsweekly *Respekt*,[1] for instance, had not updated its site's "Election" section since the national general election of 2002, posting nothing there concerning the 2004 European contest. The first-ever elections to the European Parliament in the Czech Republic were shot through with domestic politics. Expectations of low voter turnout dissuaded parties here from waging spirited campaigns, with the major parties opting to save resources for forthcoming domestic battles (a general election is due mid-2006). Nothing spoke better to the lack of contention on the part of the major parties than media coverage of the poor oratory of certain top-touted candidates.

All in all, media and communication experts – and, without a doubt, voters – found the campaign toothless and uninteresting, with the exception of a handful of humorous moments, like the Balbin Poetic Party candidates attempting to "release" the statue of a horse-mounted Saint Wenceslas on the eponymous and heavily trafficked Wenceslas Square.

The 2004 e-campaign

Czech e-campaigns during the 2004 European elections were characterized by average flows of information and generally low engagement compared to the benchmark of other European countries in the Internet and Elections Project (see other chapters in this volume). Low voter turnout (27.9 percent comparing to 58.2 percent in the 2002 Lower Chamber elections) reveals that the elections were not considered to be crucial. Unsurprisingly, neither offline nor e-campaigns featured costly or sophisticated political-marketing tools. On the cost side of parties' budgets, expenses for marketing in media decreased from CZK283.6 million to CZK105.4 million (*Strategie* 2006). Revenues declined as well; in 2002, government plus private campaign contributions amounted to CZK926.6 million, while in 2004, they were only about CZK543.9 million (CT24 2006). Non-governmental organizations showed little interest, given the limited influence of Czech members in the European Parliament (the Czech Republic is allotted 24 of 732 seats), and many found the European platform irrelevant. For example, the main site of online intellectual opposition to the EU, *Euroskeptik*,[2] neither mentioned the date of the elections nor supported nor condemned candidates. The corporate sector seemed only interested in the Czech government's EU-accession engagement such as more stringent consumer protection, and labor organizations proved reluctant to evaluate or assess parties or candidates.

In the course of monitoring electoral activity, we studied 95 sites produced by six types of political actors. We found three types of actors to be the most active: the press, political parties, and candidates. Between the latter two – that is, the direct players – parties were the e-campaign leaders. Tables 6.1 and 6.2 show the extent to which candidates and parties employed certain informational and engagement features (in percentage of sites). On the basis of these percentages, we ranked the producer types (from the first to the sixth). These ranks are used for further descriptive statistics.

For both informational and engagement features, parties score better than candidates. We obtain that result by threefold comparison of average ranks, distributions of maximums and minimums, and distributions above and below means of producer types. First, the average rank for informational features is 2.2 for parties and 3.0 for candidates, and for engagement features, 3.0 for parties and 4.1 for candidates. We secondly compare the frequencies of percentages above and below the means of producer types. In this case, parties have nine information features above the mean and four below the mean (9:4); for engagement features, the score is even better, 9:1. Candidates score only 7:6 and 0:10, respectively. Last, we calculated cases when the percentage values represent maximums or minimums among the producer types. Parties have five maximums and two minimums among both informational and engagement features (5:2). For candidates, the scores are far worse, 1:3 and 0:4.

The comparisons show that the 2004 electronic campaign was a contest of political parties, not of candidates. Candidates did not exactly take up gauntlets, and they rarely distinguished themselves on the internet.

Parties' dominance

Aside from the press, the parties led the results on a number of fronts. Nevertheless, only four had effective web presentations (see Table 6.4). Of the four, some party candidates offered very good personal websites, but only a handful of candidates from other parties took efforts to distinguish themselves on the web.

Table 6.1 Informational features on websites of EP candidates and party sites in the Czech Republic

Feature	Candidate (21)[a]	Rank[b]	Party (24)	Rank	All (95)[c]
IMAGE[d]	100.0	(1.)	95.8	(3.)	89.5
BIO	90.5	(3.)	100.0	(1.)	88.4
ANN	90.5	(3.)	95.8	(2.)	73.7
ISSUE	71.4	(3.)	100.0	(1.)	70.5
CALENDAR	33.3	(2.)	54.2	(1.)	26.3
INFOV	19.1	(4.)	20.8	(3.)	25.3
A/V	9.5	(4.)	37.5	(2.)	17.9
COMPARE	19.1	(2.)	41.7	(1.)	16.9
SPEECH	38.1	(2.)	20.8	(3.)	19.0
INFOC	0	(5.)	8.3	(3.)	9.5
TERMS	0	(4.)	0	(4.)	9.5
ENDOR	4.8	(2.)	25.0	(1.)	7.4
PRIVACY	0	(4.)	0	(4.)	4.2

Notes
a Number of sites per political actor noted in parentheses.
b Rank among six producer types for given feature noted in parentheses.
c The average proportion of scores of all coded sites.
d Proportion of scores for candidate and party sites.

Abbreviations and description of informational features
ANN: announcement of the elections present on site.
A/V: audio or video files present on site.
BIO: biography or history of party/candidate present on site.
CALENDAR: a calendar or list of events with election-related events present on site.
COMPARE: comparison of issue positions of candidates/parties present on site.
ENDOR: endorsements for a candidate/party present on site.
IMAGE: an image of a candidate or party representative present on site.
INFOC: information about the electoral campaign process present on site.
INFOV: information about the voting or registration process present on site.
ISSUE: list of issue positions held by party/candidate present on site
PRIVACY: privacy policy present on site.
SPEECH: speech by a candidate or party representative present on site.
TERMS: terms of use present on site.

Parties were also the most proactive web producers because they provided site templates, which, consequently, acted to reduce the incentives of affiliated candidates to establish their own sites. The templates allowed the candidates to fill in only curricula vitae, basic policy positions, and slogans. Parties using templates thus discouraged candidates from launching a special, perhaps more personal, and informative site. Interestingly, all parties in a coalition government – the Social Democrats, the Christian Democrats, and the Liberal Democrats – employed the templates.

As a result, candidate sites rarely supplemented the main party campaign sites. Moreover, they were few in number; in the first site-identification round, only 21 of 808 candidates created websites toward the 2004

Table 6.2 Engagement features on websites of EP candidates and party sites in the Czech Republic

Feature	Candidate (21)[a]	Rank[b]	Party (24)	Rank	All (95)[c]
CONTACT[d]	90.5	(6.)	100.0	(1.)	97.9
FORUM	19.1	(5.)	58.3	(2.)	40.0
JOIN	0	(5.)	70.8	(2.)	35.9
GETMAIL	9.5	(6.)	20.8	(4.)	20.0
OFFDIST	9.5	(3.)	41.7	(1.)	13.7
DONATE	4.8	(5.)	29.3	(1.)	13.7
VOLUNT	9.5	(2.)	25.0	(1.)	9.6
EPARA	4.8	(5.)	16.7	(1.)	9.5
REGISTER	4.8	(2.)	4.2	(3.)	5.3
SENDLINK	4.8	(2.)	4.2	(3.)	3.2

Notes
a Number of sites per political actor noted in parentheses.
b Rank among six producer types for given feature noted in parentheses.
c The average proportion of scores of all coded sites.
d Proportion of scores for candidate and party sites.

Abbreviations and description of engagement features
CONTACT: information provided on site for contacting party or candidate.
DONATE: donations are encouraged or enabled through site.
EPARA: e-paraphernalia available on the site (banners, screensavers).
GETMAIL: possibility to sign up to receive e-mail from party/candidate.
FORUM: possibility to participate in online forum or other communication space.
JOIN: opportunity for visitors to join, or become member of party.
OFFDIST: site encourages offline distribution of election-related materials.
REGISTER: site enables visitors to register to participate in election.
SEND: site enables a visitor to send a link from this site to a friend.
VOLUNT: site encourages visitors to volunteer for the electoral camping.

elections. The most prominent example was the right-of-center Civic Democratic Party (*Obcanska demokraticka strana*, ODS); its candidates, with their party leading the domestic opinion polls and with the best party site behind them, had little reason to distinguish themselves as individuals. The personal website of the 2004 ODS campaign leader, Jan Zahradil,[3] for example, included no campaign materials. Another ODS candidate, until then the vice-chairman of the Committee for European Affairs of the Chamber of Deputies of the Czech Republic, Jaroslav Zverina,[4] had not updated his personal website for several months prior to the election.

To summarize, Czech candidates were largely absent from the internet, or barely there. Those that did have a web presence rarely encouraged voter participation; on candidate websites, campaign-financing information was often absent, volunteers were rarely solicited, and the online or offline distribution of leaflets or other supportive material was rarely demanded. Some candidates admitted they had their personal websites put up only in the face of the election. And a special curiosity, the Civic Federal Democracy party,[5] mentioned only two members on its site and published a list of vacancies in the party executive board and a passive summons to "join our executive board."

On the other hand, we should note in our sample that 90.5 percent of candidate and 100 percent of party sites offered an e-mail contact means. This indicates that low-cost engagement features have been evolving rapidly and that a lack thereof may have been more a matter of technical or know-how constraints than of disincentive to engage voters.

Party analysis

Electoral results and web sphere development: case by case

In this section, we employ the web sphere development indices derived for political parties. Before proceeding to the statistical analysis, we overview electoral results and study parties' web sphere activities case by case.

Concerning electoral outcomes, Table 6.3 presents percentages of 2004 votes (E2004) of parties with electoral result above 0.1 percent, with the exception of NEZ, whose website was launched too late to be considered in the study. Percentages of 2002 votes (E2002) as well as electoral gains (GAIN) are also included.

The top four parties were the only parties that had established campaign-dedicated websites. Since the European Democrats created an electoral coalition with the Association of Independents (*Sdruzeni nezavislych kandidatu-Evropsti demokrate*, SNK-ED), there were actually only three election-specific party websites: the centrist SNK-ED coalition, the conservative ODS, and the Green Party.

Table 6.3 Top ten Czech parties in the 2004 EP and 2002 Lower Chamber elections

Party	E2002[a]	E2004[b]	GAIN
Civic Democratic Party	24.5	30.1	+5.6
Communist Party	18.5	20.2	+1.7
Association of Independents	2.8	11.0	+8.2
European Democrats	0	11.0	+11.0
Christian Democracy	9.2	9.6	+0.4
Social Democratic Party	30.2	8.8	−21.4
Green Party	2.4	3.2	+0.8
Open Society Party	0	0.2	+0.2
Labor Party	0	0.2	+0.1
Civic Federal Party	0	0.1	+0.1

Notes
a Percentage of votes in the Lower Chamber election, 2002.
b Percentage of votes in the European Parliament election, 2004.

The Green Party maintained an effective site,[6] albeit missing a feature to send links. The SNK-ED umbrella site[7] was a special case; having cross-linked the websites of two parties, it lacked further infrastructure. This was, however, sufficient to induce the parties to employ a variety of features in parallel. This only highlights the point that having a dedicated electoral e-device stimulates other online activities, here the development of features present on the party homepage.

As to the main conservative party, the ODS, their site[8] included many features; including several blogs and interactive entertainment. The key role of their website was visible across the country since all ODS billboards depicted the web address as part of a stylized, eye-catching logo. ODS candidate sites, on the other hand, were not rich in election-relevant content. As mentioned above, the top ODS candidate, Jan Zahradil, maintained a superficial site, devoid of campaign material. Even more strangely, another ODS candidate, one Jan Sequens,[9] had a site that was so elegiac and apolitical that we had to consult the official party list to be sure he was indeed a candidate; there was otherwise no mention of an election being contested on his pages.

In spite of the average (or sparse) flow of information and engagement offered, we argue that the more information and engagement possibilities offered, the larger is the success over previous elections, at least on the party basis. As suggested in the introduction, this may be attributed to signaling, rather than to instrumental use of party websites. In Table 6.4, we provide the first idea on the relation between web sphere presence and electoral outcomes. The table lists all web sphere development indices and the electoral gains, sorted by the total web sphere development variable, WT.

The relevance of e-campaigns to the electoral success can be illustrated case by case, with reference to Table 6.4. First, those less-established parties

Table 6.4 Web sphere development of the top ten Czech parties

Party	WI^a	WE^b	WT^c	GAIN
European Democrats	9	7	16	+11.0
Civic Democrats	9	5	14	+5.6
Association of Independents	9	5	14	+8.2
Green Party	9	5	14	+0.8
Christian Democrats	7	4	11	+0.4
Social Democrats	7	3	10	−21.4
Communists	6	3	9	+1.7
Open Society Party	7	2	9	+0.2
Labor Party	6	2	8	+0.1
Civic Federal Party	5	3	8	+0.1

Notes
a Index of web sphere information development (from 0 to 13).
b Index of web sphere engagement development (from 0 to 10).
c Index of total web sphere development (from 0 to 23).

who invested into their online presentations indeed enjoyed success: the Greens reached 3.16 percent, and thus crossed the threshold whereby their election expenses were eligible to be reimbursed, and the European Democrats (with a party structure located almost exclusively in Prague), in a coalition with the Association of Independents, polled an unexpected 11 percent. As for the established parties, the ODS, with an advanced website, were tops with 30.1 percent of the popular vote (up from 24.5 percent in the 2002 general election). The Christian Democrats, with an average-quality site, received an average-for-them outcome of 9.57 percent (vs 9.2 percent in 2002), while the engagement-feature-free site of the Social Democrats duly served the party's ultimately poor result (8.78 percent vs 30.2 percent in 2002). Unfortunately, the NEZ, with 8.18 percent, launched its website too late to be included in our study.

Electoral results and web sphere development: statistics

A rigorous empirical analysis would regress the final electoral outcome on web presence, party size, incumbent versus challenger, pre-electoral polls outcome, and ideology. We would have, however, only one degree of freedom if we did that for the sub-sample of EP-elected parties. Even for ten parties with the outcome above 0.1 percent, the number of degrees of freedom would be insufficient. Including small parties with negligible results (below 0.1 percent) but large variation of their web sphere indices, we would get a covariance matrix with extremely low values. Estimates on this matrix would consequently yield insignificant results unless we had reliable information on spatial position of the parties and the preferences of voters. Thus, we exclusively focus on correlation between electoral outcome/gain and the web sphere development index scores in the entire sample and its partitions.

Table 6.5 supports the claim that web presence relates to electoral success, measured by E2004 variable. For the full sample and total index,

Table 6.5 Correlation between web sphere development and the 2004 electoral result

Sample[a]	WI	WE	WT
All (22)	0.42	0.35	0.56
Established (12)	0.50	0.27	0.59
Newcomers (10)	0.47	0.71	0.71
EP-elected (6)	0.15	0	0.07
EP-non-elected (16)	0.44	0.29	0.56

Notes
a Sample size in parentheses.
b Parties that participated in both 2002 and 2004 elections.
c Parties that emerged prior to 2004 elections.

WT, the correlation is as high as 0.56. The strongest correlation appears to be in the case of newcomers, specifically in their engagement index, WE, and their total index, WT (both 0.71). Using the signaling intuition, we may conjecture that *a newcomer has an incentive to signal activity more strongly than an established party*. In contrast, the table gives strikingly low results for large, EP-elected parties. The total position of those who make it into office therefore cannot be measured by the web sphere presence. To succeed on the top level, some other qualities are necessary. We could interpret this and the previous result as follows: online activity is a necessary though a not sufficient condition for electoral success.

The picture changes when we consider the electoral gains measured by the GAIN variable. What kind of difference shall we anticipate? The electoral success, expressed by E2004, arguably has to do with the long-term attractiveness of the party, given by reputation, stability, and brand. The electoral gain, measured by GAIN, is more indicative of the short-term attractiveness of the party. We would expect that the web sphere presence stimulates rather the short-term, not the long-term attractiveness. Hence, it shall affect electoral gains more than electoral outcomes.

Yet, Table 6.6 leads to the conclusion that on average, web sphere development is *less* related to the electoral gain than to the electoral success. For the entire sample and total index, WT, the correlation is only 0.29. The low figure emerges clearly because fringe parties often offer websites with a huge variety of features, so the website presence is not a good measure for all parties. Only by focusing on sub-samples of EP-elected parties do we find the outcome we anticipated, namely the strong correlation between electoral improvement/decline, GAIN, and the engagement index, WE, respectively total index, WT. Employing the signaling intuition again, we may conjecture that *a big party can improve electoral outcome by signaling far more than can a small party*.

We arrived at two findings regarding the importance of online campaigns. First, online activity is correlated with electoral success of all parties, newcomers in particular. The electoral success is modestly indicative of the long-term position, so we get a relation between the long-term status of parties and their web presence. We cannot determine the way of causation,

Table 6.6 Correlation between web sphere development and electoral gain (2002 and 2004)

Sample	WI	WE	WT
All (22)	0.19	0.31	0.29
Established (12)	0.10	0.21	0.20
Newcomers (10)	0.47	0.71	0.71
EP-elected (6)	0.60	0.74	0.70
EP-non-elected (16)	0.74	−0.01	0.40

however; in fact, it may be such that large parties simply tend to have more extensive websites than smaller ones. Second, we find that online activity boosts electoral gains, as compared to past results. This is true for EP-elected parties and perhaps also newcomers, for whom we nevertheless cannot determine whether the first-time outcome reflects the short-term success or the long-term position.

Is it possible to generalize these findings? We hasten to claim that the direct effects of online campaigns subscribe these results. Instrumental effects of websites are doubtful due to low intensity of campaigning and low importance of elections. Yet we find the internet to be a reliable indicator of ambitions. For newcomers, it is an alternative means to more costly outlays; for large parties, it is a way to demonstrate proactivity and to address engaged constituencies. Therefore, it is not unlikely that proactive and flexible parties put an extra effort into site upkeep. On the contrary, poorly designed and outdated sites (mainly those of incumbents) reflect the low interest of the actors in boosting public support and signal potential electoral failure.

Conclusion

Even if direct electoral benefits from running an effective site are not clear from the 2004 European elections (the votes directly gained on the basis of websites were arguably few), we found that relative differences in site quality supported electoral results. The better the newcomer's site, the higher the likelihood of passing the electoral threshold; also, those parties that passed into the European parliament and were active online gained relative to other, less-active parties who also got into the European parliament. To sum up, we found that the web presence helps two groups: newcomers and large parties striving for victory. It is less relevant for established parties that are small. And it arguably does not affect the long-term standing of temporarily unsuccessful big parties.

Hence, websites must have catered to special needs. They may have pushed the loyal and the undecided alike to action. They could create, maintain, and communicate a profound sense of mission. And they could flexibly respond to evolving topics and change the direction of the campaign. Further, they facilitated activists' ability to get information useful for organizing campaigns and defending parties and candidates. From the perspective of an external observer, we argue that the websites are equally likely to signal political innovations, proactiveness, and an interest in expertise and in marginal voters. This is a hitherto neglected use of websites in electoral campaigns. A party thirsty for success simply has to be pre-emptive enough, maintain a certain degree of professionalism, and keep up to date. Failure to do as much is striking, especially considering the cost-effectiveness and relative ease of administering a website; those who aren't effectively online risk appearing as laggards.

The Czech 2004 European parliamentary election is an interesting case since the perception of "just a midterm" election proved invalid. The elections carried a tremendous impact by revealing the shockingly low support for the senior partner in the Czech coalition government, the Social Democrats. The outcome catalyzed a party crisis that culminated in the fall of the cabinet and of Prime Minister Vladimir Spidla, who also resigned as party chairman. To conclude, the online activities cited herein were definitely not of a "second order;" nor was this a "second-order election." On the contrary, the elections were decisive, and those who invested in quality e-campaigns saw successful returns.

Notes

1 www.respekt.cz.
2 www.euroskeptik.cz.
3 www.zahradil.cz.
4 www.zverina.cz.
5 www.ofd.cz.
6 www.voltezelene.cz.
7 www.ceskyuspech.cz.
8 www.eu.ods.cz.
9 www.sequens.cz.

Bibliography

Carlson, T. and Strandberg, K. (2005) "The 2004 European parliament election on the web: Finnish actor strategies and voter responses," *Information Polity*, 10, 3–4: 189–204.

CT24 (2006) "Sponzori byli loni opet nejstedrejsi k ODS a CSSD" [Sponsors again favor Civic and Social Democrats], CT24. Available online: www.ct24.cz/index_view.php?id=164403 (accessed 12 April 2006).

Kamarck, E.C. and Nye Jr, J.S. (eds) (2002) *Governance.com – Democracy in the Information Age*. Washington, DC: Brookings Institution Press.

Lusoli, W. (2005) "The Internet and the European Parliament elections: theoretical perspectives, empirical investigations and proposals for research," *Information Polity*, 10, 3–4: 153–163.

Margolis, M. and Resnick, D. (1999) "Party competition on the internet in the United States and Britain," *Harvard International Journal of Press/Politics*, 4: 24–48.

Mas-Colell, A., Whinston, M.D., and Green, J.R. (2002) *Microeconomic Theory*. Oxford: Oxford University Press.

Rainie, L., Cornfield, M., and Horrigan, J. (2005) *The Internet and Campaign 2004* (Pew Internet and American Life Project). Available online: www.pewinternet.org (accessed 3 April 2006).

Riley, J.G. (2001) "Silver signals: twenty-five years of screening and signaling," *Journal of Economic Literature*, 39: 432–478.

Schneider, S.M. and Foot, K.A. (2005) "Web sphere analysis: an approach to studying online action," in C. Hine (ed.), *Virtual Methods: Issues in Social Research on the Internet*, pp. 157–170. Oxford: Berg Publishers.

Strategie (2006) "Strany zvysi vydaje na volebni reklamu" [Parties about to increase campaign expenditures] *Strategie*. Available online: www.istrategie.cz/scripts/detail.php?id=102812 (accessed 12 April 2006).

Weber, L.M. and Murray, S. (2002) "A survey of the literature on the internet and democracy," paper presented at the Prospects of Electronic Democracy Conference, Pittsburgh, PA, September.

7 Online structure for political action in the 2004 U.S. congressional electoral web sphere

Kirsten A. Foot, Steven M. Schneider, and Meghan Dougherty

The use of the web in U.S. congressional elections has grown dramatically in each campaign cycle since the first election-oriented websites appeared in 1994. The percent of congressional candidates with websites produced by their campaign organizations dedicated to promoting their candidacy has increased in the past decade, to the point that 71 percent of Senate campaigns and 68 percent of House campaigns produced websites in 2004 (Howard 2006). The rise of candidate-centered campaign structures in the U.S. paralleled the emergence of new communication media that allowed candidates to establish direct contact with prospective supporters (Schier 2000). In addition, election-oriented web materials have been developed since 1994 by a wide range of actors such as political parties, the Federal Election Commission and other government bodies, news organizations, civic and advocacy groups, educational institutions, and individual citizens. Of course, the adoption and strategic use of information and communication technologies by political actors precedes the digital era. In some respects, the history of campaigning could be understood as the diffusion of technology into the political sphere; within the U.S., there has been tight inter-linking between advances in communication technologies and the practices of political communication (Abramson *et al.* 1988; Foot and Schneider 2006).

As is typical in presidential election years in the U.S., congressional elections in 2004 were overshadowed by the presidential race. However, investments in key Senate races were record-breaking. Many of the sites produced by Senate campaigns manifested a similar level of technical sophistication that was evident in some of the 2004 presidential primary campaign sites. News reports trumpeted the use of the web for fundraising by parties and interest groups along with campaigns in 2004 (Roberts Frith 2005). Civic and advocacy groups, as well as campaigns and parties, worked hard to get out the vote and had demonstrable success: at nearly 61 percent of the adult population, voter turnout in 2004 was the highest since 1968 (Faler 2005).

The internet was clearly a significant source of political information and a location of political action in the 2004 election. According to the Pew Internet and American Life Project (Rainie *et al.* 2005), more than a third of American adults used the internet for political purposes at some time during the 2004 election. The most common uses of the internet were getting news or information about the elections, and using e-mail to discuss politics. In a national telephone survey during November 2004, over 40 percent of internet users reported that the internet was an important source of political information for them. Some 27 percent of those who accessed political information online said it made a difference in how they voted, and nearly 10 percent reported monitoring campaign developments via the internet every day during the final weeks before the election (Rainie *et al.* 2005). One decade after its introduction into the U.S. political realm, the web has emerged as a place where many citizens look for politically oriented information and where political activity occurs to a significant extent.

Web practices

We use the term "web practices" to denote the acts of making, by which website producers create, appropriate, manipulate, link to, and/or display digital objects that can be accessed by web browsers (Foot and Schneider 2006; Foot *et al.* forthcoming 2007). We view the web as both a surface and site on which socio-political and communicative action may be structured, organized, and inscribed – through the web practices of political (and other) actors. In keeping with Giddens' (1984) structuration theory, we contend that web production practices both reflect existing offline structures and prior practices, and result in a particular online structure. These acts of making in turn enable and constrain actions in ways that may shape future iterations of practices, and thus the evolution of structures, both online and offline. More specifically, the web practices of political actors in electoral contexts are shaped by existing (offline) structures and cultural resources, reflecting political strategies and campaign practices developed over decades of electoral activity. They also manifest technology adoption patterns within socio-technical organizations or networks that may have deep historical and/or cultural roots. Concurrently, political actors' web practices instantiate an emergent and evolving set of norms, and create online structures for political action, some of which may be quite innovative (Schneider and Foot 2002). We conceptualize an "online structure" as a (co)produced electronic space, comprised of various html pages, features, links and texts, providing users opportunities to associate and act. On the web, relations between web producers, as well as between producers and users, are enacted and mediated through online structures. Furthermore, each online structure enables and constrains the potential for various kinds of political action, both online and offline.

As part of the Internet and Elections Project, this study was designed to examine the extent to which various types of political actors differentially engaged in web production practices within the 2004 U.S. congressional web sphere. Our two research questions were: (1) which practice was most/least prevalent across actor types within the sphere? (2) which types of political actors were most (least) likely to engage in specific practices? Since the online structures created through these practices enable and constrain actions in ways that may shape future iterations of the practices, and thus the evolution of structures online and offline, the answers to these questions hold significant implications for the U.S. political arena.

To understand how various types of political actors differentially engaged in web production in 2004 we analyzed four specific practices – informing, connecting, involving, and mobilizing – on sites produced by entities with a role in the electoral process. Each practice involves a distinctive type of relationship between site producers and other political actors (Foot and Schneider 2006). Site producers engage in the practice of informing by providing opportunities for site visitors to become informed about political actors or the election process. This practice invokes the classic transmission models of communication, in which a communicator or producer transmits a message to a receiver or recipient (Lasswell 1948). A biography or "About Us" text, issue position statements, information about voting or campaigning, and text or audio files of candidate speeches are features associated with the practice of informing.

Some political actors also engage in the practice of involving via their sites, in which the organization provides the online structure facilitating a connection between the user and the organization. In other words, involving is evidenced through opportunities for site visitors to interact with the site producer. This practice is indicated by features such as: invitation to join the organization; e-mail list subscription; opportunity to sign up to volunteer; calendar of events; request for financial contributions; and discussion forum. The relationship between the producing organization and the actor using the site is reminiscent of the swapping between roles of source/encoder and receiver/decoder envisioned by Schramm (1954) in his model of communications (McQuail and Windahl 1981).

The web practice of connecting is seen in the creation of an online structure that serves as a bridge between the user of the site and a "third" political actor. In other words, the producer uses its web presence to "connect" a site user with another political actor, such as a campaign, press organization, political party, government agency, or even an electoral opponent. In social network theory, these bridges are the ties between nodes of the network (Granovetter 1973); in our analysis, any other political actor, whether offline or online, constitutes a node to which a site in the electoral web sphere may be connected, and the online structure facilitating the connection acts as the tie between nodes. The practice of connecting on the web is most familiarly invoked using the technique of linking, but our conception is considerably broader in that we suggest campaigns create both cognitive and transversal bridges between users and third actors. Transversal connections provide the online structure to facilitate movement through cyberspace, from one place (e.g. a web page) to another (Saco 2002), while cognitive connections provide only the mental or psychological bridge, relying on users to complete the connection through their own action, either online or offline.

Additionally, some web producers engage in the practice of mobilizing – providing online structure that enables supporters to become advocates for a campaign, party, or cause. In this type of practice, the producer has moved beyond involving itself with the user and beyond making it possible for the user to become connected with a third party actor. Mobilizing is evidenced in structures that allow the visitor to send web pages to friends, print brochures for offline distribution, access promotional e-paraphernalia, or make public support statements (e.g. letters to editors, interaction with polls, talk radio stations, and other local media).

In summary, these four practices can be viewed as supporting a variety of relationships among three types of political actors: the site visitor, the site producer, and another political actor(s). The practice of informing is a one-way relationship in which the site producer functions as the sender, and the site visitor functions as the receiver; no exchange relationship is invited or intended. The practice of involving is an attempt to establish interactions between the producer and the visitor. The practice of connecting, positions the producer as a facilitator attempting to establish some form of communication between the site visitor and other actors. The practice of mobilizing takes this one step further, and positions the producer as a facilitator attempting to establish some form of communication between site visitors and potential supporters of a campaign, party, or cause.

Web production practices are inscribed in particular site features (Foot and Schneider 2006; Foot *et al.* forthcoming 2007). While the mapping of practices to features described above is neither exhaustive nor mutually exclusive – we certainly recognize that other features could have been identified and/or associated with the practices under review, and that some of the features could arguably be said to be indicators of practices other than those we have suggested – we nevertheless believe our mapping to be a useful starting point to assess the extent to which four web production practices were employed by different types of political actors in the 2004 congressional electoral web sphere.

Methods

To conduct this study, websites comprising the U.S. congressional electoral web sphere were identified as systematically and comprehensively as possible in correspondence with the overall methodological framework employed in the Internet and Elections Project. Websites corresponding with sampled URLs were coded in accordance with a common protocol to generate structured observations that could be compared across web spheres over time. Researchers identifying sites and coding sites also created a set of field notes with unstructured observations about particular sites and the electoral web sphere in general, to document phenomena of particular interest or significance to online structure and political action within the web sphere.

Systematic identification of sites within the U.S. electoral web sphere took place between 30 and 85 days before the election; however, researchers continued ongoing *ad hoc* identification and annotation of election-related sites until the day of the election. Researchers used the WebArchivist Resource Identifier to add the URLs of identified sites to a project database and aid in generating catalogue data for URLs added to the database. To facilitate consistent identification of sites among members of the U.S. research team and across the Internet and Elections Project, the research team used a "sleuthing guide" to guide the identification of sites produced by a range of political actor types involved in the election.

Researchers ran search queries in two internet search engines (Google.com and one other major search engine such as Yahoo.com) and followed the first 50 links from the search results page to identify resources within the web sphere. Web resources from all political actors relevant to the election were identified as part of the web sphere regardless of whether election-related content appeared on the site at the time of identification. Once a site was identified, researchers followed links appearing on the site to sleuth out other sites by the same producer.

A very large number of campaign sites (1097) were identified in comparison with other producer types within the sphere, due in part to the ease through which they could be identified as well as the large number of contested congressional seats. In the U.S. House of Representatives, all 440 seats (435 representatives, five delegates) were up for election. In the U.S. Senate, 34 of the Senate's 100 seats were at stake in November 2004, as well as the 11 states which held governor races. Thus a total of 485 seats in the general election were open. Given time and resource constraints, we identified as many sites as possible within each of the other producer types, adding the URL for each site and associated metadata about the site and its producer to a shared project database. Different members of the research team took responsibility for identifying sites produced by the press, political parties, government bodies, and citizens. Election-related government and party sites were prolific and easy to find; we identified 155 party sites (including national and state-level party organizations). Several federal government sites were identified using the search string: 2004 + congressional + elections. From this initial query many of the federal government sites provided valuable links to other government agencies containing general election information. Secretary of state sites were found by searching for "secretary of state" on Google. For states for which a secretary of state site did not surface using this technique, a more specified Google query was used including the actual name of the state. Many secretary of state sites which did not provide election-related information (usually because it was outside of their jurisdiction) provided a link to the states' board of elections site.

The search strategies used for identifying citizen sites were far different than those employed for identifying party and government sites. Many citizen sites were identified from links provided on the political blog directories ETalkingHead.com, or ChangeforAmerica.com. It was quite common for citizen blogs to provide links to their favorite sites, which were typically produced by other citizens or NGOs/political action groups; such linked-to sites were included in the Identifier. Searching for "news media" on Google led to a directory of press sites at abyznewslinks.com. The directory contained a listing of "all media in state" for each state in the U.S.; however, many of the press sites located via this directory were local newspaper sites, which did not have a page for national election coverage. Identification focused on press sites in larger metropolitan regions which were more likely to provide national news coverage.

Identifying sites produced by other types of actors with a role or voice in the election process was more challenging. Various combinations of the following terms were searched on Google, as well as on Yahoo, Lycos, Ask Jeeves, Netscape, MSN, and Excite.com: "religion and politics", "political action committees", "religious organizations or groups", "George Bush," and "John Kerry". A Yahoo directory led to NGO and labor sites with election content. Since sites produced by NGOs or religious organizations are less likely to address elections, the first 20 sites returned from each search were examined, and included in the database only if it had content relevant to the U.S. congressional elections. Links on some pages returned from searches were followed when they appeared promising. Major press sites such as those produced by U.S. television networks (e.g. ABC, NBC, CBS, and FOX) as well as international news service sites such as Reuters were consulted for links to election-related sites by other producers.

Four weeks prior to the election, a sample of 100 sites, based on the sampling frame employed across the Internet and Elections Project, was drawn from the sites identified in the U.S. congressional electoral sphere. Systematic coding of the sample of identified sites took place during a period of two weeks ending three days prior to the election. Annotation, like identification, was a process that continued throughout the campaign period – during the identification process, during the coding process, and up to the day after the election. Through regular, repeated observations, and drawing on insights developed through studies of previous elections, team members also noted phenomena of particular interest or significance to the 2004 U.S. congressional electoral web sphere. Open-ended field notes about online structure and political action informed our analysis of the coding data for this study.

Findings

Our analysis of the prevalence of specific features grouped by web practice in relation to each type of political actor is presented in Table 7.1. The

Table 7.1 Feature prevalence

Practice	Feature	Campaign	Government	NGO/Labor	Party	Press	Other
Informing	About the producer	0.93	0.67	1.00	0.79	0.50	0.81
	Issue positions	0.81	0.17	0.46	0.71	0.50	0.21
	Information about campaign process	0.33	0.75	0.21	0.50	0.25	0.00
	Information about voting process	0.41	0.75	0.36	0.79	0.42	0.10
Involving	Discussion forum	0.22	0.00	0.14	0.50	0.67	0.52
	Join/become a member	0.07	0.00	0.21	0.14	0.00	0.19
	Get e-mail from site	0.56	0.00	0.36	0.50	0.42	0.19
	Information about donating money	0.89	0.00	0.57	1.00	0.08	0.29
	Opportunity to sign up to volunteer	0.74	0.00	0.21	0.86	0.00	0.14
	Calendar of events	0.33	0.67	0.07	0.71	0.00	0.19
Connecting	Endorsement of candidates or party	0.48	0.00	0.15	0.14	0.50	0.14
	Comparison of candidates or parties on issues	0.33	0.08	0.21	0.07	0.58	0.14
	Voter registration information	0.44	0.75	0.43	0.86	0.17	0.10
Mobilizing	Offline distribution of online materials	0.30	0.17	0.14	0.21	0.00	0.05
	Send link to page	0.11	0.00	0.14	0.00	0.50	0.14
	E-paraphernalia	0.11	0.00	0.07	0.14	0.00	0.14
	Facilitating statements of public support	0.30	0.00	0.21	0.36	0.42	0.10
Number of cases		27	12	14	14	12	21

presence or absence of each of the 17 features assessed is indicated for the sites produced during the 2004 election season by campaigns, government agencies, non-governmental organizations/labor unions, press organizations, and others.

Our assessment of the prevalence of each feature associated with the four practices on sites developed by different types of political actors served as the foundation of our primary analysis. We were especially interested in establishing the extent to which each type of producer engaged in the four web campaigning practices, rather than the likelihood of any specific feature appearing on a particular type of website. To complete this analysis, we calculated a cross-site index (see Table 7.2) by dividing the sum of features present across all sites developed by a given producer type by the product of the number of features observed and the number of sites examined within each producer type. For example, if every website examined for a given producer type was found to have each feature associated with a given practice, the cross-site index would equal 1.0. The cross-site index is most useful in a comparative context, when sets of sites across two or more producer types are assessed.

Across all producer types, informing was the most prevalent practice and mobilizing was the least prevalent practice. For most producer types, involving followed informing in prevalence. Unsurprisingly in view of their respective roles in the electoral process, government and press site producers posed exceptions to this pattern with involving scores that were lower than their connecting scores.

Parties engaged in informing and involving more extensively than any other producer type; campaigns were second for both of these practices. Campaigns and press organizations tied for the highest score in the connecting practice, followed by parties. Press organizations had the highest index score for the mobilizing practice; however, since the prevalence of features associated with this practice was low across all producer types, it is important to note that the presence of all four features across the sites of a particular producer type is arguably more significant as an indication of the type of online structure created by that producer type than the index score. Thus, although press sites received the highest score for mobilizing, Table 7.1 reveals that was driven by the relatively high frequency of two features:

Table 7.2 Cross-site index

	Campaign	Government	NGO/Labor	Party	Press	Other
Informing	0.62	0.58	0.50	0.70	0.42	0.27
Involving	0.47	0.11	0.26	0.62	0.19	0.25
Connecting	0.42	0.28	0.26	0.36	0.42	0.13
Mobilizing	0.20	0.04	0.14	0.18	0.23	0.11
n	27.00	12.00	14.00	14.00	12.00	21.00

sending links and facilitating public support statements. None of the press sites included in our sample employed the offline distribution feature as it was operationalized for this study, or e-paraphernalia. In contrast, some campaign sites manifested all four features associated with mobilizing. Although the campaign producers' index score for mobilizing was slightly lower than the press producers' score, online structure for mobilizing was actually more robust on the campaign sites. When the index scores for each practice were summed for each producer type, parties were found to have created the most extensive online structures. This finding was a bit surprising to us, in view of the candidate-centered nature of U.S. elections.

In summary, within the U.S. 2004 congressional web sphere, web producers were more likely to provide opportunities for web users to become informed and involved than they were to provide opportunities for connecting and mobilizing. Practices of informing and involving may be more prevalent across producer types in the electoral web sphere because they are adaptations of traditional, offline, political practices, whereas practices of connecting and mobilizing require strategic and technological innovation. Informing and involving are core practices for campaigns, parties, and NGOs offline, and these organizations incur minimal cost and risk in adapting them to the web. The use of metaphors such as "brochure-ware" and "digital yard signs" in the studies of campaign sites in the 1996 and 1998 U.S. elections (Hill and Hughes 1998) demonstrate that informing was the first campaign practice adapted to the web, and it is certainly the easiest from a technical perspective. Public perception of the web as an information source may also help explain why campaigns and other political actors engage extensively in informing.

Similarly, the practice of involving is a long-standing political strategy, and adapting it to the web does not require a rethinking of strategy or a release of control. The relatively high level of involving across producer types in 2004 may also reflect the donor-driven political culture of electoral politics in the U.S. The contributions of volunteers, both financial and in labor, are fundamental to the life of campaigns, parties, civic, and advocacy groups in the U.S. Offering e-mail updates to site visitors allows an organization to collect e-mail addresses and often other kinds of personal information from site visitors. This information enables organizations to tailor future requests for donations and volunteer labor in ways that might increase their persuasive power. Thus, development of website features associated with informing may represent investment in the organization, whether for the present or the future.

Connecting and mobilizing, on the other hand, represent the emergence of more innovative forms of political activity on the web. We suggest that the extent of connecting was relatively low in 2004 for several reasons, including producers' desire to maintain control of site traffic and presentation, concerns about repurposing of materials by opponents or even supporters, legal concerns, and a general aversion to risky behavior on the part of many political actors. Some political actors may desire to maintain site "stickiness" (Lewin 2003), based on the sense that site visitors, once captured by a specific site, are too valuable to "give away" to another site via a link. It is also conceivable that from one political actor's perspective, connecting to other political actors gives rise to the possibility that the material ultimately viewed by site visitors clicking on the link will not be the same as was intended when the connection was created. The uncertainty created by a link to another political actor's site may be sufficient to discourage its implementation by some organizations. Also, the practice of connecting through the technique of linking can place organizations on somewhat uncertain legal terrain. Some may be wary of copyright infringement, either on their own part or on the part of those organizations to which they connect. Connecting to organizations whose tax status forbids political activity could lead to questions and allegations threatening the independence of those organizations. The possibility of providing links to organizations that may be registered as lobbyists for foreign governments is another legal barrier.

A significant reason for campaigns' and other actors' wariness in regard to both connecting and mobilizing may be that these practices are perceived by some organizations as risky. Campaigns are inherently risk-averse organizations (Selnow 1998). This risk-aversive behavior is particularly applicable to environments in which the opportunities for rewards are perceived as low. Given a lack of perceived rewards, many political actors have been cautious in their experimentation with connecting and mobilizing. The 2004 presidential primary campaign of Howard Dean seemed to have changed this calculus. One of the lasting outcomes of the phenomenal success Howard Dean's campaign experienced online in the lead up to the 2004 primary season may be its catalyzing of both connecting and mobilizing. The online component of the Dean campaign was created as a distributed web presence, involving multiple sites, many of which were produced by people outside of the official campaign. For example, one part of the Dean campaign's web presence, the fordean.org network of sites, included a single site that connected more than 500 discussion groups, state and local Dean action coordinators, and Dean supporters' websites. This extensive use of connecting and mobilizing as web practices set a new standard for web campaigning that was, in part, emulated by other campaign organizations in the 2004 presidential primary, and which we should anticipate being replicated in future election cycles.

Implications

Our findings hold several implications for the U.S. electoral arena. First, when internet users go to different parts of the sphere (depending on the type of actor whose site they visited) they are more/less likely to encounter online structures reflecting particular practices. For instance, visitors to party and campaign sites are much more likely to find online structures for both informing and involving, whereas visitors to government sites are unlikely to find online structures for either involving or mobilizing. The forms of online structure provided enable and constrain the kinds of political engagement that are encouraged, and may shape the nature of political engagement that occurs.

Second, the relatively low prevalence of connecting and mobilizing across producer types indicates that political actors producing the 2004 U.S. congressional electoral web sphere under-utilized the web's affordances for enabling multi-actor engagement. In other words, web applications make it relatively easy for producers to create cognitive and transversal bridges between actors, which can be employed in politically strategic ways by both producers and users. Levels of connecting and mobilizing may have a constraining influence on web users' individual participation in the electoral process, and on the robustness of the electoral web sphere in general.

Third, by emphasizing involving over connecting and mobilizing, site producers may have created online versions of "gated communities". That is, producers sought the support of visitors for their particular organizations, but did so without providing bridges for visitors to other sites and actors. As noted above, this may indicate a preference for retaining control of scarce political resources and an aversion to the risks associated with connecting and mobilizing. The consequences for civic engagement of online structures that could be considered gated communities is an area ripe for future research.

It is useful to situate the productive behavior of the various actors in an electoral web sphere. For example, future research on the web in U.S. elections could contrast the web production experience of those recruited into political participation by candidate-oriented organizations (i.e. campaigns) from those recruited by issue-oriented organizations (i.e. advocacy groups). Alternatively, assessment of the potential strategic values of the various decisions made by web producers might shed further light on the decisions involving the deployment of features associated with the practices of connecting and mobilizing. For example, will citizens as producers increasingly seek to differentiate themselves and form *ad hoc* communities, or will campaigns and organizations increasingly structure the online democratic activities of citizens? A focus on these kinds of questions might also yield insights regarding the status of the citizen-as-producer in a digital world, and the tensions between campaign organizations and advocacy groups for control of resources and messages.

References

Abramson, J.B., Arterton, F.C., and Orren, G.R. (1988) *The Electronic Commonwealth: The Impact of New Media Technologies on Democratic Politics.* New York: Basic Books, Inc.

Faler, B. (2005) "Election turnout in 2004 was highest since 1968". *Washington Post*, January 15, p. A05.

Foot, K.A. and Schneider, S.M. (2006) *Web Campaigning*. Cambridge: MIT Press.

Foot, K.A., Schneider, S.M., Xenos, M., and Dougherty, M. (forthcoming 2007) "The influence of political-structural factors on candidates' Web practices in the 2002 U.S. House, Senate and gubernatorial elections", *Journal of Political Marketing*.

Giddens, A. (1984) *The Constitution of Society: Outline of the Theory of Structure*. Berkeley: University of California Press.

Granovetter, M.S. (1973) "Strength of weak ties", *American Journal of Sociology*, 78: 1360–1380.

Hill, K.A. and Hughes, J.E. (1998) *Cyberpolitics: Citizen Activism in the Age of the Internet*. Lanham, MD: Rowman & Littlefield.

Howard, P.N. (2006) *New Media Campaigns and the Managed Citizen*. New York: Cambridge University Press.

Lasswell, H.D. (1948) "The structure and function of communication and society", in L. Bryson (ed.), *The Communication of Ideas*, pp. 203–248. New York: Harper and Row.

Lewin, J. (2003) Is your site sticky? *Computer World*, 18 March.

McQuail, D. and Windahl, S. (1981) *Communication Models for the Study of Mass Communications*. Harlow, UK: Longman.

Rainie, L., Cornfield, M., and Horrigan, J. (2005) *The Internet and Campaign 2004*. Washington, DC: Pew Internet and American Life Project.

Roberts Frith, C. (2005) "Candidates on the stump online: framing the Internet in the early stages of the 2004 presidential election", paper presented at the International Communication Association, New York, NY, 27–31 May.

Saco, D. (2002) *Cybering Democracy: Public Space and the Internet*. Thousand Oaks: Sage.

Schier, S.E. (2000) *By Invitation Only: The Rise of Exclusive Politics in the United States*. Pittsburgh: University of Pittsburgh Press.

Schneider, S.M. and Foot, K.A. (2002) "Online structure for political action: exploring presidential web sites from the 2000 American election", *Javnost (The Public)*, 9, 2: 43–60.

Schramm, W. (1954) "How communication works", in W. Schramm (ed.), *The Process and Effects of Mass Communication*. Urbana: University of Illinois Press.

Selnow, G.W. (1998) *Electronic Whistle-stops: The Impact of the Internet on American Politics*. Westport, CT: Praeger.

Part III

Reaching diverse constituencies via the web

8 Philippines: poli-clicking as politicking

Online campaigning and civic action in the 2004 national election

Kate A. Mirandilla

Introduction

New media technologies are transforming political campaigns across the globe (Gibson and Ward 2001; Norris 2001). Recent studies on politics and new media, particularly the internet, present arguments that follow two overarching and opposing perspectives. Norris (2003) presents these two distinct views. On the one hand, "cyber-optimists" believe that as internet access spreads across nations and into societies, new opportunities are created for direct access to politically relevant information and for unmediated communication between the political organizations and the electorate (Norris 2003). For this group, the internet introduces changes in civic participation. On the other hand, non-believers, or "cyber-skeptics," perceive the internet as simply reflecting and reinforcing – rather than transforming – the existing structural features of each country's political system. For these skeptics, the internet enhances democratic action and participation only among those who are politically active by nature. The more able or powerful ones dominate the usage of the internet; the less able ones are put in (even) more isolation. The technology merely promulgates existing trends in politics. Thus, for these individuals, the internet is basically an extension of traditional media; it does not change people so much, but it rather allows them to do what they usually do *and* to do it better to some extent.

In recent years, the Philippines has joined the cyberspace bandwagon. The Philippine government spearheaded initiatives on IT infrastructures that spawned greater online presence across sectors, especially the government, educational institutions, media, and non-government organizations. Although still in its infant stages of adoption, internet usage in the country has started penetrating into the socio-cultural (e.g. e-mails, blogs, online discussion forums, online video streaming), economic (e.g. online payment of bills), and political (e.g. political advertising) dimensions in the society.

This current study[1] on the role of the internet in the Philippine political arena can better be contextualized by providing a brief overview of how politics works in the country. The political system of the Philippines is a democratic, presidential form of government. National political players include the president, vice-president and 24 senators. The country is divided into geographical regions that are further segregated into districts and municipalities. Members of the House of Representatives serve at the district level, while the city mayors, councilors and village leaders encompass the rest of the officials of the local government units (LGUs) in the country.

Following the restoration of democracy by former president Corazon Aquino in 1986, the presidential and vice-presidential elections have been held every six years, while a separate election for the second half (last 12) of the 24 senatorial seats is done every three years (often coinciding with the elections for the LGU positions). Voting for elections is done directly by the electorate, and the candidate who gets the most number of votes wins the election. All eligible voters vote for all positions and the electoral system is one of plurality or a first-past-the-post system (Leones and Moraleda 1999).

The media play a vital role in Philippine elections. Various media vehicles are used for image building, information dissemination, and the development of public opinion (Meinardus 2004). Political campaigns maximize the use of mass media like television, radio, and print to provide the voting public with more exposure to their respective candidates. Election campaigns have become more creative and sophisticated with candidates looking for extensive media coverage by visiting talk shows, appearing on television sitcoms, dispensing advice over the radio, and buying advertisement spreads in newspapers. Such practice further establishes an image-oriented election campaign, which puts more importance on a candidate's popularity rather than on his or her political platform. Internet use for political purposes is still in a preliminary phase, primarily because issues of internet access, resources, costs, and literacy keep many Filipinos from effectively using the technology.

However, there is little doubt that the internet is playing a role in Philippine politics. The first prominent usage of the internet as a political communication tool occurred in 2001 when activists used websites to post exposés and charges against former president Joseph Estrada (Cuevas 2004). The growing discontent with the Estrada administration provoked people – mostly from the middle and upper income levels – to post anti-Estrada content in online political forums, news groups, blogs, as well as to forward "hate" campaigns using e-mail and short messaging services (SMS or "text messaging") of mobile phones (Cuevas 2004). Ultimately, these online protests contributed to the eventual impeachment of Estrada in a move that later came to be dubbed as the "People Power II." These nascent applications of the technology show that the internet is slowly having an impact through the bold but steady initiatives taken by the government, the private sector, and academia in the Philippines.

In spite of the role of technology in Asian politics, however, most of the studies documenting political uses of the internet have been conducted in western developed societies (Gibson and Ward 2001; Norris 2001; Mianni

2001; Farnsworth and Owen 2003; Pace 2003), and only a few in Asian countries (Kluver 2004; Ducke 2002; Wang 2002; Hong and Chang 2002; Tkach-Kawasaki 2003). In the Philippines, evidence of the impact of the internet on political action remains anecdotal and largely undocumented.

This study attempts to fill this literature gap. The current chapter employs a descriptive-exploratory assessment of the role of political websites in the Philippines during the May 2004 national election from the reference point of the "election stakeholders." The findings of this study demonstrate how political campaigning via the internet provides fresh opportunities to politicians, on the one hand, and newer modes for political participation to the Filipino electorate, on the other. Most importantly, the findings of this project will help to document the possible effects of the internet, if any, in the political campaigning and civic participation in the Philippines.

I particularly focus on the use of two distinct types of web features in the Filipino web sphere – engagement and information provision – during the recent election campaign. My analysis focuses on the range of election-related activities encouraged by political websites during the campaign season.

Research questions

My goal in this study is primarily to draw conclusions regarding the primary *function* of the internet in the 2004 Philippine national election. In particular, I pose the following questions: (1) what/who were the primary political actors which used the internet for campaigning?; (2) what were the most prominent website features of the 2004 Philippine web sphere?; and (3) what was the main function of the internet in the 2004 election?

Study framework

This chapter employs the Internet and Elections Project approach to web sphere analysis, similar to the other chapters in this volume. In addition to the methodological framework embodied in this approach, the study also draws upon a model of internet engagement proposed by Norris (2001) for theoretical grounding. Norris' model takes the perspective of internet users and examines the ways in which content producers of websites design content. It should be mentioned that the factors inherent in the model are broad concepts that may have various meanings in different contexts.

In this model, Norris (2001) posits three general factors that may interact and influence the use of the internet in various societies: namely, the *resources* needed to establish the infrastructure, the *structure* of the technology itself, and the *motivation* to use the technology. In Norris' model, these factors are presented non-hierarchically. *Resources* refer to the availability of time and money set by a society to invest in infrastructures needed to establish new communication technologies such as the internet. The discourse on *resources*

touches larger concerns about the digital divide, which suggests the dispar-
ity in usage patterns of the technology is influenced by users' relative access
to the technology. Similarly, *motivation* is anchored by the political will of
the society's leaders.

Further, Norris (2001) argues that the *structure* of the technology itself
may invite various usage patterns from the users. In the case of political
campaigns and new media, the structure of the latter is significant in initiat-
ing greater civic participation among the electorate. In this study, the choice
of the content producers to offer specific online features, the primary units of
analysis of the study, may show how they view the social dimension of the
internet as a technology. Consequently, Norris argues that if online political
participation indeed is a reality, how different – or reflective of – is this from
what we consider "offline" political participation?

Last, according to this model, citizens must possess a certain degree of *motivation* to avail themselves of the services offered by the internet. In online
political campaigns, one of the primary challenges is creating interest among
the electorate to use the technology, regardless of how well the resources are
made available to them. On the one hand, the motivation of the content producers to use the internet for their campaigns may stem from the gratifications
of web use among the site visitors by maximizing the structure of opportunities found in these sites. On the other hand, the site visitors' decision to
participate in these varied online activities may be influenced by their level of
trust and confidence in the online system provided by the content producers.
In addition, the level of technical "savvy-ness" required to access the internet
and its features remains another consideration. This observation may explain
why the sophisticated features of the websites are not fully maximized –
mainly because site visitors are not familiar with them.

As part of the overall methodological orientation, this study identifies the
Philippine election web sphere for the 2004 national election, or the group
of potential content producers who might have had a stake in the election,
including: (1) business/commercial enterprises; (2) political candidates; (3)
citizens; (4) educational institutions; (5) government offices; (6) non-government organizations; (7) political consultants; (8) political parties; (9) portal
sites; (10) press organizations; and (11) religious groups.

The data collection was conducted in two stages. First, the identification
stage aimed to develop a database of Filipino websites that posted content
related to the May 2004 Philippine election. I identified 235 relevant sites
during this stage (see Table 8.1). In the coding stage, based on a stratified
random sample, I examined 100 of the 235 sites (N = 100), which constituted the sampling frame of the study.

Online features

For the purposes of the research, I regrouped the information and engagement web features used by the overall project into two groups based on: (1)

Table 8.1 Types of site producers in the Philippine political web sphere

Types of site producers	Frequency
Government	30
Political candidates	29
Citizens	33
NGOs	35
Political parties	3
Political professionals/consultants	5
Portal sites	26
Press organizations	72
Religious organizations	2
Total	235

Note
* There were no sites identified for the business, educational, and labor categories.

content, and (2) web design elements. Tables 8.2 and 8.3 illustrate the initial data on the assessment of the information and engagement site features.

For the content features, I adopted the categories used by Cuevas (2004) in a study on the internet in Philippine elections. Here, specific website features and links were reclustered into five sub-groups that describe the various functions of the internet as a tool for political campaigns. These content feature sub-groups are: (1) information provision; (2) candidate/party promotion; (3) voter participation; (4) political education; and (5) political talk. The web design elements include: (1) images or still photos, and (2) audio-visual clips uploaded and streamed in the websites. The interactive capacity of the internet crosses over both the content and web design features of the websites.

The information provision category contains those features that provide basic information about the identity of the site producer, political positions, or other types of election-specific information. Information provision facilitates limited interaction between the political candidates/parties and the voting public. These features contain more information about the candidates and their parties as compared with the data found in the "offline" environment, that is, in traditional media. In this cluster, the Biography/History/About Us, Speeches, Endorsements, and Issue Positions features are included.

The second content feature category, candidate/party promotion, contains site features that directly promote candidates and parties. My study attempts to assess whether the websites encouraged offline distribution of electoral campaign or election materials downloaded from them. Other site features included in this category are: (1) send-a-link; (2) public statements of support; and (3) e-paraphernalia (e.g. desktop wallpapers and screen-savers).

Table 8.2 Information-related features on websites of site producers in the Philippines

Site producers	Case (f)	Elec (f)	Bio (f)	End (f)	Issue (f)	Sp (f)	Cal (f)	Com (f)	InfC (f)	InfV (f)	IM (f)	AV (f)	Priv (f)	Ter (f)
Candidate	26	26	21	4	16	12	3	0	0	21	26	9	0	0
Government	10	7	6	0	0	1	2	0	3	4	10	0	0	0
NGO/Labor	9	9	9	0	2	1	3	1	0	4	9	1	1	1
Party	3	3	2	2	3	3	2	0	2	0	3	1	0	0
Press	9	7	6	0	1	0	0	1	1	1	9	1	0	0
Others	35	31	21	5	8	7	9	0	6	6	30	9	6	26
Total	92	83	65	11	30	24	19	2	12	36	87	21	7	27

Abbreviations and descriptions of features:
AV: audio or video files present on site.
BIO: biography/history of party/candidate present on site.
END: endorsements for a candidate/party present on site.
CAL: a calendar/list of events with election-related events present on site.
COM: comparison of issue positions of candidates/parties present on site.
IM: images present on site.
INFC: information about the electoral campaign process present on site.
INFV: information about the voting/registration process present on site.
ISSUE: list of issue positions held by party/candidate present on site.
SP: speech by candidate or party representative present on site.
TER: terms of agreement present on site.

Table 8.3 Engagement-related features on websites of site producers in the Philippines

Site producers	Cases	Cont (f)	Join (f)	Regis (f)	E-mail (f)	Don (f)	Forum (f)	Offdist (f)	Slink (f)	Pubsup (f)	Epara (f)	Volunt (f)
Candidate	26	19	7	0	3	4	9	8	21	6	5	9
Government	10	9	0	0	0	0	1	1	0	0	0	0
NGO/Labor	9	8	2	0	3	0	5	3	2	1	0	1
Party	3	3	1	0	2	1	2	2	1	1	1	2
Press	9	8	0	0	1	0	3	1	1	2	0	0
Others	35	25	10	0	9	6	21	7	5	21	4	4
Total	92	72	20	0	18	11	41	22	28	31	10	15

Abbreviations and descriptions of features:
JOIN:	join-the-organization or -campaign present on site.
REGIS:	registered voting present on site.
EMAIL:	e-mail back features present on site.
CAL:	a calendar/list of events with election-related events present on site.
DON:	donate for the campaign present on site.
FORUM:	communication space present on site.
OFFDIST:	offline distribution of online material present on site.
SLINK:	send-this-link present on site
PUBSUP:	statements of public support on party/candidate present on site.
EPARA:	downloading of e-paraphernalia present on site.
VOLUNT:	volunteer for the organization present on site.

The voter mobilization/participation category comprises online features inviting commitment among the site visitors. These features encourage site visitors to: (1) volunteer for the campaign activities; (2) join/become a member of the organization; (3) sign-up to receive e-mails from the site producer; (4) read updates of the prospective election-related events posted in the calendar or list of activities of the political actor; and (5) donate monetary support to the political candidate or organization (offline or online).

The fourth content feature category is political education. The features included here concern the official campaign and election procedures. I reviewed the websites and determined whether information on the Philippine elections in general, as well as on the actual voting processes (for example, registration precincts), was available in the websites prior to the election day (10 May). Here, I inspected whether the websites included online information about the campaign process (electoral campaigning rules and governmental regulations in the country), and whether the websites provided information about the pre-election day announcements such as the eligibility of voters, voting dates, and corresponding precinct information. In addition, this category also included features offering comparisons of the similarities and differences of the issue positions held by various political actors.

The content category sub-group contained features that provided a venue for political discussion. Some candidate and political party websites allowed immediate two-way communication from the voters to the candidates or parties, or vice versa; as well as communication between and among the members of the electorate themselves. Examples of these venues were comment sections, message boards, weblogs, forums, chats, polls, or other types of communication spaces. Similarly, this category includes features that provide the site producer's contact information (for example, their e-mail address, postal address, and telephone number).

This study also examined site design elements, and multimedia features. Some examples of these were election-related images, such as photographs, flags, icons, logos, and downloadable audio or video campaign materials.

Results

Table 8.4 shows the top five most represented election stakeholders in the population of the study. This included 26 candidate websites, the largest group of election stakeholders represented in the sampling distribution. In this list, political parties obtained the least representation because only three party websites existed for the national elections.

It is apparent from the distribution of the sites that the political candidates were overly represented as compared with the other stakeholders included in the study. I attribute this to the fact that the candidates were more active in creating their own websites during the campaign period than the other sectors. Only a few sites representing other producer types posted election-related content, excluding them from the initial coding.

Table 8.4 Top five election stakeholders with online presence in the 2004 Philippine election

Election stakeholders	Frequency
Political candidates	26
Government	10
Press	9
Non-government organizations (NGOs)	9
Political parties	3

Table 8.5 Distribution of candidates and party websites in the 2004 Philippine election

Political actor	Candidates/parties	Candidates/parties with websites
Presidential candidates	5	5
Vice-presidential candidates	4	2
Senatorial candidates	48	14
Political parties	11	3
Total	68	24

Note
* Study sample.

During the campaign season, all of the *presidentiables* (presidential candidates), as well as two of the four vice-presidential candidates, maintained their own official websites. Out of the 48 senatorial candidates, only 14 allotted resources for the creation and maintenance of sites. Moreover, only three out of the 11 parties fielding candidates maintained an online presence. Of the three official party sites, one party owned two.

During the election campaign, candidates and political parties generally created more sophisticated websites than other stakeholders did, based on an analysis of the number of online and interactive features posted. The campaign websites of Eddie Villanueva, an evangelical pastor and *presidentiable* also known as "Brother Eddie," appeared most complete and sophisticated, in terms of the number and type of features he included. One of his websites was more politically oriented, whereas his religious followers created the other. The former provided a clear outline of his specific standpoints on selected issues. He provided a wide range of features encouraging participation from the site visitors such as asking them to volunteer, join, or donate to the campaign. This site also provided multimedia clips providing downloadable campaign video clips, jingles and other campaign materials. Content on Villanueva's site set a pattern later followed by the other candidates. Importantly, this was one of the first few, if not only, websites that

Table 8.6 Frequency distribution of the online features studied

Online features	Frequency
A Content	
Information dissemination	132
Political talk	113
Voter participation	82
Candidate/party promotion	55
Political education	31
B Web design	
Multimedia capacity	109

recognized the potential of SMS technology (for example, "Support the presidential bid of Bro. Eddie Villanueva by texting BRO. EDDIE to 46333").

Meanwhile, election stakeholders seemed to be the least interested in providing online political education to voters. Accessing the audio-visual files normally entails another command from the site visitors, thus making it appear more "interactive" than the uploaded still images that are readily seen on the websites.

Coding revealed that the most commonly included feature on these sites was a "Contact Us" section, followed by "Biography/About Us/History" sections, and some sort of communication space. Least frequently present on the sites were issue comparisons between parties or candidates. The findings also indicate that, generally, the websites offered venues for offline voter participation. Most sites invited visitors to join their organizations or political campaigns. However, few asked for donations.

Most sites did not promote candidates or parties. On those that did, however, candidate/party promotion mainly took the form of downloadable campaign materials, which could be distributed offline. The fact that downloading e-paraphernalia was not available on most sites may illustrate that producers preferred to promote candidates and parties using traditional offline means.

Few sites offered political education features, such as a Comparison on Issue Positions. Instead, the websites mostly provided the site visitors with a link containing information on the voting process. In terms of multimedia offerings, the data revealed that while the websites provided still photos and other graphical images, they did not generally maximize the potential of the technology to offer clips of campaign jingles and other audio-visual materials of the candidates. Thus, the sophistication of the web design of the coded sites was determined more by the principles of aesthetics instead of the capacity of the internet to store abundant information aside from still photos and images.

Discussion

By looking into the interplay of the *resources*, *structure of findings*, and *motivation of users* in the Philippine context, we can obtain a more holistic, systematic and logical picture of the role the internet played among the election stakeholders during the 2004 election season in the Philippines.

Resources

The digital divide in the Philippines is illustrated by the growing gap between those who have access to the information technologies such as the internet and those who do not. The users – both the content providers and consumers – are bound by financial and physical constraints, which may suggest why content providers are placing less emphasis on their internet presence than their use of traditional media.

The priorities of the Philippine government in building sufficient infra-structures for widespread utilization of the technology will affect its rate of diffusion in the country, thereby limiting what is available for political usage. From a resource perspective, the issue of the access to the internet is a significant logistical concern, and will determine the ultimate affordability, accessibility, and availability of this technology.

Structure of opportunities

From the perspective of the Filipinos who are non-believers or "cyber-skeptics," the political role of the internet reflects and reinforces, rather than transforms, the existing structural features of the country's political system. For them, the internet enhances democratic action and participation only to those who are already politically active. Thus, the internet, for cyber-skeptics, is basically an extension of traditional media; it does not change people, but rather, it tends to allow them to do what they usually do, *and* to do it more effectively.

At the other end of the spectrum are the Filipinos who are believers or the "cyber-optimists." For these individuals, as internet access spreads across the globe, and becomes more deeply integrated into societies, it brings new opportunities for direct access to politically relevant information. It also offers opportunities for unmediated communication between and among political organizations and the electorate.

When viewed from this perspective, the Philippines is structurally con-strained, which may explain why Filipino society has experienced a slow adoption rate and poor maximization of the internet. Some of these issues include: equipment costs; language barriers, in terms of not only the content but the technical language expertise required to use the technology; the low promotion of IT use among many members of the society; and the different internet development policies and strategies of the Philippine government.

Motivation of users

Even if the economic and technological resources are present and the structure of opportunities are provided, if the users do not possess the motivation to use the technology, then it will still be poorly used. The Filipinos must be educated on the benefits of the internet, through professional training or schooling, and IT subjects need to be integrated into the academic curricula.

There also needs to be a change in the attitude of the Filipinos towards the technology, which would allow citizens to realize newer ways to participate politically. Eventually, this may result in the feeling of being a part of an "empowered" voting public. Of equal importance is an issue of Filipino political culture, which is characterized by large numbers of passive citizens who do not engage in civic participation.

Thus, from this perspective, I agree with Saunby, as cited by Dutton *et al.* (2003), when he argues:

> social and economic divides could not be closed by just providing broadband access or specific broadband content, but only by also ensuring the "quality" of content of education and other social and business institutions is sufficient to encourage people to care enough to want to interact with, and through, broadband.
>
> (Dutton *et al.* 2003: 9)

Conclusion

Because it is a new medium for political campaigning, the internet was not extensively exploited in the 2004 Philippine national elections. Political candidates, parties, and their website developers (the primary political actors who used the internet for campaigning) missed opportunities afforded by the highly unregulated online environment in the country. In such an environment, one would expect an increase in election-related websites with information and engagement features that encouraged political participation on the web. The data reported in this chapter, however, suggest the opposite.

Despite the potentially wide range of content that can be made available on websites, most of the political sites under examination limited themselves to basic information provision – the primary function of the internet in the May 2004 Philippine elections. In fact, many of the websites could be best described as merely "virtual" or "electronic brochures" (Kamarck 1998) of the campaign materials that were distributed in the offline environment. As with the offline printed brochures, these sites were highly graphical, as indicated by the prevalence of the colorful images or still photos posted. This study reveals that the primary political actors who utilized the internet in the previous national election are the political parties and candidates. Amongst the website features, providing contact and biographic information were commonly found on election-related sites during the campaign period.

The potential of the internet for interactivity or public engagement was likewise under-utilized. Most of the sites offered only the most basic of the interactive features in the form of discussion boards and forums. Other interactive features, such as the downloading of e-paraphernalia or the ability to donate monetary support to the campaigns via online bank transactions, were almost non-existent.

Similarly, the internet's multimedia capacity was not fully utilized on these websites. By merely uploading still photos and other graphical images, site producers failed to maximize the technology's audio and visual streaming capabilities. The "sophistication," therefore, of their respective web designs was based more on aesthetics instead of the sites' multimedia offerings.

It appears that political internet usage in the Philippines is reflective of the overarching Philippine political culture. In the "offline" environment, Philippine politics is more personality based than issue based. Philippine political parties are often viewed as electoral mechanisms that can be easily formed, dissolved, or grouped into convenient coalitions so candidates can easily switch from one party to another, whenever they see it fit to do so (Arugay 2004). Elections in the Philippines are principally won through personalities, and not because of the political goals of their respective parties. Candidates, apart from their personalities, are drafted into lists of party candidates based on their potential to win, which in turn is based on their ability to extend personal favors to supporters. After elections, Philippine politicians often become detached from their parties and proceed to work as "independent" public seat holders.

Such a candidate-focused orientation that frequently neglects party platforms is manifest in the online environment. Rather than encouraging active online discussions on important political concerns and issues, and thereby maximizing interactivity, websites thus far have simply offered basic information about the political candidates and parties. Moreover, most of the websites were created on the initiative of the individual political candidates instead of the parties to which they belonged. This is considered another consequence of the personality-based orientation of Philippine politics.

Although the internet may have a strong potential for bridging offline and online political activities, in the Philippines it will take some time for the internet to become an effective tool for political participation. It can only happen when there is the right combination of resources, access, opportunities, education, and civic motivation. New media should not always be construed as a radical departure from previous practices, but rather as an extension. It is not a case of the online environment prevailing over the offline environment, or vice versa. Instead, the former simply offers newer opportunities than the latter.

This study suggests that given the development of sophisticated infrastructures over time, internet usage will become more meaningful in the political arena. In spite of the low internet penetration rate in the country and a high dependence on traditional media at present, the internet has the potential to become an important tool for political campaigns due to its interactivity, room for individualization and disintermediation, and its cost efficiency. The Philippines has yet to realize that: (1) other election stakeholders in the country can utilize the internet apart from the political candidates and their parties; (2) sites can offer more significant materials than simply contact and biographical information; and, most importantly, (3) there is more to this technology than mere basic information provision.

The web does seem poised to contribute to a shift in the structure of political opportunities in the country that could then pave the way for significant social and/or political changes. This assessment of the websites of selected political actors in the 2004 Philippine national election has pointed to several possibilities through which the internet – as harnessed by electoral candidates – may alter the nature of Philippine political discourse. It did not look into the other half of the discourse, that is, how citizens use the internet for their own political empowerment. The full picture of *poli-clicking* as politicking in the Philippines, then, is yet another area of inquiry that needs to be pursued.

Note

1 The author is grateful to Arleen Cuevas for invaluable help in gathering data on the Philippines during this project.

References

Arugay, A. (2004) "Coalitions of convenience," *Institute for Popular Democracy*. Available online: www.ipd.ph/elections/opinion/convenience.htm (accessed 25 May 2004).

Cuevas, A. (2004) "The internet and 2004 Philippine elections: analysis of election campaign websites," unpublished MA Thesis, Nanyang Technological University, Singapore.

Ducke, I. (2002) "Use of the Internet by political actors in the Japanese–Korean Textbook Controversy," paper presented at Media in Transition 2, Massachusetts Institute of Technology, May. Available online: www.dijtokyo.org/doc/UseofInternet.pdf (accessed 20 January 2004).

Dutton, H., Gillet, S.E., McKnight, L., and Peltu, M. (2003) "Broadband internet. The power to reconfigure access," paper presented at Broadband Divides Forum in Oxford Internet Institute, University of Oxford, August. Available online: itc.mit.edu/itel/Docs/2003/Bill-Dutton-Oxford.pdf (accessed 31 January 2004).

Farnsworth, S. and Owen, D. (2003) "Internet use and the 2000 presidential election," *Electoral Studies*. Available online: www.sciencedirect.com/science/journal/02613794 (accessed 4 October 2003).

Gibson, R. and Ward, S. (2001) "Virtual campaigning: Australian parties and the impact of the Internet," *Australian Journal of Political Science* 37, 1: 99–129.

Grossman, L. (1995) *The Electronic Republic. Reshaping Democracy in the Information Age.* New York: Viking.

Hong, Y.H. and Chang, R. (2002) "Who's on and why are they there? A study of visitors to electoral candidates' websites in Taiwan," *Asian Journal of Communication*, 12, 2: 31–48.

Kamarck, E. (1998) "Campaigning on the Internet in the elections of 1998," in E. Kamarck and J. Nye (eds), *Democracy.com*, pp. 100–123: Hollis, NH: Hollis.

Kluver, R. (2004) "Political culture and information technology in the 2001 Singapore general election," *Political Communication*, 21: 435–458.

Leones, E. and Moraleda, M. (1999) "Philippines," in W. Sachsenroder and U. Frings (eds), *Political Party Systems and Democratic Development in East and Southeast Asia*, Vol. 1, pp. 289–342. Aldershot: Ashgate.

Meinardus, R. (2004) "The Media in Elections," *Foundation for Liberal Politics in the Philippines.* Available online: www.fnf.org.ph/liberalopinion/2004-02-03.htm (accessed 7 July 2004).

Mianni, M. (2001) "The usage of the Internet in the 2001 Italian elections," paper presented at the Second International Conference of the Association of Internet Researchers, University of Minneapolis, October. Available online: www.mattiamiani.it/pubblicazioni/paper_mattia_revised.doc (accessed 5 November 2004).

Norris, P. (2001) *Digital Divide: Civic Engagement, Information Poverty and the Internet Worldwide.* Cambridge: University of Cambridge Press.

—— (2003) "Preaching to the converted? Pluralism, participation and party Websites," *Party Politics Journal*, 9, 1: 21–45.

Pace, C. (2003) "Web usability and politics: a content analysis of campaign websites during the fall 2002 elections," unpublished Doctoral Dissertation, Regent University, Virginia Beach, VA.

Tkach-Kawasaki, L. (2003) "Politics@Japan: party competition on the Internet in Japan," *Party Politics Journal*, 9, 1: 105–123.

Wang, T. (2002) "Whose 'interactive' channel? Exploring the concept of interactivity defined in Taiwan's 2000 presidential election online campaigns," *Asian Journal of Communication*, 12, 2: 50–77.

9   The internet in the 2004 Sri Lankan elections

Shyam Tekwani and Randolph Kluver

Introduction

In developed countries and vibrant democracies, it seems clear that the internet is increasingly playing a role in political processes and outcomes. In a number of countries, the internet has been used either as an effective campaign medium or as a vehicle for political mobilization of the populace. In Sri Lanka, however, the political context suggests that the findings of other studies might not be applicable. As a nation divided by years of civil war, and with a population that is generally unable to access the internet, Sri Lanka would seem to be an unlikely place to make a significant investment in developing an election-oriented web sphere. The purpose of this chapter is to explore the Sri Lanka web sphere and to determine how the internet is deployed during an election campaign. According to Joshi (2004), Sri Lanka's 2004 parliamentary elections saw the internet emerge as a tool for campaigning for the first time in the country. E-mails disseminating candidate and party information and canvassing for votes were widely circulated in the run-up to the campaign. Our purpose is to determine the nature of this web sphere and the likely purposes of election-oriented websites given the context of Sri Lanka's political culture and the unique circumstances of the nation.

In this chapter, we examine the 2004 electoral web sphere for the Sri Lankan election, with a particular focus on examining two phenomena: the ways in which various political actors, including the proxies for the separatist Liberation Tigers of Tamil Eelam (LTTE), deployed web-based resources to influence external, international opinion during the 2004 election; and the ways in which those same actors sought to use the internet to bolster their political standing, even as the internet remained inaccessible to much of the voting population. We argue that even though much of the web sphere in the 2004 election was oriented towards an international audience, we find that certain elements of Sri Lankan political culture remained present in the sites examined.

In contrast to Joshi (2004), our findings suggest that in the 2004 electoral web sphere was not so much a tool for campaigning but rather that the electoral web sphere became a space for trying to articulate and reify the nationalistic tensions within Sri Lanka to a global audience. Castells (1997) argues that the rise of global information technologies seems to be happening in congruity with the rise of powerful nationalistic forces seeking to define communal identity. As information technologies have become a relatively inexpensive and convenient manner of disseminating information, they also allow local identity movements to achieve a global footprint, as illustrated by Castells' analysis of the *Zapatista* movement in southern Mexico. Moreover, technology becomes a primary platform for the definition of communal identities, as the use of language, hyperlinks, and other features can help to establish reference points for ethnic, religious, and even geographical boundaries.

Political culture in Sri Lanka

Like other former British colonies, Sri Lanka inherited a Westminster model of parliamentary government, with universal suffrage established in 1931 and full general elections in 1947. In 1978, the Sri Lankan government moved from a parliamentary system into a French-style executive presidency to accommodate ethnic diversity (Reilly 1997). In spite of its open democracy, Sri Lanka lags far behind the developed world in terms of development, with a GDP per capita at approximately U.S.$4000 (CIA Factbook 2005). There remains a tremendous inequality of access to both wealth and information technology resources, and the "information society" is still limited largely to traditional elites, those with the socio-economic and educational backgrounds that enables them access to information, and, particularly, the internet. Internet diffusion in Sri Lanka stands at approximately a quarter of a million people, or only about 1.3 percent of the population, according to the International Telecommunications Union (Internet Worldstats 2005). Internet access, while freely available, is still expensive at an average charge of approximately U.S.$15 for 20 hours of connection. In a country with only 47 phone lines per 1000 inhabitants, internet access is limited primarily to the educated, wealthy elite. The internet is becoming an important source of information for a very small, but inordinately influential, portion of Sri Lanka's population, primarily students, governmental officials, and business persons. The majority of the population participates in elections only through other media, such as print, radio, and television.

Given the low rate of internet penetration and the obviously elite nature of its use in Sri Lanka, a question emerges as to why political actors used the internet at all during the election campaign. These traditional campaign styles, including personal appearances, rallies, flags, and pamphlets are the primary means of political campaigning, especially in the rural areas, where the great majority of Sri Lankans live. Obviously, Sri Lanka's electoral web sphere was not devoted to reaching a mass of the nation's voters, as most would find English language information inaccessible anyway. These factors lead us to conclude that in contrast to many other nations, the deployment of the internet in this Sri Lankan election had little to do with internal political considerations or strategies, but rather was an attempt to represent the election, and Sri Lankan politics more generally, to a global audience, rather than a domestic one.

In 2004, Sri Lanka faced its third election in less than four years, spurred mainly by a power struggle between President Chandrika Kumaratunga of the Sri Lanka Freedom Party (SLFP) and Prime Minister Ranil Wick-remesinghe of the United National Party (UNP). The dissolution of the previous parliament and the calling of fresh elections were precipitated by those who led the campaign to form the United People's Freedom Alliance (UPFA) coalition by bringing together the Sri Lanka Freedom Party (SLFP) and the Marxist Janatha Vimukthi Peramuna (JVP). The 2004 election was unique in that it was the first time the LTTE actually took part in the elections, even if by proxy, and used its propaganda machinery as part of the campaign. Previously, the LTTE had urged the people of the northeast to boycott local or national elections on the grounds that participation in elections under a unitary constitution would undermine the Tamil claim for self-determination. Moreover, in a significant development in these elections, the LTTE announced that it would support the Tamil National Alliance (TNA), a coalition of four Tamil parties, which resulted in unfettered election coverage by the Tamil diaspora sites and an enthusiastic use of the community's online resources to campaign for its candidates.

Politics in Sri Lanka are inevitably driven at least partially by the long-running conflict between the Sinhalese-majority government, based in Colombo, and the Tamil separatist movement concentrated in the country's northeast. The insurgency, led by the LTTE, or Tamil Tigers, aims to carve out a Tamil homeland in the northeastern part of the Sinhalese-majority island. This conflict, which has devastated the island for over two decades, killed thousands, and ruined the country's economy, is always a key issue during election campaigns. Moreover, in spite of the fact that it has never before directly participated in Sri Lanka's democratic process, the LTTE has sought to influence the outcome of every presidential or parliamentary election in the country, either through intimidation or boycotts. The LTTE directs the political choice of Tamil voters in northern Sri Lanka, as well as influencing Tamil voters, directly and indirectly, in other parts of the country. At times, the group has openly backed a candidate or a political party, such as 1994, when it supported Chandrika Kumaratunga for president, and in 1999, when the movement supported Ranil Wickremesinghe.

In previous campaigns, opponents of the movement have been targeted for attacks, presumably by the LTTE itself, resulting in the killing of Gamini Dissanayake, and sending a suicide bomber to attack Kumaratunga, who lost an eye in the attack. In 2001, its cadres canvassed support for a Tamil National Alliance (TNA). In 2004, it went a step further, killing and intimidating candidates opposing the TNA, and on voting day, broke all the rules to ensure its clients won. The tactics varied but the criterion for support remained the same: which candidate would better serve the long-term goal of establishing a separate state.

Another significant consequence of the Tamil movement is that the Tamil homeland in the northwest part of the island, known as "Eelam" in the Tamil language, functions as a more or less autonomous region under the authority of the rebel group, and the Sri Lankan government has little influence over this region. This "nation within a nation" is characterized by a sense of national identification with Eelam more than by a sense of Sri Lankan national identity. However, although the region functions autonomously and for most purposes is considered by its residents to have little to do with "Sri Lanka," citizens there do vote in the national elections. For a number of years, nationalistic Tamils have sought to create a "virtual nation" through a strong Eelamese web sphere that uses the internet to reinforce a strong sense of Eelamese identity (Tekwani 2003). These groups have used the internet as a tool for spreading propaganda and supporting the violent separatism of the LTTE through fundraising and recruitment. In fact, the LTTE and associated groups were most likely the first political organizations in Sri Lanka to make use of the internet, as their use goes back at least to 1994. In contrast, the first governmental website in Sri Lanka dates from only around the year 2000.

Method

In early 2004, campaigning began for the Sri Lankan legislative election, which was held on 2 April of that year. In order to develop a representative web sphere, a research team identified all relevant websites which could be located using available search engines. In contrast to some of the other nations examined in the Internet and Elections Project, in which sites were identified, and then a representative sample was then selected and coded, a short time frame meant that the identification and coding of websites happened at the same time for the Sri Lankan sites.

Foot *et al.* (2003) define a web sphere as a "hyperlinked set of dynamically defined digital resources spanning multiple websites deemed relevant or related to a central theme or 'object', with boundaries around a shared object orientation and a temporal framework." For the Sri Lankan electoral web sphere, all websites that listed information, advocated candidates, or otherwise provided materials relevant to the elections were included in the web sphere. In addition, we included a number of sites that focused on Sri Lankan politics, identified either by the terms "Sri Lanka" or "Eelam." We included Eelamese nationalistic sites because those sites, even if they did not contain specifically election-related material, do help to define the political reality of the nation.

The search parameters included identification of websites in English, Sinhalese, and Tamil, and included all the types of site producers common to the studies in this volume. In spite of this expansive set of parameters, however, we were only able to identify 53 sites, considerably less than those present in other web spheres reported in this book.

There are two important notes concerning the coding of sites by site producers. The first is that one of the sites that we have coded as "governmental" is in fact an independent commission established by the government to conduct elections in a fair and impartial manner. We classified it as governmental primarily because of its role in administering the election, which typically is a governmental role.

Second, the "NGO" category was used to refer to the LTTE and associated groups, and its group of supporters both within and largely outside of Sri Lanka. Although it is not customary to refer to this group as an NGO, that in fact is how the groups position themselves and, thus, we have coded these sites in that manner. From this analysis, the Tamils produced one-quarter as many of the sites produced by the more mainstream political parties. The category NGO was not used to code Tamil-based political parties, however.

After coding, we analyzed the findings based on the Internet and Elections Project common coding template and further analyzed the web sphere to determine what other unique characteristics may have been present. We also noted the presence of "information" features and "engagement" features in this particular web sphere. Information features are those that are primarily informative in nature, while engagement features are those which give the web surfer an ability to participate in some way in the election process by providing mechanisms such as sending e-mails, posting to a forum, adding content to a particular website, and so on. In particular, we highlight the ways in which the features present on the sites demonstrate the goal of internationalizing the Sri Lankan conflict as well as illustrate certain other aspects of Sri Lanka's political culture. Due to the small number of sites included in the sample, our analysis must of necessity be considered primarily an impressionistic accounting of the presence and absence of features.

The 2004 electoral web sphere

In Sri Lanka, a number of traditionally powerful institutions did not use the internet at all during the election. For example, none of the over 200 candidates contesting had their own website. It is pertinent to note that, unlike their counterparts in the West, candidates in Sri Lanka depend almost entirely on the party apparatus for electioneering and are not yet prone to canvassing for votes on their own. Thus, we would not necessarily expect to find individual candidate web pages in that context. The dominant type of site producer in the Sri Lankan election, as illustrated in Table 9.1, was the press, with approximately 45 percent of the sites, indicating the dominant role of the press in Sri Lanka as a vehicle for political communica-

Table 9.1 Coded websites within the Sri Lankan election web sphere

Producer type	Number of sites
Government	9
NGO/(LTTE)	3
Party	12
Press	24
Citizen	5
Portal	1
Total	54

tion and the relative weakness of other political entities, including political parties. The next most prominent site producer, political parties, only produced half as many sites, a total of 12. Although it is possible that we were unable to identify all of the party websites, it is revealing that less than one-quarter of the 50 political parties in the nation produced websites (Sri Lanka Department of Elections 2005). As most of the parties in Sri Lanka, including the Tamil parties, are based in the capital city of Colombo, connectivity would not be an obstacle to producing a website. However, most parties, faced with limited budgets, most likely made the choice that internet campaigning would provide little real electoral benefit.

Many producer types prominent in other elections did not contribute to Sri Lanka's web sphere, such as educational organizations, labor organizations, religious organizations, businesses, and political professionals. This left only six distinct types of site producers, as seen in Table 9.2. This is surprising, given the social and political role many civil society and religious groups, especially Buddhist groups, play in Sri Lankan society.

The one portal site that was identified, the Lanka Academic Network, is a specialized portal, run by volunteers, and seeks to serve the information needs of Sri Lankan students, teachers, and professionals. It is widely perceived as non-partisan. We were unable to identify commercial portals, such as localized versions of Yahoo, during the campaign period.

As we have already noted, it seems that the Sri Lankan electoral web sphere stands in stark contrast in terms of web campaigning to nations with higher internet penetration. The sites that were identified included relatively few information features and even fewer engagement features.

Images were the most consistent feature present in websites among the different producer types. All of the governmental, NGO, portal, and citizen sites contained images, and all but two press sites contained images. Images have a unique political importance in rural and underdeveloped nations such as Sri Lanka and India, primarily because literacy rates have traditionally been low and visual images thus become important icons of political significance. With an image, a party attempts to communicate its ideological and policy preferences in easy-to-remember ways. The importance of

Table 9.2 Information features present on website across different producers within web sphere

Political actor*	Election	Biography	Issues	Speech	Calendar	Issue comparison	Campaign info	Voting info	Images	Audio visuals	Privacy policy	Terms of use
Government (9)	7	7	0	4	2	3	2	1	1	9	2	0
NGO (3)	1	2	0	1	1	0	0	0	0	3	0	1
Party (12)	12	9	1	5	1	3	2	0	0	11	4	0
Press (24)	24	8	1	1	0	1	2	1	1	22	2	3
Citizen (5)	1	1	0	0	0	0	0	0	5	0	0	0
Portal (1)	0	0	0	0	0	0	0	0	1	0	1	1

Note
* Number of political actors per category indicated in parentheses.

the party symbol is demonstrated by the list of officially approved parties by the Department of Elections. On this list, along with the party name and address, each party is assigned an "official symbol," which is the shorthand brand identification for that political party; such symbols include everyday objects such as flower vases, bicycles, fountain pens, electrical lamps, and clocks (Sri Lanka Department of Elections 2005). The parties are clearly identified with a symbol, and they consistently use these images in all party materials, regardless of the audience.

The feature that was least present in this web sphere was a feature that provided site visitors with information about the voting process in Sri Lanka. Only one government site out of nine provided this information. In addition, one press site also provided such information. This content was absent in citizen, party, NGO, and portal sites. Information about campaigning was also not prominent during this election cycle. This content was present on only a small number of sites – two of 12 party sites, two of nine government sites, and two of 24 press sites. The paucity of information about the actual campaign process demonstrates that the internet was not a significant means of disseminating information to the actual political actors during the election. The fact that these features were not present seems to point to a conclusion that the goal is, in fact, not to engage a voting public, but rather to engage a non-voting public, international public opinion.

Biographies of political leaders were found on many of the sites, including all of the party sites, and on a majority of government sites (eight out of nine) and NGO sites (two out of three), illustrating the role of charismatic leadership in Sri Lankan political culture, given cultural attitudes towards authority. Pye and Pye (1985) argue that in the Hindu and Buddhist-influenced states of Southeast Asia, such as Sri Lanka, politics continued to exhibit strong indicators of an idealized authority vested in the "god-king," or charismatic religious-political leader whose task was the preservation of the *sangha*, or community of believers. This king-like figure is typically seen as a possessor of extraordinary virtue who would maintain the strength of the state by virtue of his own piety. This remains true, if in a secularized form, in contemporary politics, as illustrated by the experience of the SLFP. This party had only two leaders from 1951 to 1994, and they were both members of the same family. In 1994, the party passed to the control of Chandrika Kumaratunga, who was also a family member, thus demonstrating that control over the dominant political party was held by a single family over a period of decades (De Silva 1998). In a number of ways, the campaign biographies provided on the Sri Lankan websites tended to demonstrate exactly this kind of expectation and to present images that link the leadership to a sort of secularized "divine mandate." At the time of this writing, the SLFP had a campaign site that showed a picture of the new party leader, with the title "president for righteous rule." This explicitly religious language demonstrates continuity of traditional political culture into the era of the internet.

In spite of the relative dearth of party-related sites, it is interesting to note that the party sites that did exist tended to have a greater range of information available. Across political party sites, all information features with the exception of terms of use and information about voting were present. Government sites also provided an extensive amount of information. These sites provided all informational features with the exception of information on privacy. However, governmental sites typically had fewer features than political party sites. One of the key purposes of the governmental sites was to provide information for international observers rather than to the nation's voters.

In terms of the presence and role of engagement features in the Sri Lankan web sphere, it seems that there is little attempt made to engage the audience. Generally speaking, none of the site producers provided much in the way of engagement features at all. The one feature provided consistently is the ability to contact the site producer, which was present across all the different producer types and in most of the sites that were coded. NGO sites and citizen sites also had a feature enabling viewers to join, but no other engagement feature appeared in more than one-third of the sites we coded; the highest percentages of engagement-oriented features were provided by governmental sites. Among the citizen and portal sites, five out of the six sites had contact information for the site producer, half enabled visitors to become members of their organization, while only one allowed visitors to participate in online discussions or forums and to download electronic paraphernalia.

The engagement feature that was least likely to appear across websites was a feature that allowed site visitors to express their support for a candidate or party. This was noticeably absent across all sites, including the party sites. In addition, only one party had a feature that enabled site visitors to volunteer in the campaign process.

Government organizations were the site producers that offered the most varied types of engagement features. All government sites had information that would enable visitors to contact the site producer. In addition to this, one-third of these sites allowed visitors to register to vote, to receive mail from the site producer, to make donations, to participate in forums, and to send links from the site to other people.

The one portal site that was coded had the least varied engagement features. Only one feature, the ability to contact the site producer, was present on this site. Contact Producer was the engagement feature that was most commonly featured across websites produced by different political actors within this web sphere. This is not surprising, as providing contact information is the starting point in engaging visitors in the process.

However, as can be seen from Table 9.3, features that required a higher level of interaction between the site producer and site visitor were not common within this web sphere. This seems to suggest that within the Sri Lankan political context, the internet is seen primarily as a form of provid-

Table 9.3 Engagement features present on websites across different producers within web sphere

Political actor*	Contact	Join	Register	Get mail	Donate	Forum	Offline dist	Send links	Publish support	E-paraphernalia	Volunteer
Government (9)	8	0	0	2	0	1	0	1	0	3	0
NGO (3)	3	0	1	1	1	1	0	1	0	0	0
Party (12)	6	2	0	1	1	1	3	0	0	3	1
Press (24)	21	5	0	5	0	6	1	2	0	2	0
Citizen (5)	4	3	0	0	0	1	0	0	0	1	0
Portal (1)	1	0	0	0	0	0	0	0	0	0	0

Note
* Number of political actors per category indicated in parentheses.

ing information and is not (yet) viewed as a meaningful exchange between citizens and political actors.

Discussion

Our analysis of the Sri Lankan web sphere seems to confirm the argument that we made earlier in this chapter, that the content on election-related websites seems to reflect an attempt to define a political reality for an international audience, rather than a local one. This is reflected in the use of language, the presence of information and engagement features, and the types of information presented. At the same time, these sites also exhibit characteristics of Sri Lankan political culture, in which ethnic identity is a major issue, parties are represented by graphic symbols, and cultural attitudes towards authority are made manifest. This is not inconsistent with our thesis that the web sphere is oriented towards an international audience, as we would expect that site producers would produce content and features, or an online structure, that reflects the political attitudes and values that arise from that nation.

When we isolate the most noteworthy player in this election, the LTTE or related websites, we also see some interesting elements. The LTTE and the Tamil diaspora used their substantial internet resources to promote the Tamil National Alliance and actively campaign for its platform and candidates. The TNA's election manifesto was carried word-for-word in the leading diaspora and LTTE websites, and as the election campaign unfolded, reports were updated and highlighted. Some Tamil sites even offered links to non-partisan election-related international sites such as Election-world.org.

However, the LTTE sites tended to be sparse in terms of information, providing only a bare minimum, including election information, biography, issue positions and speeches, and images. One site provided a privacy policy. Overall, the LTTE sites provided little in terms of the actual election, but did provide politics. In other words, the website reflected an authoritarian approach to providing political information and offered little information that would be helpful to create an informed choice.

There is another unique feature of the Sri Lankan web sphere that demonstrates our contention that the purpose of the sites was primarily to engage an international rather than a Sri Lankan audience, and that is the use of the English language. Sinhalese is the dominant language in Sri Lanka, spoken by about 75 percent of the population, while Tamil is the language of most of the people in the troubled northeastern part of the nation, spoken by approximately 18 percent of the nation's citizens. English, however, plays a dominant role in government, although it is spoken by only about 10 percent of the population. Wilson argues that among those educated in the northeast of Sri Lanka, "This generation of pupils had all their education in the Tamil medium ... the last generation who studied in the English medium is now well into middle age" (2000: 172). However, we found that all election-related websites were written in English, with only a small percentage of the site content in either Sinhalese or Tamil. Typically, the only content in these languages would be slogans or catchphrases.

The fact that English is the dominant language in the web sphere illustrates our contention that the primary purpose of the websites is to engage an international audience, including the proportion of Sri Lankans residing abroad. For the TNA, in particular, which staked a tremendous amount on its participation in the election, it would seem that Tamil-language websites would be imperative. And yet, it chose instead to put up English-language websites instead. This can only point to the conclusion that the sites are primarily propagandistic in nature, and are intended to influence international public opinion far more than to engage Sri Lankan voters. This goal was made very explicit on a web page associated with the Tamil movement, which declared that "the TNA has decided to make use of the opportunity presented by this election to bring forcefully to the attention of the world, and Sri Lanka in particular, our resolve for self determination" (Tamilnet.com).

Election results, reactions, and analysis were widely featured on the diaspora sites, and the TNA's success (it won 22 seats, making it a major player in the political balance of the new Sri Lankan government) was widely touted as indicative of the support of the country's Tamil population for the leadership of the LTTE. Thus, the overseas sympathizers tended to provide a highly interactive and engaging feature, probably arising from years of experience of using the internet to build political cohesion.

Conclusions

We have argued so far that the primary function of the web presence of political parties during the 2004 Sri Lankan election was to "internationalize" the internal conflict, as reflected in the language used, the types of informational and engagement features presented, and the content. The paucity of engagement features in the Sri Lankan web sphere could be partially explained by the fact that Sri Lanka is a developing country, with little indigenous internet content yet. Another potential factor is that within the national context, websites are seen primarily as digital calling cards, ways to be "known" to the outside world. Within the Sri Lankan context, the value of political websites is not in the classic mode typically seen in the West, such as mobilization, fundraising, or participation in a campaign, but rather in terms of demonstrating a certain technical savvy, thereby hopefully creating a sense of legitimacy or credibility to an international audience.

The presence of engagement features on a website indicates that the site producer expects some interaction from the audience and enables a certain openness about what the political reality is. If a surfer can insert a comment, for example, it potentially alters the meaning of the site itself. However, in a top-down political environment, in which leaders provide the political reality for the citizens, there is no reason to expect that there would be any means for citizens to redefine or negotiate that reality. If, as we have argued, the primary purpose of the web sphere in Sri Lanka is to define the political reality for an international audience, as well as for an elite, English-educated audience within the country, then we would expect that there would be little, if any, opportunity to alter it.

Overall, what do the coding data indicate about the characteristics and structure of this electoral web sphere and the kinds of political action it enabled on the part of the citizens? We suspect that most of the websites that were present in the campaign were primarily produced for the purposes of establishing a web presence, as this is perceived as modern and sophistic-ated. As a result, little attention was paid by site producers to the types of information or features that would prove valuable to potential voters. More-over, we have argued that Sri Lankan political culture is indeed reflected in spite of this, through an emphasis on propagandistic, rather than engage-ment, types of features, and that these features illustrate continuity with Sri Lanka's political traditions (Kluver 2005).

From this analysis, it is clear that within Sri Lanka, the information revolution has a limited base. Its access and its advantages are restricted to the urban and educated, and the elite who do not represent the majority of the electorate and who still view politics and elections as a one-way street. Information flow is restricted to and controlled by government sources and sites who put out data and news, with little expectation of citizen participa-tion or response. The online versions of Sri Lankan print media were a major presence in the web sphere, with the detailed election coverage posted online in a timely fashion. Online media were found to be important sources of background information on parties, candidates, and issues and were a forum for a discussion of election issues.

Besides the government and the largely government-controlled mass media, the other significant internet user group found was the Tamil rebel network, and even among this grouping, much of the participation was from overseas Sri Lankan Tamils rather than from Tamil voters in Sri Lanka whose participation on the internet might have carried any weight in the electoral process. Ironically, it is this last grouping that represented the most dynamic and interactive online component of the web sphere. The Tamil diaspora has sustained and extended the Tamil separatist movements for decades, circumventing media restrictions that exist within the island, by using the online networks to define the nature of the separatist struggle for an international audience. Similar dynamism on the part of the Sri Lankan government and citizens could potentially significantly increase citizen par-ticipation in public life and elections.

In addition, the biggest revelation in this election was the use of the internet by the Sri Lankan government itself. The increased attention paid to the dissemination of information on the internet by the government and political parties bodes well for the future of the electoral process in the country. Government departments and agencies, as well as leading political parties, used the internet to reach out to the electorate, but they did not do so to the extent that one might expect. Moreover, the culture of internet use has not taken hold such that the average voter would expect information to be more interactive. If the peace holds and prosperity returns at the same steady pace, increased internet access can only mean that one can expect to see the information road as it is now turn into a two-way street – if not a highway – in Sri Lanka.

References

Castells, M. (1997) *The Power of Identity. The Information Age: Economy, Society, and Culture*, Vol. 2, Oxford: Blackwell Publishers.

CIA Factbook: Sri Lanka. Available online: www.cia.gov/cia/publications/factbook/geos/sn.html (accessed 29 November 2005).

De Silva, K.M. (1998) *Reaping the Whirlwind: Ethnic Conflict, Ethnic Politics in Sri Lanka*. New Delhi: Penguin Books.

Foot, K., Schneider, S., Dougherty, M., Xenos, M., and Larsen, E. (2003) "Analyzing linking practices: candidate sites in the 2002 US electoral web sphere," *Journal of Computer Mediated Communication*, 8: 4.

Internet Worldstats (2005) Available online: www.internetworldstats.com/stats3.htm (accessed August 2005).

Joshi, P. (2004) "Sri Lankan parties get wired for votes," *Hindustan Times*, 11 March.

Kluver, R. (2005) "Political culture in online politics," in M. Consalvo and M. Allen (eds), *Internet Research Annual*, vol. 2, pp. 75–84. Newbury Park, CA: Sage Publications.

Pye, L, and Pye, M. (1985) *Asian Power and Politics: the Cultural Dimensions of Authority*. Cambridge, MA: Belknap Press.

Reilly, B. (1997) "Sri Lanka: changes to accommodate diversity," *Administration and Cost of Elections Project*. Available online: www.aceproject.org/main/english/es/esy_lk.htm (accessed 1 November 2005).

Sri Lanka Department of Elections (2005). Available online: www.slelections.gov.lk/parties.html (accessed 30 November 2005).

Tekwani, S. (2003) "The Tamil diaspora, Tamil militancy, and the Internet," in K.C. Ho, R. Kluver, and K. Yang (eds), *Asia.com: Asia Encounters the Internet*, pp. 175–192. London: Routledge.

Wilson, A.J. (2000) *Sri Lankan Tamil Nationalism: Its Origins and Development in the 19th and 20th Centuries*. London: Hurst and Company.

10 Addressing young people online

The 2004 European Parliament election campaign and political youth websites[1]

Janelle Ward

Addressing young people online

Advances in technology can enable a restructuring of the political system. Political actors can now use websites to supply the original message that they want to present to citizens. With a unique combination of textual, auditory, and visual components, new technologies show the potential to present political and civic material to citizens. For example, online content allows for possible interaction between the sender and receiver, provides an inexpensive means of supplying large quantities of information, and offers many forms of communication that both political elites and citizens can use. According to Norris (2003a), the internet can be viewed as a channel of interactive communication in that it furnishes a vital connection between citizens and government. Government information and services can be delivered "downwards" to citizens; citizens can provide feedback "upwards" to government.

A key focus here is how political elites are utilizing these new communication technologies. Various actors, including political parties and grassroots movements, are attempting to engage citizens online by addressing the general population, or focusing on specific groups such as young people. Numerous types of political actors are exploiting the internet in many remarkable ways. Foot and Schneider (2002) argue that using online technologies as a political tool encourages several significant developments with enduring implications for electoral politics. These include new forms of collaboration between competing political actors and parties, novel and improved methods of extensive citizen mobilization (like community networks or online petitioning), and shifts in types of campaign practices. Such advances hold possible implications for electoral politics (Bimber 2003; Bimber and Davis 2003).

Due to these developments, ICT use is providing an online structure for citizens, or a "structure of political opportunity" (Eisinger 1973: 11). Online structure is defined as "an electronic space, comprised of various html pages, features, links and texts, within which an individual is given an opportunity to act" (Schneider and Foot 2002: 5). Examples of "offline" or traditional structures for political action include offices where campaign workers promote a specific electoral campaign or town halls where candidates can gather the public in an attempt to raise support. Online structures, such as political websites, now combine the availability of both online (such as e-mail contact or links to other, related political sites) and offline (for example, opportunities to distribute campaign materials) action. They can encourage political interest by providing opportunities to find information, though usually consistent with both citizens' specific political interests and their partisan preferences (Mutz and Martin 2001; Sunstein 2001).

Young people are the most "wired" of all age cohorts and are online and active more than their older counterparts are. In addition, internet access in Europe is on the rise, predominantly with younger users (Norris 2002). On the other hand, youth are also the most politically disengaged group of citizens, at least within a traditional definition of engagement (Youniss *et al.* 2002). Thus, the younger generation is a key group to focus on when uncovering these websites' roles as online opportunity structures.

An increasing amount of academic literature concentrates on political websites, both in Europe and worldwide. Some studies have chosen a more global approach and look at how political parties are using new ICTs. They do this by examining party competition and campaigning online, internal party democracy and the role of political parties within democracies (Gibson *et al.* 2003). Some analyzed the websites of Dutch political parties along with the concept of digital democracy (Van Selm *et al.* 2001; Voerman 2000; Voerman and Boogers 2002). while others examined candidate websites in recent Finnish election campaigns and found that some candidates – mainly incumbents, female, and relatively young – seldom use the web to offer interactive features, instead providing more traditional campaign material (Carlson and Djupsund 2001). Through the use of branch surveys and content analysis of political party websites, recent U.K. research observes how politicians are using the internet (Gibson and Ward 1998) and describe the use by candidates during the 2001 general election campaign as inconsistent and similar to traditional political leaflets (Ward and Gibson 2003).

With a focus on the U.S., other research has identified a range of online features present on political websites, including interactivity, links to other political sites, and various opportunities for both on and offline political participation (Foot and Schneider 2002;, Klinenberg and Perrin 2000; Schneider and Foot 2002; Schneider and Larsen 2000). All are not optimistic, however. Some conclude that political sites are simply "brochure-ware," consisting of little more than online adaptations of offline material (Kamarck 1999). One study discovered a pervasiveness of such substance in an analysis of the websites for the eight major candidates in the 2000 U.S. presidential election (Schneider and Larsen 2000).

This study will examine the function of political websites in the recent European Parliament (EP) elections. With a specific focus on websites geared towards young people, it considers the online potential to engage this age cohort through the "online structures for political action" (Schneider and Foot 2002) provided on election-related websites. The primary research question is, during the 2004 European Parliament election campaign, how are both youth party and youth organization websites addressing young people, and how do these websites compare in their information provision for and enabling of engagement with online users to participate in the election campaign?

The research here will help to uncover how websites addressed the 2004 EP election campaign. The analysis will also contribute to a more general inquiry into how online content is addressing young people and encouraging youth political engagement.

Youth and political engagement

Many agree that the strength of representative democracy rests on its degree of citizen engagement; such citizen engagement is found in voting, political engagement, and civic involvement (Almond and Verba 1989; Pattie *et al.* 2003). From this perspective, young people are often charged with being disengaged from conventional politics. Examples of such disengagement are common throughout the Western world. For instance, British youth are increasingly detached from governmental and party politics (Wring *et al.* 1999). Others go so far as to assert that young people are the most politically disengaged of all citizens, and this disengagement contributes to a growing sense of apathy and even alienation (Jowell and Park 1998; Norris 2003b; Parry *et al.* 1992). Such trends are noticeable when examining voting behavior. For example, in the 2002 15-nation European Social Survey, 75 percent of those surveyed in the middle-aged and older groups had voted in the past 12 months. In contrast, only half of those under 30 – of those eligible to vote and those that had the opportunity to vote – had voted (Norris 2003b). Due to their age and intellectual and social maturity, young people stand at a critical point of development for their civic and political skills. Such skills are predictive of future political behavior, including voting (Miller and Shanks 1996). This documented detachment from traditional political participation, together with young people's notable online presence and extensive use of new technologies, calls for inquiries into the potential of youth-geared websites to address this apparent indifference. Online initiatives may be able to influence the motivations, capacities, and opportunities of young people to become involved in public life. This is partly possible due to the unique characteristics of the internet, as it encourages an interest- rather than geographic-based community. In addition, it confronts conventional characterizations of authority and information gatekeepers, and it alters who consumes and who produces the content (Delli Carpini 2000).

Recent research has specifically concentrated on the online presence of organizations that attempt to mobilize young people. Bennet and Xenos (2004) examined youth engagement sites and election campaign sites during the 2002 U.S. elections, finding that the former provided a satisfactory amount of political content and supplied interactive content complete with youth lingo. Nevertheless, such content was more seldom present on websites run by political candidates. Similar research has taken place in Scotland, where e-initiatives that aim to make contact with youth are under investigation; recent work focuses on describing a system of e-democracy designed especially for young people of pre-voting age (Macintosh *et al.* 2002). Initiatives such as these give young people the opportunity to discuss significant political issues online and young participants typically respond with interest to online debating and voting (Smith *et al.* 2003). In a thorough examination of youth civic organizations in the United States, Montgomery, Gottlieg-Robles and Larson (2004) report that such websites, often based on offline organizations but sometimes a function of purely "digital" groups, encourage young people to vote, volunteer, become socially active, and be aware of racism and tolerance.

Civic and political engagement is as much dependent on the ability and enthusiasm of citizens to participate as on their actual engagement behavior (Verba *et al.* 1995). Although online initiatives such as those previously discussed have the potential to affect both cognitive and attitudinal aspects of participation, the greatest potential is their ability to provide structures that enhance pre-existing political behavior (Bimber 2003; Ward *et al.* 2003). Similarly, this study focuses on whether and how the websites of traditional mediators offer structures that facilitate youth engagement.

2004 European Parliament elections

Although notorious for their widespread lack of public and media interest, the 2004 EP elections were, at least on paper, a highly symbolic event. In May 2004, when the EU was enlarged to include ten new member states, almost 350 million Europeans were eligible to vote in 25 countries (the second-largest democratic electorate in the world after India), and in June 2004 they selected 732 Members of the European Parliament (MEPs). However, voter turnout has consistently decreased since the first EP elections, from 63 percent in 1979 to just above 48 percent in 2004, the lowest turnout in the election's history. However, a different picture emerges when individual countries are considered. In fact, turnout in the U.K. rose to 38.9 percent during the 2004 elections – the highest ever – and up from 24 percent in the 1999 elections. In addition, 59.7 percent of the Irish public exercised their right to vote, their second-highest turnout since joining the EU.[2] This higher-than-normal turnout may be a result of the EP elections coinciding with local elections. In Ireland, both local elections and a highly contested referendum on immigration happened concurrently with the EP elections. Furthermore, Ireland maintained the EU presidency for the first half of 2004, thus overlapping the election campaign period. In Britain, local elections coincided with the EP elections.

Method

By focusing on the 2004 EP elections for this study, attention is given to an election with historically low interest and turnout; choosing to concentrate on youth points to an age cohort with even lower interest and turnout. For the current project, two types of organizations were chosen that addressed young people during this election campaign: youth sections of political parties and youth-oriented organizations. Bennett and Xenos (2004) provide a related comparison between candidate and youth engagement sites. Youth branches of political parties exist in order to attract young, politically active or curious citizens and to encourage political engagement; youth organizations appeal to young people for comparable but often less political reasons.

In this study, websites were examined for their provision of both information and engagement features. Information features consist of election content, biographical information, candidate endorsements, issue positions and comparisons, speeches, election-related calendars, and information about the electoral or voting process. The presence of such features allows the online user to gather relevant information about the election campaign, thus permitting an expansion of their knowledge about the political process. Engagement features let website users interact with the producer or other visitors and provide participation opportunities for activities and actions both online and offline. The following engagement features were coded: the ability to contact the producer or receive an e-mail newsletter; to become a member of the organization; to engage in previously offline activities, such as donating to the party or organization or registering to vote; to contribute to a forum space; to write a public support statement for a candidate, party, or other relevant organization; to send links and e-paraphernalia to others; to distribute materials offline; and to volunteer. This research was conducted as part of the Internet and Elections Project, an international research effort to compare political websites (Foot *et al.* 2003).

Using a two-step approach, websites in Britain and Ireland were identified in the months leading up to the EP election campaign. Initially I chose websites that explicitly cater to youth. For the purposes of this study, "young people" of voting age were between the ages of 18 and 30 years old. This definition was chosen inasmuch as selected websites generally identified a target group within this age range. As a further prerequisite for inclusion, websites must have had a realistic potential to contain information about the 2004 EP election campaign; a preliminary examination of their content and focus determined whether this was present.

I used two separate sources to compile the website list used in this research (Norris 2003a): "Governments on the WWW"[3] and "Political Science Resources."[4] "Governments on the WWW" provided an online, comprehensive list of political parties' websites in Britain and Ireland. From this directory, party youth branches with an online presence were included in the sample. Youth organization websites were located using the United Nation's listing of youth and student coordinating bodies in Ireland and the U.K.[5] In addition, well-known search engines were employed to perform additional queries in order to ascertain that all relevant sites were identified within the two specific producer definitions.

The identification of youth websites transpired during the six months prior to the election campaign. In order to ascertain that they remained operable, the chosen sites were checked several times throughout this time period; if any other relevant organizations had obtained a web presence they were included. Website identification was completed on 7 May 2004. In total, 46 youth sites were selected for analysis, including 31 sites in the U.K. and 15 in Ireland. Of these, 21 belonged to youth branches of political parties (13 British and eight Irish) and 25 to youth organizations (18 British and seven Irish). The websites were coded two weeks prior to the EP elections using a frame employed by all Internet and Elections Project researchers.

Results

Youth websites active during the EP election campaign provided a broad range of offerings, from high-tech, high quality websites representing the main political parties to the cheaply designed or rarely maintained web presences of other, less financially endowed organizations. In the following two sections, I provide a summary of the information (Table 10.1) and engagement (Table 10.2) features identified on youth websites in Britain and Ireland. Overall, 15 out of 46 sites in the sample contained election-related content. As other elections occurred simultaneously with the EP elections in

Table 10.1 Information features on youth websites during the 2004 EP election campaign

	Youth organization websites (n = 25)	Political party websites (n = 21)
Election content	*4	*11
Biography/history/about us	24	21
Endorsements	*_	*8
Issue positions	*_	*14
Speeches	*_	*5
Calendar/List of events	*_	*4
Comparison of issue positions	1	2
Info-electoral campaign process	*_	*4
Info-voting process	5	5

Notes
* = sig.
$p < 0.01$.

Table 10.2 Engagement features on youth websites during the 2004 EP election campaign

	Youth organization websites (n = 25)	Political party websites (n = 21)
Contact producer	22	21
Join/become a member	*8	*17
Register to vote	3	4
Get e-mail from site	5	9
Donate	*2	*10
Contribute to forum space	4	5
Offline dist. of material	1	4
Send links	2	3
Public support statement	–	–
E-paraphernalia	1	2
Volunteer	4	5

Notes
* = sig.
$p < 0.01$.

both the U.K. and Ireland, there consequently may have been more information on local elections than the EP elections.

A strong association was found between producer type and election content ($p < 0.01$). That is, political party sites ($n = 11$) provided election content more frequently than youth organizations sites ($n = 4$). This is in many ways to be expected, as political parties have a direct stake in the election. All U.K. youth party websites, except for the Young Greens and the Young Socialists, and the Young Fine Gael and Irish Labour Youth in Ireland, provided information about the candidates running for their party. This feature often linked to the candidates' homepages; some also provided candidates' photos. The U.K.'s Conservative Party youth site[6] offered one explicit example of election promotion. A pop-up "sticky note" appeared when accessing the homepage, dimming the rest of the content and reminding visitors to vote on Election Day, encouraging participation, and urging the guest to enter the site.

Other websites did not specifically feature EP election information although they did focus on Europe in other ways. Two U.K. youth organizations dealt with Europe directly: the Euro-skeptic Youth for a Free Europe[7] and the pro-European Young European Movement.[8] Although both websites clearly positioned themselves in relation to Britain's role in Europe, neither mentioned youth participation – nor its avoidance – in the election campaign.

Issue positions, or statements of viewpoints the organization holds about relevant issues, could be reflections of party manifestos for the election campaign. Fourteen of the political party sites listed issue positions, but none of the youth organizations presented this feature. However, the Young Communist League[9] had a "What we stand for" link on its homepage, directing visitors to a bulleted list of its beliefs, discussing its democratic and revolutionary nature, and highlighting its autonomy from the Communist Party. Theoretically, sites could list a comparison of issue positions between themselves and other political parties or organizations. However, only three websites in the sample provided this feature, and the only youth organization to do so was the Union of Students in Ireland, which showed initiative in questioning parties on their stances on issues of importance to students.

Both youth organizations and political party sites did relatively little to provide information about campaign logistics. Only four of the political party sites provided information about the electoral campaign process. Information about the voting process, such as how to register to vote and where and when to vote, turned up relatively more often – five political parties and five youth organization websites supplied this information.

Endorsements, defined as explicit support for a candidate for the European Parliament, were present on eight political party sites. However, there were many other mentions of candidates, but not in the traditional way often found on main party or press sites. Several political parties endorsed young candidates from their organizations, and in doing so promoted certain events where these candidates would be present and available for questions.

In general, information features were found more often on political party youth websites than on those related to youth organizations. Traditionally, political parties are more involved in the election, so this result was not unexpected. A strong association ($p < 0.01$) was found between producer type (party versus organization) and various information variables (excluding biographies, comparison of issue positions, and information about the voting process).

Engagement features are website characteristics that offer visitors the opportunity to participate actively in the organization and the campaign, both online and offline (see Table 10.2). The defining characteristic of these features is their interactive nature, which allows communication with the political party/organization and others by sending material of interest either on or offline. All websites – excluding three youth organizations – listed simple contact information, like a contact name, mailing address, phone number, and e-mail address. Some sites hyperlinked the word "contact" and supplied an addressed e-mail for the user to fill out; other sites provided an address and phone number and still others had a link to a separate page of detailed contact information. Nine party sites and five youth organization sites offered the option to sign up to receive e-mail from the website informing recipients of upcoming events or news. On the Young Green's[10] homepage, a prominent "Get Involved" banner listed involvement opportunities, including registration for one of the "Young Greens Email Lists" that consisted of local groups involved in everything from "green" website design to policy making.

A relative large number of websites provided the option to join or become a member (eight youth organizations and 17 party sites). On the Young Labour site,[11] visitors were encouraged to become members after reading an appeal to shared values with the party itself as well as with other young people. The site also offered other ways to become involved, such as helping the Labour campaign and assisting in candidate choice.

Voter registration is a feature that provides explicit means for the user to register to vote; this differs from voter information, which focuses on offering information about the voting process rather than enabling registration. Voter registration was made available by only a few websites (three youth organizations and four political party sites). One online Irish youth organization, Youth.ie, not only provided a link to voter registration forms, but also explained why many young people do not vote, the reasons for voting – as an Irish citizen – in the EP elections, and candidate/current politicians' biographies and contact details.

Visitors could contribute to a forum or other communication space on four youth organization sites and five party sites. Although providing a forum is one of the best ways for organizations to make use of the internet's interactive qualities, it was rarely available on the sites included in this study. The Institute for Citizenship website[12] contained many different political discussion forums, some specifically regarding European citizenship. Another type of communication space, polls, allowed site visitors to voice their opinion about election issues. Throughout the campaign, the Scottish Youth Parliament website[13] boasted a "Euro voting" poll on its front page. Visitors were asked, "Will you be voting in the European Election in June?" and were given the option to choose between three alternatives: "Elections . . . NO WAY!," "I would but I'm under 18," and "Yeah, I'll be voting."

Websites can also promote the offline distribution of campaign material, by enabling visitors to send campaign-related links and download e-paraphernalia supporting the campaign. However, the opportunity to participate in this kind of distribution took place on only one youth organization and four political party sites; the chance to send links to friends or others was present on only five sites. Only one youth organization and two youth branches of political parties provided e-paraphernalia on their sites. The Young European Movement[143] announced on its homepage "Send your friends an e-card" and showed a sample of a postcard-shaped greeting that read "Euro Yes!" After one more click, the visitor could preview six card options, some of which were animated. After making a choice, the card could be e-mailed to a recipient.

Volunteer opportunities appeared on four of the youth organization sites and five party sites. This feature often encouraged site visitors to submit a form with contact information or promoted volunteering for specific issue campaigns. For example, the British Youth Council,[154] an organization dedicated to promoting the rights of young people, contained a list of current campaigns linked from its homepage. These campaigns, dealing with such topics as getting the vote out or lowering the voting age to 16, were often sponsored in conjunction with other, similar organizations.

In a majority of the sites examined, European citizens were not heartily encouraged to become active online in the EP election campaign. The generally limited offering of engagement features, suggests that, at least here, websites are considered more suitable for providing informational content than for encouraging participation. However, in comparison to more information-rich youth political party sites, youth organizations offered greater possibilities for young people to become more involved in the campaign or organization itself. When examining two specific engagement features (the ability to join/become a member online and the opportunity to donate to the party or organization), a notable difference between party and organization websites became apparent. A strong association ($p < 0.01$) was found between producer type and these two features.

Discussion

In the context of the EP election campaign, this chapter compared youth political party and organization websites in regard to information and engagement features present on the sites. The information feature accessible most often on both types of sites was biographical content about the organization; the most notable difference regarded the presentation of issue positions, which was entirely absent for youth organizations and present on almost three-quarters of political party sites. Variations in engagement feature provision were less prominent – contacting the producer was almost always possible, but the largest difference was the ability to become a member of the party or organization.

Only 15 websites provided explicit election information; its presence on party sites was noticeable higher than on youth organization sites. This minor focus on the EP elections may be a cause for concern. With European integration moving forward, it is vital that young Europeans understand their role in the political process, particularly in relation to the EP elections. However, it is important to note that differences may exist in how young people are addressed during a non-electoral time period. Namely, a point in time that is not characterized by increased political activity might reflect different strategies of addressing and engaging with young people. The question of whether methods of information provision and engagement opportunities change outside the context of election campaigns should be addressed in future research.

Whether dealing with local or EP elections, an equal number of both types of websites provided information about the voting process. Likewise, offering the option to register to vote was found on a similar number of sites. Youth organizations left specific election information provision to the political parties, instead focusing on getting young people more involved with various campaigns and activities. Despite a number of promising counter examples, the websites examined in this study suggest, as Bennet and Xenos (2004) argue, "the potential of digital technologies as media for greater youth mobilization have yet to be fulfilled" (p. 28).

This study analyzed the ways in which political websites addressed young people during the 2004 EP election campaign. However, to understand better the philosophy behind the website content, it is important to query the site producers themselves – a task for a future study. Based on the analysis presented here, youth organizations appear to believe that political engagement entails more than simply voting every few years for a representative. Although they find traditional political participation important, they also believe that engagement can occur in broader, more unconventional activities through volunteering or participating in political discussion. On the youth organization websites, engagement was framed according to general, organizational participation, rather than explicit encouragement or enablement of election campaign participation. This is best illustrated by some of the more frequently coded features. For example, joining an organization definitely provides an opportunity for young people's participation, but it does not obviously relate to their electoral participation, or specifically relate to the European Parliament elections. It may be seen as equally important to provide more generalized information to build a pattern of engagement among young people. Such an observation, however, is based solely on the *content* of the websites we examined. In order to ascertain the specific motivations of the organizations, and the intentions of their producers, other methods of inquiry such as interviews with key persons are necessary.

This analysis suggests that, while scarce, sites are offering many information and engagement provisions to young visitors. Seeing an increase in these features is just a matter of organizations that lack an online presence imitating those that have already created these methods to address young people. Of course, such a strategy is useful only if youth are actually visiting these sites and using these features. Therefore, speaking to young users about their views concerning political engagement as well as their online preferences would help explain how youth will likely react to new initiatives.

Future research should examine the style of communication present on these websites, and its relevance to the young audience that such initiatives are seeking to attract. Additionally, youth-oriented websites could be compared to and contrasted with their adult counterparts. For instance, does Young Labour address its constituency in a different manner than the primary Labour party website does? Based on the analysis presented here, it is not clear whether websites catering to an older target audience provide different types of information and engagement features, or a different style of communication. Additional research will help to understand whether such online initiatives are engaging young people, and how such websites should address young people's political inclinations in the future.

Notes

1 An earlier version of this chapter was published in *Information Polity* 10 (3/4).
2 Comprehensive statistics available online: www.euractiv.com/Article?tcmuri= tcm:29-117482-16&type=LinksDossier.
3 www.gksoft.com/govt/.
4 www.psr.keele.ac.uk/parties.htm.
5 esa.un.org/socdev/unyin/country5.asp.
6 www.conservativefuture.com/.
7 www.free-europe.org.uk/.
8 www.yem.org.uk/home.php.
9 www.ycl.org.uk/.
10 www.younggreens.org.uk/Home.
11 www.younglabour.org.
12 www.institute_for_citize\speakout\index.html.
13 www.scottishyouthparliament.org.uk/.
14 www.yem.org.uk/home.php.
15 www.byc.org.uk/.

References

Almond, G. and Verba, S. (1989) *The Civic Culture: Political Attitudes and Democracy in Five Nations*. Newbury Park, CA: Sage Publications.

Bennett, W.L. and Xenos, M. (2004) "Young voters and the web of politics: pathways to participation in the youth engagement and electoral campaign web spheres," CIRCLE Working Paper 20, the Center for Information and Research on Civic Learning and Engagement. Available online: www.civicyouth.org/PopUps/WorkingPapers/WP20BennettExecSumm.pdf (accessed 6 September 2006).

Bimber, B. (2003) *Information and American Democracy: Technology in the Evolution of Political Power*. Cambridge: Cambridge University Press.

Bimber, B. and Davis, R. (2003) *Campaigning Online: The Internet in U.S. Elections*. Oxford: Oxford University Press.

British Youth Council (n.d.) Available online: www.byc.org.uk/ (accessed 24 May 2004).

Carlson, T. and Djupsund, G. (2001) "Old wine in new bottles? The 1999 Finnish election campaign on the Internet," *Harvard International Journal of Press/Politics*, 6, 1: 68–87.

Conservative Party (n.d.) *Conservative Future*. Available online: www.conservativefuture.com/ (accessed 28 May 2004).

Delli Carpini, M.X. (2000) "Gen.com: youth, civic engagement, and the new information environment," *Political Communication*, 17, 4: 341–349.

Eisinger, P.K. (1973) "The conditions of protest behavior in American cities," *American Political Science Review*, 67: 11–28.

EurActiv (n.d.) "European parliament elections 2004: results." Available online: www.euractiv.com/Article?tcmuri=tcm:2911748216&type=LinksDossir (accessed 29 April 2005).

Foot, K. and Schneider, S. (2002) "Online action in campaign 2000: an exploratory analysis of the U.S. political web sphere," *Journal of Broadcasting and Electronic Media*, 46, 2: 222–244.

Foot, K., Jankowski, N.W., Kluver, R., and Schneider, S. (2003) "The Internet and elections: an international project for the comparative study of the role of the Internet in the electoral process," unpublished manuscript.

Gibson, R. and Ward, S. (1998) "U.K. political parties and the Internet: 'politics as usual' in the new media?," *Harvard International Journal of Press/Politics*, 3, 3: 14–38.

Gibson, R., Ward, S., and Nixon, P. (2003) *Political Parties and the Internet: Net Gain?* London: Routledge.

Governments on the WWW (n.d.) Available online: www.gksoft.com/govt/ (accessed 12 January 2004).

Institute for Citizenship (n.d.) Available online: www.citizen.org.uk/ (accessed 28 May 2004).

Jowell, R. and Park, A. (1998) *Young People, Politics and Citizenship: A disengaged Generation?* London: Citizenship Foundation.

Kamarck, E.C. (1999) "Campaigning on the internet in the elections of 1998," in E.C. Kamarck and J.J.S. Nye (eds), *Democracy.com? Governance in the Network World*, pp. 99–123. Hollis, NH: Hollis.

Kimber, R. (n.d.) "Political parties, interest groups and other social movements." Available online: www.psr.keele.ac.uk/parties.htm (accessed 12 January 2004).

Klinenberg, E. and Perrin, A. (2000) "Symbolic politics in the information age: the 1996 Republican presidential campaigns in cyberspace," *Information, Communication and Society*, 3, 1: 17–38.

The Labour Party (n.d.) "Britain is working in Europe." Available online: www.labour.org.uk/news/20reasonswhyeuropeworks (accessed 29 May 2004).

Macintosh, A., Robson, E., Smith, E., and Whyte, A. (2002) "Electronic democracy and young people," *Social Science Computer Review*, 21, 1: 43–54.

Miller, W.E. and Shanks, J.M. (1996) *The New American Voter*. Cambridge, MA: Harvard University Press.

Montgomery, K., Gottlieg-Robles, B., and Larson, G.O. (2004) *Youth as E-citizens: Engaging the Digital Generation*. Washington, DC: American University, Center for Social Media.

Mutz, D.C. and Martin, P.S. (2001) "Facilitating communication across lines of political difference: the role of the mass media," *American Political Science Review*, 95: 97–114.

Norris, P. (2002). *Digital Divide: Civic Engagement, Information Poverty, and the Internet Worldwide*. Cambridge: Cambridge University Press.

Norris, P. (2003a) *Deepening Democracy via E-governance*. Available online: ksghome.harvard.edu/~pnorris/ACROBAT/e-governance.pdf.

Norris, P. (2003b) "Young people and political activism: From the politics of loyalties to the politics of choice?," paper presented at the Council of Europe Symposium, Young People and Democratic Institutions: From Disillusionment to Participation, Strasbourg, France, November.

Parry, G., Moyser, G., and Day, N. (1992) *Political Participation and Democracy in Britain*. Cambridge: Cambridge University Press.

Pattie, C., Seyd, P., and Whiteley, P. (2003) "Citizenship and civic engagement: attitudes and behaviour in Britain," *Political Studies*, 51, 3: 443–468.

Schneider, S. and Foot, K. (2002) "Online structure for political action: exploring presidential campaign web sites from the 2000 American election," *Javnost – The Public*, 9, 2: 43–60.

Schneider, S. and Larsen, E. (2000) "The 2000 presidential primary candidates: the view from the web," paper presented at the meeting of the International Communications Association, Acapulco, Mexico, June.

Scottish Youth Parliament (n.d.) Available online: www.scottishyouthparliament. org.uk/ (accessed 24 May 2004).

Smith, E., Macintosh, A., and Whyte, A. (2003) "Culture and context in an online voting system for young people," paper presented at the IFIP Summer School: Risks and Challenges of the Network Society, Karlstad, Sweden, August.

Sunstein, C.R. (2001) *Republic.com.* Princeton: Princeton University Press.

Union of Students in Ireland (n.d.) Available online: www.usi.ie/ (accessed 2 June 2004).

United Nations (n.d.) "United Nation's listing of youth and student coordinating bodies in Ireland and the UK." Available online: esa.un.org/socdev/unyin/ country5.asp (accessed 12 January 2004).

Van Selm, M., Jankowski, N.W., and Tsaliki, T. (2001) "Political parties online: digital democracy as reflected in three Dutch political party Web sites," *Communications: The European Journal of Communication Research*, 27, 2: 189–210.

Verba, S., Schlozman, K.L., and Brady, H.E. (1995) *Voice and Equality: Civic Voluntarism in American Politics.* Cambridge, MA: Cambridge University Press.

Voerman, G. (2000) "Elektronisch folderen: de digitale campagne," in P. van Praag and K. Brants (eds), *Tussen beeld en inhoud. Politiek en media in de verkiezingen van 1998*, pp. 193–213. Amsterdam: Het Spinhuis.

Voerman, G. and Boogers, M. (2002) "Users of Dutch political websites during the 2002 national elections," paper presented at the Euricom Conference, Nijmegen. Netherlands, October.

Ward, S.G. and Gibson, R.M. (2003) "Online and on message? Candidate websites in the 2001 general election," *British Journal of Politics and International Relations*, 5, 2: 188–205.

Ward, S., Gibson, R., and Lusoli, W. (2003) "Participation and mobilisation online: hype, hope and reality," *Parliamentary Affairs*, 56, 3: 652–668.

Wring, D., Henn, M., and Weinstein, M. (1999) "Young people and contemporary politics: committed skepticism or engaged criticism?," in J. Fisher, P. Cowley, D. Denver, and E. Russel (eds), *British Elections and Parties Review*, Vol. 9. London: Frank Cass.

Young Communist League (n.d.) Available online: www.ycl.org.uk/ (accessed 24 May 2004).

Young European Movement (n.d.). Available online: www.yem.org.uk/home.php (accessed 29 May 2004).

Young Fine Gael (n.d.) "About Young Fine Gael." Available online: www.yfg.ie/about.php (accessed 28 May 2004).

Young Greens (n.d.) "Young Greens: doing more than dreaming." Available online: www.younggreens.org.uk/Home (accessed 24 May 2004).

Young Labour (n.d.) "Our Aims." Available online: www.younglabour.org/ (accessed 28 May 2004).

Youniss, J., Bales, S., Christmas-Best, V., Diversi, M., McLaughlin, M., and Silbereisen, R. (2002) "Youth civic engagement in the twenty-first century," *Journal of Research on Adolescence*, 12, 1: 121–148.

Youth for a Free Europe (n.d.) Available online: www.free-europe.org.uk/ (accessed 28 May 2004).

11 Two Indias

The role of the internet in the 2004 elections

Shyam Tekwani and Kavitha Shetty

Introduction

Politics and popular culture have long been intertwined in Indian public life and in its elections. The internet and new media technology add another dimension to this complex yet commonplace interaction. In the 2004 election, the rapid diffusion of information technology was incorporated into the normally raucous political environment in ways that reflected the unique characteristics of Indian political culture, both in terms of the artifacts of campaigns, as well as in the deep and abiding persistence of the divide between rich and poor in India. The purpose of this chapter is to explore the characteristics of the Indian electoral web sphere for the 2004 election, and the ways in which the rise of the internet as a campaign device reflected and reinforced these aspects of India's political culture.

Our concern here is with the role of the internet as a campaign medium. We are interested in exploring the ways in which the electoral web sphere reflected and reinforced certain aspects of Indian political culture, notably to what extent it reinforced the class divide which is such a prominent characteristic of Indian life. In this chapter, we will demonstrate the ways in which the 2004 electoral web sphere both demonstrated the characteristics of offline media campaigns and reflected and reinforced the class divide. In effect, the internet, rather than empowering the marginalized players in Indian elections, reinforced a "two Indias" reality in which the middle and upper classes are given greater political efficacy through the use of information technology and the lower classes are reliant almost entirely upon traditional, low-cost media for election information.

Elections in India

"India enjoys elections," Butler and Roy argue (1991: 1), describing Indian democracy as "not only the largest but the most triumphant example of democracy." India has been described often as the world's largest democracy, not just because it is home to the world's largest population but also because of the enormity of the electoral process in India and the high level of voter participation in all aspects of elections. According to Chandra *et al.* (2000), the greatest achievement of independent India has been its secular, federal and multiparty political system. Despite its backward economy and impoverished masses, its violent social conflicts and high defense expenditures since independence, the political system has endured and flourished. In fact, the firm entrenchment of political democracy and civil liberties are considered by many to be India's most remarkable post-1947 accomplishment. To quote Chandra *et al.*:

> Indians enjoy today a free press, the freedom to speak, travel and form associations, the right to freely criticize the government, they have competitive elections, unrestricted working of political parties, an independent judiciary, the right to participate in political life and to change the government through the ballot box, and freedom from fear of arbitrary arrest.

> (2000: 491)

India consists of 28 provinces and seven Union Territories, extending over a geographic area of three million square kilometers (approximately equivalent to Western Europe). The population in this area speaks in 22 official and 1600 minor languages and dialects. The country has a population density of 310 persons per square kilometer; a quarter of the population resides in urban areas, about 260 million people live below the poverty line, and two-thirds of the population is dependent on agriculture for its livelihood. India is home to the world's largest population and is living on less than U.S.$1 a day, considered to be the international standard for poverty.

Elections in India are huge affairs and occur every five years, in the form of an enormous, raucous, colorful festival. Of the total population of 1.09 billion, 688 million Indians were eligible to vote in the 2004 parliamentary elections. Of these, nearly 60 percent (about 380 million people, or 10 percent more than in the 2000 American presidential election) turned out to vote, making the electoral exercise one of the largest undertakings in political history – and one of the most expensive, costing the Indian exchequer 13 billion rupees (approximately U.S.$288 million).

The Election Commission of India (ECI), which is responsible for conducting the elections in the country, calls this task the "management of the largest event in the world." The Election Commission is a permanent constitutional body, established in accordance with the Constitution on 25 January 1950. India's unique linguistic and cultural plurality makes the task of conducting an Indian election immensely challenging. While the logistics and expense involved in conducting such an exercise in electoral politics are phenomenal, the calculations and permutations involved in contesting elections, and the necessity of campaigning to a population divided along diverse social, cultural, religious, linguistic, and political lines, turn the entire exercise into a Babel-esque festival. While new technology has made tremendous inroads into electoral campaigns, with internet advertising and text messaging reaching huge swathes of the fast-expanding urban middle classes, previous technology – the old fashioned billboard, with bright visual depictions of contestants and campaign messages, along with posters, pamphlets, and other low-end political propaganda materials – still have their roles to play in largely rural and illiterate India.

But in this election the billboards were the sideshow, at least according to popular perception. India is a country awash with the mantra of high technology and new technology. It is saturated with stories of the Indian technological revolution and the emergence of the savvy Indian techie, who dominates all Indian markets from the matrimonial market to the job market to the stock market, and, many believed, even the election market. With this election, the big difference was to be the technological one. After all, this was the first major election in the new-technology India, the India of booming economic growth and a rising educated middle class.

Methodology

Using methods common to chapters in this volume, the authors identified websites relevant to the Indian election six weeks prior to the 2004 election. A sample of 100 sites was coded systematically for the presence of informational and engagement features according to the common template prepared for this project. Information features are those website features which seek to provide information about politics, the election period, or political actors in an election, while engagement features are those which seek to provide users with opportunities to take an active role in some aspect of the election. These ranged from such simple procedures as sending e-mails or registering for further information to more involved activities such as joining a party or sending party materials to others.

In addition, we sought to consider the role of the internet within the larger context of how political actors within India traditionally used various types of media, including folk media, mass media, and other forms of campaign materials. Thus, we rely on a more qualitative assessment of the role of information technology, specifically drawing upon newspaper accounts and other secondary analyses of the deployment of information technology.

Internet deployment in the 2004 elections

Given the novelty of the internet in Indian elections, there is little regulation in place to govern internet political campaigns specifically. The same was not true of other forms of media, with recent rulings by the Election Commission of India restricting election campaigning on television and imposing severe penalties for defacing public property with posters. Moreover, these rulings put limits on the spread of cut-outs and billboards for campaign purposes. Thus, Indian politicians used their resources instead to

Table 11.1 Internet diffusion in India

Population (2005 est.)	1,094,870,677
Internet users (year 2000)	5,000,000
Internet users, latest data (year 2005)	39,200,000
User growth (2000–2005)	684.0%
Penetration (% population)	3.6%

Source: Internet Usage in Asia (2005)

exploit the internet and other communications technologies to get their message to the voters. The growing number of mobile phone users and increasing use of the internet (see Table 11.1) provided the parties with a new campaign platform, and most of them used it extensively, if not successfully. In addition, most political parties jumped on the internet bandwagon using websites and portals, along with telephone messaging services (e.g. SMS) and e-mail campaigns to reach voters directly. Print and electronic media also used their online versions to disseminate news and analysis on the elections to reach India's burgeoning group of internet users.

The Election Commission of India had perhaps the most comprehensive website assessed in this study, providing information on every aspect of the elections, including information about the electoral system and the election process in India, elections schedules, results, news, lists of all political parties and their symbols, links to their websites, lists of all candidates, and lists of various alliances across the political spectrum, as well as discussions on key election issues and personalities. Besides the Election Commission website, the Chief Electoral Officers (CEOs) in each state had their own websites putting out information on state-level elections, parties, alliances, candidates, and election issues.

Political parties were also strongly represented in the electoral web sphere. For example, The Mission 2004 website, a product of the Bharatiya Janata Party (BJP) media center, was the launching pad for the party's internet campaign. The BJP's website[1] even had a downloadable Prime Minister Vajpayee screensaver in which the portly prime minister read poems which he had written. The Indian National Congress (Congress) Party set up a website that was used like a war room to coordinate the electioneering and even a site to denounce the campaign of the ruling party with the intriguing URL of www.nationbetrayed.com.[2] The Congress Party in Karnataka included IT skills as a required qualification for election volunteers.

In the IT capital of India, Bangalore, the Congress Party, led by Chief Minister S.M. Krishna, had, in keeping with its image, an aesthetically pleasing site.[3] Likewise, Congress Party candidate Kiran Choudhry's website listed her political, educational, and family background as well as her achievements and that of the party. Visitors to the site could send feedback as well as address questions they wished answered by the candidate herself.

Table 11.2 Websites in sample per producer type

Producer type	Number of sites
Candidate	7
Government	33
NGO	7
Party	26
Press	11
Citizen	4
Portal	8
Political Professional	1
Business	2
Education	1
Total	100

It was not just the major political parties with significant finances, such as the BJP and Congress that used the internet. Underlying the perception that technology was the key to success in every field, including politics, was the widespread use of new communication technologies, including the internet, by regional political parties whose support base is largely non-English speaking and rural based. The Samajwadi Party (SP) and Bahujan Samaj Party (BSP), heartland parties, both of which are perceived as representing the poor and uneducated, also put up official party websites and used the internet to spread campaign messages. In all, there was so much IT hype that even the communist parties did not want to be left behind.

However, notwithstanding the fact that even parties focusing on the poor used the web, it does seem that the widespread use of technology perpetuated class differences during the election. For example, many of India's new elite (investment bankers, IT companies, consulting companies) with advanced degrees from the revered Indian Institute of Technology (IIT), Indian Institute of Management (IIM), and top universities in the U.S. and Europe, groups that have not traditionally been associated with Indian politics, helped out the various party machinery, their contributions visible in their communication messages, style, site design, and campaign strategies.

Media headlines during the campaign also indicated the changing nature of campaigning and the growing popularity of the internet as medium. "Manifesto-E" was the title for the BJP's online manifesto; "Politicos and their web dreams" (Kalbag 2004) and "Powerpoint Pashas" (Bhaumik 2004) were just a few of the articles in mainstream media that described the online advertising blitz that accompanied the elections.

Our analysis of the distribution of informational and engagement features on websites in the Indian electoral web sphere suggest a limited deployment of information and engagement features. Informational features on websites may facilitate the democratization process by providing visitors with information related to various aspects of the election. Thus, providing high quality information on different issues can be seen as the first step towards internet deployment for democratic purposes. Table 11.3 provides a summary of the information features present across websites produced by political actors within the Indian parliamentary election web spheres. Websites most consistently featured biographies, a common characteristic of Indian politics, reflecting an emphasis on charismatic leadership. Issue positions of the various political actors were found on most party and candidate sites, but were much less likely to be found on sites produced by political portals or political professionals. On the other hand, very few sites feature speeches or audio-visuals. Political party sites provided the most varied types of information. As the web sphere included sites related to the parliamentary elections, it is perhaps not surprising that political parties provided the most varied type of information; amongst the different political actors, they would have the most at stake.

Turning now to an assessment of engagement features, the feature most consistently present across the different producer types was contact information for the site producer. An engagement feature that was noticeably absent from all the websites coded within the web sphere was a feature that enables visitors to volunteer. This is in contrast to Schneider and Foot's (2002) findings in the 2000 U.S. election as they found that all candidate sites had this feature. The presidential website had a feature that enabled visitors to volunteer to help in the campaign process. The producer type that offered the most varied amount of engagement features was political parties. Of 26 political party sites, 21 had contact information, although none of the party sites had a feature that enabled site visitors to help with the campaign process or to register to vote in the elections. The sites with the least varied type of engagement features were those produced by election candidates. Engagement features that were most prominent across candidate sites were contact, which was present on four out of seven sites. None of the candidate sites had features that enabled visitors to register to vote, distribute campaign material offline, express support for a party or candidate, download e-paraphernalia or volunteer. Government sites were the next least likely to offer a variation of features to engage visitors. The engagement features present on government sites were contact producer, register to vote, solicit for donations, contribute to a forum or online discussion, and distribute relevant material offline.

Analysis

Elections and election campaigns are an important part of public life in India and election campaigns in India are a reflection of the deep-rooted political culture of the nation. In this context it is interesting to observe how India's political culture affected the use of the internet in the 2004 elections.

Table 11.3 Information features on websites per producer type

Political actor*	Election	Biography	Issues	Speech	Calendar	Issue comparison	Campaign info	Voting info	Images	Audio visuals	Privacy policy	Terms of use
Candidate (7)	7	5	6	2	1	3	0	0	0	0	7	4
Government (33)	33	32	19	0	0	2	19	0	31	6	32	1
NGO (7)	7	3	7	0	1	0	0	0	0	0	7	0
Party (26)	26	22	22	11	16	9	2	2	3	2	24	7
Press (11)	11	11	8	1	3	0	5	1	2	2	10	4
Citizen (4)	1	3	1	0	1	0	3	0	4	1	0	0
Portal (8)	1	4	1	1	2	2	4	3	7	1	2	5
Political Professional (1)	0	0	0	0	0	0	0	1	0	0	0	0
Business (2)	0	2	2	0	0	2	0	0	2	1	0	0
Education(1)	1	1	1	0	1	0	0	0	1	0	0	1

Note
* Number of political actors per category indicated in parentheses.

Table 11.4 Engagement features on websites per producer type

Political actor*	Contact	Join	Register	Get mail	Donate	Forum	Offline distribution	Send links	Publish	E-paraphernalia	Volunteer
Candidate (7)	4	1	0	1	1	3	0	1	0	0	0
Government (33)	32	0	13	0	1	2	17	0	0	0	0
NGO (7)	4	3	0	3	0	3	0	0	1	0	0
Party (26)	21	10	0	3	3	16	2	8	4	4	0
Press (11)	10	5	0	1	1	3	3	2	0	2	0
Citizen (4)	4	3	0	1	1	2	1	0	1	0	0
Portal (8)	7	2	0	0	0	7	0	3	1	1	0
Political Professional (1)	1	0	0	0	0	0	0	1	0	0	0
Business (2)	2	2	0	0	0	2	0	0	0	0	0
Education (1)	0	0	0	0	1	0	0	1	0	0	0

Note
* Number of political actors per category indicated in parentheses.

Our first observation from this data, as well as from general media coverage of the elections in India, is that technology in these elections was more of a symbol than a mechanism. The ruling BJP emphasized the "India Shining" slogan in the election, proclaiming the resurgence of India as an emerging software and new technology hub, and touting the accompanying economic boom as its leading accomplishments in government. Given this theme, it was only appropriate for the party to deploy the internet and other new media technologies in a significant manner in its election campaigns. But the electronic campaign was largely targeted at the urban, educated, elite, expatriate Indians (who are not eligible to vote), and at the media in general. The internet campaign, then, was more important in creating or extending the image of BJP than it was in canvassing for votes. The Congress Party also used the internet extensively, and although the party's central election campaign was focused on the grassroots – and the huge swathes of urban poor and rural voters left out of the technology boom and its accompanying economic "miracle" – it used the internet in the same way as the BJP, to be in-step with public perceptions of India as a high-tech nation and the Congress as a party that was instep with the times.

In many countries the internet is a crucial aspect of election campaigns and is growing more important. In contrast, in India, despite the general environment of high- and new-technology use, the country's growing reputation as a nation of technology users and producers, and the much-hyped use of internet by political parties, the internet did not influence the outcome of elections in any significant way. The reasons for this have as much to do with the political culture in India as with the economic and social realities of the country. The huge digital divide in India is one of the major factors.

India has always been a nation of large contrasts. The economic divide between rich and poor, between haves and have-nots, in India is wide, and the recent technology-inspired economic growth has not helped bridge this gap. It may, in fact, have widened it further. Research suggests that IT growth can often cause income inequality to rise if incomes in the IT industry rise faster than other sectors – and if the IT sector does not have strong linkages with other sectors, which limits the trickle-down effect (Morley 2001). Many of the technology hubs in India, such as Bangalore, are indicators of this trend. Globalization in India has caused a divergence between Bangalore and the rest of the country and a simultaneous convergence between core markets, advanced capitalist centers, and Bangalore (D'Costa 2003). As D'Costa concludes, "In the absence of countervailing forces, class based polarization based on income, education and social connections is inevitable" (p. 63).

Unequal access to education owing to social biases stemming from the caste system is responsible in large part for the continuing digital divide in India. Other related factors include internet penetration in India, the low rate of which is itself an outcome of the rich–poor divide, where internet access is confined to the educated urban middle class and the elite. This leaves out the large mass of voters who live in rural India and the huge segment of the urban poor. Nearly 70 percent of Indian voters live in rural India and over 50 percent are illiterate.

In 2004, the total number of internet users in India was probably around 6.5 million. Despite a national focus on e-governance and information and communication technology for development, few initiatives have really taken off, and "most States remain in the primary phase of disseminating information using the worldwide web, without moving on to offer services online" ("Towards Internet for All 2004"). This description of the internet industry in India is particularly appropriate for the use of the internet and elections, as this web sphere seems to be designed primarily for disseminating information rather than for engaging potential voters or political activists.

The low rate of penetration can be attributed to several factors, such as low literacy levels and poor communication infrastructure across the country. In this context it is important to point out the role played by the linguistic plurality of India both in the uneven development of infrastructure across the country and in the slow and uneven uptake of the internet. Language plays a key role in Indian politics, and just as states in India are divided along linguistic lines, often political parties are divided along the same lines. And internet uptake in turn is determined by the language abilities of the party supporters in different states. The internet in India is largely an English-language phenomenon, and this is one of the major reasons for its limited role in Indian electoral campaigns, where most of the voters are rural and illiterate and non-English speakers. While the BJP and the Congress as national parties use English to target urban voters across the country, regional or state-level political parties use the language of that locality to communicate with supporters and the electorate. While the internet has been making an entrance in several Indian languages, such as Hindi, Malayalam, and Tamil, it is largely an educated urban phenomenon favored by English speakers, putting it beyond the reach of a majority of eligible voters.

Large-scale illiteracy is another reason for the subdued impact of the internet in this election. In a developing country such as India, with the multiple burdens of poverty, underdevelopment, and illiteracy, the role played by visual images in political communication is significant. In this regard the internet had little to offer Indian political parties and candidates. In order to reach the huge segment of the rural and the illiterate and to mitigate the barriers created by the complex linguistic diversity of the country, politicians in India have always relied on visual images to carry their messages to voters. Billboards, cut-outs, posters, and direct communication are the most popular form of political campaigning in India, even in this era of digital technology, internet advertising, and text messaging.

For the largely rural and illiterate voter in India, party symbols are the key to election choice. For those who cannot read, the party symbol is key, and in order to familiarize constituencies with party symbols in order to persuade them, political parties in India have long relied on billboards and posters plastered across cities and villages and the fanfare of election meetings held on parade grounds, in village centers, and town halls. These traditional media maintained their critical role in the 2004 election. Further, given the tradition of party-driven campaigning in Indian elections, where the concept of volunteerism itself scarcely exists (party work is done by paid workers or party members) citizen participation is still in its infancy. Some inroads have been made by the internet in this election, however, and given the general trend towards increasing technologization in India, it is perhaps a matter of time before activists and average citizens adopt a more proactive role in the political process.

Conclusion

In the 2004 election, the ruling BJP party was ousted, and the traditional secular Congress Party was returned to power in a surprise result. Polls had consistently pointed to the BJP as the victor, largely due to its popularity among the young, urban, and highly educated voters, those who were most likely to access the internet as a medium for political information. As these results demonstrate, the information revolution in India has a limited base. Its access and its advantages are largely restricted to the urban, the educated, and the elite – who do not represent the majority of the Indian electorate. One analyst concluded:

> The IT-savvy campaign of BJP-led NDA that included phone-ins by the Prime Minister, SMS and e-mails miserably failed to woo the electorate. A bulk of voters failed to "feel-good" and preferred the age-old "jansampark" (roadshow) style of the Italian-born Congress President. The grueling campaigns and personal street corner meetings during her road shows and the overwhelming response to her visits indicate that a two-way communication scores much more than "carpet-bombing."
>
> (IT Blitz 2004)

The limited impact of the internet in the 2004 elections in India does not mean that the internet has no potential as a political tool for elections and political participation. The technology is still new, both to political parties and to most of the Indian public. Practical factors such as access, poverty, and poor infrastructure and illiteracy played a major role in its low impact in 2004. It is also important to note that a very large percentage, nearly 70 percent, of the Indian population is under 35 years of age. These are the voters who indicated their preference for the apparently pro-technology BJP and its allies in polls throughout the campaign period. In the end, however, it was the urban–rural divide that cost the ruling party the government.

However, the fact that this critical population of young voters is growing, in combination with sustained internet growth and increased connectivity in India, can only mean that the internet will have a greater role to play in coming elections in India. Further, the perceived role of the internet in these recent elections and the interest it has generated in the Indian media have nevertheless sown the seeds for a more interactive approach to politics. In this election, politicians reached out to the public in a one-on-one basis through e-mail and mobile phones; perhaps in the next, the average citizen will reach out to the government, political parties, and interest groups to drive the election in a way more reflective of the concerns and agendas of the non-elite segment of India's population.

Notes

1 www.bjp.org.
2 Many of these websites have since shut down.
3 www.smkrishna.com.

References

Bhaumik, S.N. (2004) "Powerpoint pashas," *Outlook India*. Available online: www.outlookindia.com/full.asp?fodname=20040308&fname=Cover+Story+%28F%29&sid=1 (accessed 1 June 2004).

Butler, D., Lahiri, A., and Roy, P. (1991) *India Decides: Elections 1952–1991*. New Delhi: Living Media.

Chandra, B., Mukherjee, M., and Mukherjee, A. (2000) *India after Independence 1947–2000*. New Delhi: Penguin.

Congress and the Gandhi Dynasty (2004) Available online: www.indian-elections.com/editorials/editorial-2.html (accessed 1 August 2005).

D'Costa, A. (2003) "Catching up and falling behind: inequality, IT, and the Asian diaspora," in K.C. Ho, R. Kluver, and K.C.C. Yang (eds), *Asia.com: Asia Encounters the Internet*, pp. 44–66. London: Routledge.

Indian National Congress Party Profile (2004) "Indian Elections Portal." Available online: www.indian-elections.com/partyprofiles/congress.html (accessed 1 August 2005).

Internet Usage in Asia. Available online: www.internetworldstats.com/stats3.htm (accessed 1 August 2005).

IT Blitz Didn't Move Indian Voter (2004) "Sify News." Available online: sify.com/news/politics/fullstory.php?id=13474695 (accessed 26 April 2006).

Kalbag, S. (2004) "Politicos and their web dreams," Mid-Day.Com. Available online: web.mid-day.com/news/nation/2004/february/77029.htm (accessed 27 April 2006).

Morley, S.A. (2001) "Working Paper No. 184," *Distribution and Growth in Latin America in an Era of Structural Reform: The Impact of Globalisation*. Paris: OECD Development Center.

Schneider, S.M. and Foot, K.A. (2002) "Online structure for political action: exploring presidential campaign web sites from the 2000 American elections," *Javnart – The Public*, 9, 2: 43–60.

Sen, A. (2003) "India's new age election campaign," *BBC News/South Asia*. Available online: newswww.bbc.net.uk/1/hi/world/south_asia/3223646.stm (accessed 26 April 2006).

Srivastava, S. (2004) "Indian elections: the high-tech way," *Asia Times Online*. Available online: www.atimes.com/atimes/South_Asia/FD08Df04.html (accessed 26 April 2006).

Tekwani, S. (2003) "The Tamil diaspora, Tamil militancy, and the internet," in K.C. Ho, R. Kluver, and K.C.C. Yang (eds), *Asia.com: Asia Encounters the Internet*, pp. 175–192. London: Routledge.

"Towards Internet for All" (2004) "The Hindu Online." Available online: www.the-hindu.com/2004/04/08/stories/2004040803731000.htm (accessed 8 April 2004).

Part IV

Political culture and the diffusion of technologies

12 Web-based citizen engagement in the 2004 Australian federal election

Pieter Aquilia

Studies on the use of internet in the Australian political arena indicate that the site producer, rather than the user, is the benefactor of internet technology. Traditionally, the use of the internet in Australian state and territory elections has been, in the words of Gibson and Ward "top-down information provision" (2003: 140). Political websites were primarily an "adjunct to existing communication devices," offering limited interactive experiences (2003: 140–141). During the 2004 Australian federal election, however, this study reveals that political websites were as likely to provide features facilitating public engagement as they were to provide political information, suggesting that the internet is closing the gap on what Putman (2000) calls the "civic deficit."

In this chapter, we first examine the extent to which the internet, as it was deployed during the 2004 Australian federal election, is changing from a top-down provision of an information model towards one in which web-based citizen engagement is facilitated. Following this analysis, we take a close look at three websites that fostered public engagement in the 2004 Australian federal election – a political party, a media institution, and a citizen website. We also look beyond the definition of "e-democracy" as the privilege of the site producer alone, investigating the potential for the internet to enhance cyber-citizenship through enhanced user participation in the electoral process.

Defining the role of the citizen in internet engagement

Theorists often disagree on the role web technology plays on public engagement. Clarke (2004) and Balnaves *et al.* (2004) applaud the internet as a tool of cyber-democracy, while others such as Gray (2002) warn against the potential dangers to real citizenship if only those with "knowledge, control or access as a result of their relationships to complex technologies" are privileged to participate in the political process (2002: 24). Web-based citizen engagement in this study may be defined as the provision of website characteristics that encourage citizen participation in the political process. These include online functions that allow users to join or volunteer with the organization, distribute materials related to the election campaign, and register to vote. Engagement may also be promoted by embodying interactivity through the inclusion of web forums, web mail services, and other functions that make citizens feel politically empowered (Stromer-Galley and Foot 2002). Sites that exclude such features may be dismissed as top-down or authoritarian (Kluver 2005).

However, citizen engagement on the internet is not just a matter of whether online features are present. Kluver (2005) argues that political culture plays an important role in setting boundaries for the deployment of the internet, emphasizing that social factors are often more important than technological factors in determining the use of technology. Gray (2002: 24) believes that as citizens living in a technological society, we "continue to technologically transform ourselves" and this social process will play an increasingly important, eventually fundamental role in politics. Gray's fear is that real citizenship may be accorded to only those individuals who gain knowledge, control, or access because of their relationships to complex technologies. Gray argues that a "citizen bill of rights" should be created which would include the right to political equality, and advocates the political power of every citizen determined by "the quality of his or her arguments, example, energy and single vote" and not based on "his or her economic holdings or social standing" (2002: 28). Gray's argument resonates with studies by Balnaves *et al.* (2004), which recognize that the distance between the citizen and democratic structures is growing in the age of interactive communication.

This relationship between the evolution of technology and the development of political citizenship is not a new phenomenon. Television, radio, and now the internet with the capability to facilitate political communication, have inspired greater participation of citizens in the democratic process. Diamond and Freeman (2002) researched the impact of internet technologies on trade unionism, paralleling the impact of the internet with that of television in the 1950s. They highlight the ability of chat rooms, discussion forums, and listservs to create virtual communities outside official settings. Diamond and Freeman (2002) cite one such case at IBM as an example of citizens gaining political empowerment using the internet. In 1999, in response to IBM's decision to change the company's pension system, workers protested in chat rooms and discussion boards online, which eventually pushed IBM to restore some of its pension benefits. This online activism was also responsible for the formation of the Alliance@IBM. The Alliance continued a strong online presence, collecting a large pool of e-mail subscribers, providing discussion groups, mailing lists, and links to related sites and information about workers' issues. A one-day e-mail campaign to contact a manager responsible for rising travel costs for engineers, resulted in an increase in the workers' mileage allowance. Alliance@IBM's use of online action is a positive example of the potential democratizing power of citizen interaction against a corporate power.

The 2004 Australian federal election web sphere

This study examined the web sphere created by various types of site produc-ers, including candidates, parties, press organizations, NGOs, government agencies, and citizens during the 2004 Australian federal election. Through systematic site identification involving the examination of political portals and searches using two search engines, 157 political websites were identified as part of the Australian federal election web sphere. A separate process esti-mated the proportion of various types of actors in the web sphere, which formed the basis for the selection of a stratified sample of 99 websites from those identified. Political parties comprised almost a quarter (24 percent) of this sample, followed by non-government organizations (16 percent), candi-date sites (13 percent), citizen sites (15 percent), press (7 percent), and government organizations (2 percent). The remaining sites constituted edu-cational sites, business sites, religious sites, or portals. We analyzed the sampled sites using a coding framework developed by the Internet and Elec-tions Project to generate comparable data across different data sets. The coding protocol was provided by the project team, based on previous work by two of the study coordinators. The coding frame included measures for the presence or absence of particular types of features. Each of the 99 sites in the Australian study was examined for the presence of 18 features. Eight fea-tures were considered information features, including the presence of elec-tion-related information, biographical information about candidates, issue position statements, information about voting, speech texts, event calendars, comparative information about candidates and parties, endorsements, and information about the campaign. An additional ten items constituted engagement features, including provision of contact information, ability to sign up for e-mail lists, join the campaign, donate money to a political cause, participate in a discussion forum, register to vote, print online mater-ials for distribution offline, send links, and contribute statements of public support.

Findings from previous research on Australian political web spheres, and changes in the political culture, led us to anticipate fewer engagement fea-tures than information features. Since 2000, there had been a significant increase in the number of regulations surrounding the use of the internet for political purposes. This legislation might be expected to have a negative impact on the presence of engagement features. For example, website pro-ducers might be reluctant to offer the "get e-mail" feature that provides vis-itors with an opportunity to sign up and receive e-mail from an organization, a feature that had been previously used to build databases of e-mail addresses. However, the practice of political parties sending unso-licited e-mails ended with the passage of the Australian Federal Spam Act 2003, which did not include an exemption for political parties to distribute unsolicited e-mails (Clarke 2004). As a result, in the 2004 Australian federal election web sphere, only 43 percent of the press sites and 59 percent of the political parties in the sample made use of this feature. Only government sites supported e-mail alerts and press-clipping services, possibly as an extension to their traditional library functions. Similarly, all election materials had to be registered with or endorsed by a member of a political party before being published or broadcast, which effectively limited the number of sites that offered offline distribution materials and e-paraphernalia. Finally, regulations surrounding the disclosure of donations and membership fees resulted in an under-exploitation of related engagement features on most websites. Both the legislation and regulations surrounding the distribution of information and products limited the use of many engagement features. In addition, peripheral reasons, such as the low number of broadband users in Australia – as of May 2004, only 28 percent of internet users subscribed to broadband services (Department of Communications 2005) – were expected to lessen the distribution of engagement features.

As shown in Table 12.1, an examination of the features available in the sampled sites indicates that the distribution was similar among information and engagement features. A few of each type of feature were widely deployed, appearing on 80 percent or more of the sites. The most common information offered on these sites was biographical. The most common engagement feature was the ability to contact the site producer. Several other features of both types were deployed less broadly, appearing on between one-fifth and one-half of the sites. Information features at this level included information about issue positions, voting, speech texts, a calendar of events, and comparative information. Engagement features included e-mail list sign up, joining an organization, donating money, participating in a forum or discussion, and signing up to volunteer. There were somewhat more engagement features found on websites than information features. Only information about the campaign was found on less than one-fifth of the sites examined. Among engagement features, voter registration, offline distribution of online materials, sending links to friends, downloadable e-paraphernalia, and adding public statements of support to a website, were all found on less than one-fifth of the sites. In summary, websites in the Australian federal election web sphere were nearly as likely to facilitate political engagement as to provide information about candidates or the campaign.

To explore further the emerging trend of providing engagement features, we selected three websites produced by different political actors that provided significant opportunities for public engagement for closer analysis. These included a press site, the Australian Broadcasting Commission's (ABC) federal election website; a major left-wing party site, the Australian Green Party; and a weblog administered by a political radical entitled *Darpism.com*. These three sites were significant players in a political culture that was marked by an unusually high number of candidates and heightened security fears after a terrorism attack on Australians in Indonesia. Nationally, a record number of parties and candidates stood for election. The Australian Electoral Commission reported 59 registered parties and 1091

Table 12.1 Presence of information and engagement features on 2004 Australian federal election websites

Information feature	No. of sites (n = 99)	% of sites	Engagement feature	No. of sites (n = 99)	% of sites
Election	89	90	Contact	94	95
Bio	81	82	getmail	43	43
Isspos	52	53	join	38	38
Infov	28	28	donate	28	28
Speech	26	26	forum	27	27
Calen	25	25	volunt	21	21
Compar	22	22	regis	18	18
Infoc	8	8	slinks	15	15
			epara	12	12
			pubsup	9	9

Abbreviations and descriptions of site features:
ELECTION: content relating to the election.
BIO: biography/history of party/candidate.
ISSUE POS: list of issue positions held by party/candidate site.
INFOV: information about the voting/registration process.
SPEECH: speech by candidate or party representative.
CALENDAR: a calendar/list of events with election-related events.
COMPARE: comparison of issue positions of candidates/parties.
INFOC: information about the electoral campaign process.
CONTACT: contact information for the site producer.
GETMAIL: sign up to receive e-mails from the site producer.
JOIN: join or become members of the organization.
DONATE: donations encouraged or enabled through the site.
FORUM: participate in online communication.
VOLUNT: encourage visitors to volunteer for the electoral campaign.
REGIS: register to participate in the election.
SLINKS: enable site visitor to send a link from the site to another party.
EPARA: enable user to engage in digital promotion of electoral activities.
PUBSUP: make a public statement supporting a political actor or issue.

candidates for the House of Representatives and another 330 candidates for the Senate (Virtual Tally Room 2004). On 9 September, a month before the election, a car bomb outside the Australian Embassy in Jakarta, Indonesia, killed 11 people and left 151 injured. It was a timely reminder to the general public of the incumbent Liberal Party's allegiance to the U.S.–Iraq war effort. In response to the bombing, the major political parties temporarily suspended campaign activities for several days.

Engagement features on the ABC, Green Party, and *Darpism.com* sites, encouraged a comparison of election parties and issues, as well as public discussion of national security issues and Australia's role in the Iraq war. The ABC 2004 federal election website effectively operated as a weblog and was the most active and linked-to site in terms of public engagement. The Australian Green Party's site allowed users to interact and participate in electoral activities. *Darpism.com*, a radical citizen site, typified citizen sites that promote political activism but potentially contravene the law by providing behind-the-scenes information about the election. By exploiting the use of engagement features in the Australian electoral web sphere, these sites created a level of social and political discourse that was similar to the traditional media, and demonstrated the potential to foster civic engagement in the electoral process via the internet.

Web-based citizen engagement and the traditional media

Traditional media outlets have always played a significant role in Australian election campaigns, educating and informing the public of election procedure. In Australia ABC's radio and television services have provided premier public service coverage of state and federal elections, with commercial networks providing coverage of varying degrees. Historically, the news media have had considerable influence over governance (Abramson *et al.* 1998). While there has been much speculation about the role that interactive media may play in civic participation (Balnaves *et al.* 2004), television, print, and radio remain the main mediums for citizen engagement in politics.

As Clarke (2004) argues, the rise of the internet has shown little sign of displacing talk-back radio in Australia as the barometer of public opinion. However, the desire for more interaction with a traditional news outlet, which had an established reputation for populist election coverage, was evident in the success of the 2004 ABC election site. Due to the constraints of airtime and layout, television, radio, and print can only deal with limited citizen feedback. This sophisticated and usable site captured audiences who wanted to participate in further discussion or register their opinions in a way radio and television limited. The ABC site offered a comprehensive forum for discussions, moderated by a well-known political commentator, and used straw polls to measure political support. This site demonstrated that unlike the system of heavily centralized broadcast television, the web can decentralize political discourse and has the potential to give citizens greater choice and access to information (see also Gilder 1992: 25–27).

The ABC 2004 federal election website was a useful example of how a proven traditional media forum may converge with new technologies. On first impression, the site seemed simple to use with a limited number of options. While it had images, links to speeches, registration to vote, and ancillary information, the public engagement characteristics were restricted to a forum for discussion. However, the site successfully encouraged public engagement. The forum moderator was political analyst Antony Green, who was already familiar to site visitors from his reputation in newspapers, and on radio and television. Green has been the ABC's election analyst for 15 years, having covered every federal, state, and territory election since 1989. Prior to appearing on television in 1993, he was a radio commentator. A computer scientist, Green designed the ABC's election-night computer system, which predicted results with speed and accuracy. This created a sense of confidence with the public, as it seemed that there was literally no question about the elections that Green could not answer. The website provided a document known as the "Green Guide" which covered topics as diverse as "how preferences work" and "how to make your vote count." In addition, the site made it easy for voters and the media to find information and keep track of debates. As new, controversial, or contentious issues about the elections were introduced in the media, Green would add editorial and information about the issues online. Print, television, or radio audiences could then log onto the media website to find out more.

In line with the broadcaster's mission, the site had to adhere to the goals of educating, informing, and entertaining the public, while fostering national identity and cultural diversity among Australians living within and outside of Australia. However, the ABC 2004 election website was limited by its political affiliations. The site producer, the Australian Broadcasting Commission, is wholly owned and operated by the federal government. While it contained no endorsements, nor did it include issue positions, it was still perceived as an organ of the two-party federal government system. Officially, the Australian Broadcasting Commission was not necessarily aligned to the government in power, but informally it has been connected to the Australian Labor Party, under which it has received more funding than the current Liberal government. The broadcaster had been accused of political bias in the 2004 election, when the *National Observer* suggested that employees of the ABC were either supporters of the Labor Party or the Greens. It illustrated a widespread contention that the ABC's bias was left-of-center.

Web-based citizen engagement and minority politics

Just as press sites such as the ABC 2004 federal election website extended citizen engagement in the political process beyond the scope of the traditional media, minority political groups utilized the web as means of circumventing traditional press restrictions. Left-wing minority political parties such as the Australian Greens and the Australian Democrats struggled for press coverage in a system that is carefully delineated along major party lines. Most Australian news organizations allocate parliamentary journalists to specific portfolios and ministries in the government and shadow cabinet, soliciting minority parties on an as-needed basis – usually for marginal issues such as the "environment" and "native title" rights (ownership of land by local indigenous Australians). However, as argued by Diamond and Freeman (2002: 577) the use of the internet by political groups "creates an opportunity to directly influence journalists, 92 percent of whom go online to research articles. The flexibility of the website to host press releases and archives makes it easier than ever for journalists to access information." Using internet technology, intermediary organizations and minority groups generate greater exposure and dissemination of their concerns in the media.

In 2000, the Australian Greens commenced its successful internet campaign, through its www.greens.org.au website. A study by Gibson and Ward (2003) about political websites during the 2000 Australian federal and state elections positioned the Australian Greens' website as the best all-round performer, especially in the area of interactivity. The study concluded that the Australian Greens' website was successful in "reaching out to supporters and inviting them in" (Gibson and Ward 2003: 152) through search engines, forums, and links to party branches, international sister organizations, like-minded pressure groups, and campaigns.

The Australian Greens continued their significant web presence in the 2004 Australian federal election web sphere. Visitors to the site were able to contact the organization, sign up for membership, get e-mails, and donate to the party. The Green Party also hosted its own web forum, provided links, and administered its own volunteer effort. The site was well organized and site administration was effectively in the hands of the organization, which enhanced its integrity and security. It effectively provided a holistic and safe environment for users.

The 2004 Australian Greens' site was one of the few to present a regularly updated straw poll on its homepage. Clarke (2004) believes these sorts of formalized approaches, are a major advantage of web-based politics. For example, hosting a straw poll on a party's homepage helps users have their say, and gives the party a way to gather information about what a selected subset of the public might think. Prior to the internet, polling of the constituency had been the domain of corporate marketing companies such as ACNielsen. Website polling is a more affordable option, allowing parties to tap into the needs of the voting public and an important tool for minority parties to capture swinging voters who are undecided on who to vote for. The website as a platform for independent polling is one positive outcome of the engagement features on the election web sphere.

Minority political parties in Australia have benefited from the low-cost benefits of the internet. For example, the technology offers the ability to present the organization's position on various issues, the advantage of targeting members or potential members with targeted messages, and engage in discourse through forums or similar interactive features (Diamond and Freeman 2002: 577). Domain names, such as "green.org.au," "democrats.org.au," and "bobbrown.org.au" have assisted in the promotion of both parties and personalities as brand names. With the internet, smaller organizations can bypass the costs of expensive advertising using traditional media outlets.

The internet has provided minority parties with a new platform to communicate to citizens on a wide range of issues. The website as a document that can be viewed, analyzed, and questioned provides greater credibility and authority to minority groups who were previously neglected in major press coverage. On a tactical level, minority political parties have used search engines and archives on the web to unearth past actions and statements by opposition politicians to illustrate their inconsistency. The web holds the potential for non-dominant groups to express alternative views to the dominant ideology.

Web-based citizen engagement and citizen-activists

Balnaves *et al.* (2004) argue that weblogs reflect a relatively minor, but still significant outlet for individual expression, where citizens can express and share their opinions of politics. In the 2004 Australian election web sphere, many citizen sites provided an inside look at the political process, often providing stories about the day-to-day running of the campaign, and links to other relevant groups or organizations. These sites, such as *Drew Hutton*, and *Bastards Inc.*, were often a satirical look at the daily events and behind-the-scene stories of candidates and campaigners. One of these sites, *Darpism.com* (www.darpism.com), attracted both notoriety and criticism.

Darpism.com is the weblog (blog) of Darp, a campaign volunteer for Andrew Wilkie, who was a candidate for the left-wing Australian Greens. Darp is a minor celebrity in left-wing politics. It is the pseudonym of 30-year-old Matthew Henderson, a former law student and so-called "anti-racist" and "anti-fascist" social activist since the mid-1990s. Before publication of his blog in 2003, Henderson had been reliant on news coverage about his public antics or citations in letters and editorials in Australian newspapers. In 2004, on the reputation of his weblog, he was asked to contribute a series of articles in the *Sydney Morning Herald*.

The website is simple: it offers basic information and images; the opportunity for readers to respond to blog postings through a third party pop-up host; and active links to other sites, including the Australian Green Party and the controversial *John Howard Lies* blog. The site also functions to coordinate social action through a calendar of events and the sale of unofficial t-shirts and paraphernalia. The website was the recipient of the 2004 Australia–New Zealand Weblog of the Year and the winner of 2005 Best Blog from the state of New South Wales in the Australian Blogging Awards.

During the 2004 election, *Darpism.com* provided an individual's point of view of the day-to-day campaign for a minority group candidate. Unlike political party, candidate, or press sites, *Darpism.com* did not publish official issue positions, only anecdotal evidence such as the underhand tactics employed by the supporters of the incumbent Liberal Party. Two weeks before the election, *Darpism.com*'s homepage featured a full-size photo of Matthew Henderson, in a boxing gym, with his hands strapped up and his middle finger raised in defiance. The caption underneath the photo read: "This is what a pissed off Darp looks like." The blog entry continued with an expression of the author's personal thoughts and opinions on the election trial:

I am ready to fucking kill. I have spent the better part of this week erecting Andrew Wilkie posters in people's front yard's only to have EVERY FUCKING SINGLE ONE OF THEM ripped down sometime this evening. Geeeez... hmmmm... you think it could be the Libs?

(Darpism.com, 18 September 2004)

The site engaged in the Australian cultural practice of "polly-bashing" (the criticism of political actors). Parody was an important element of the site, allowing it to deal with potentially contentious issues through humor. Here, the weblog demonstrates the power of the internet to express ideas not communicated through the traditional media for fear of indecency or defamation litigation.

A similar citizen site in the 2004 Australian federal election web sphere was *JohnHowardLies.com*, published by a former Australian Labor Party staffer. This anti-government site utilized a comprehensive spectrum of engagement features such as forums, downloads, volunteer registration, and online donations to appeal to visitors. *JohnHowardLies.com* was a serious website, presenting a less personality-based approach to politics than *Darpism.com* did. However, both site producers came under attack by political actors for openly criticizing opposition parties.

While *Darpism.com* and *JohnHowardLies.com* demonstrate that the distance between citizen and institutions is narrowing because of internet activity, the sites also highlight institutional challenges to e-activism. Balnaves *et al.* (2004: 16) argue that e-activism on the net is important as the participants "use the technology for non-institutionalized forms of power, or at the very least they operate at the margins of institutionalized power, challenging it in both positive and negative ways."

Darpism.com challenged mainstream ideology by harnessing the power of the web, but in so doing, it provided both information and misinformation. For example, the site strongly criticized the Australia First Party, which endorsed a predominantly white Australia. Consequentially, the Australia First Party accused Darp (Matthew Henderson) of libel and defamation (Australia First, n.d.). Increasing legislation targeted to limit libel and defamation online is one of the potential pitfalls for informal websites such as *Darpism.com*.

In the 2004 election, citizen websites still managed to operate within the cracks of federal legislation. By the 2001 federal election, the Broadcasting Services Amendment (1999) aligned the use of internet for political purposes with other electronic broadcasting media. This development grew out of the 1996 Australian federal election, the first election in which political producers used the internet, raising issues related to copyright, defamation, and privacy. However, this legislation did not have a significant impact on citizen websites. The federal government is currently reviewing criticism that arose out of internet use during the 2004 election campaign, such as the authorization of electoral advertising, misleading and deceptive publications, and the publication by an organization that a candidate supports its views without the authorization of that candidate. It is expected that new government legislation restricting online media would move political activity on the internet in line with traditional broadcast media. In the United States, for example, bloggers and news organizations risk punishment for unauthorized links to a campaign's website or even the forwarding of a political candidate's press release to a mailing list (Ferguson 2005).

Conclusion

Despite the achievements of the 2004 ABC's election website, the Australian Greens' website and *Darpism.com*'s website in providing citizen engagement, most sites in the 2004 Australian federal election web sphere were more likely to feature public information characteristics rather than public engagement features. The internet did not threaten to displace traditional media as a means for citizen participation in the political process. However, the sites analyzed in this chapter do indicate the potential of the internet to become a dominant agent in election campaigns. First, the use of forums and weblogs on the 2004 ABC's election website, the Australian Greens' website and *Darpism.com*'s website, acknowledge the benefits of internet technology to the expression of the citizen voice in the political process. Unlike, television, print, and radio, forums and weblogs can accommodate citizens' comments and feedback on the political process. Second, the internet provides an important promotional tool for minority political groups, affording web visitors accessibility to the parties' mandates. For example, the 2004 Green Party site welcomed citizen engagement by providing visitors opportunities to participate in a straw poll, comment in a forum, or sign up to volunteer or become a party member. Citizen sites, such as *Darpism.com* and *JohnHowardLies.com* were more controversial in nature, but introduced the feasibility of promoting alternative points of view alongside mainstream parties. The analysis of sites of public engagement in the 2004 Australian federal election suggests that e-democracy holds the potential for both citizen interaction and empowerment.

Relevant to the above, Gray (2002: 24) suggests that the development of websites with engagement features promotes a "technologically transformed" citizenship, and this social process will play an increasingly important, eventually fundamental role in politics. Indeed, the attention directed to sites such as the Australian Green Party, *Darpism.com*, and the ABC 2004 federal election site show that Australians may gain greater access to political power through the internet than through the traditional media. However, the results of this web sphere analysis must acknowledge the social and political culture within which these websites operate. Importantly, Australian citizens do not have access to broadband services to access fully public engagement features on the internet. In addition, the large numbers of political parties and candidates in the 2004 Australian federal election web sphere made it difficult for political actors to have equal access to the internet. Most importantly, fears over national and personal security heightened the legal restrictions on public engagement in the political process. The increasing amount of federal government legislation to restrict online political freedom is a potential threat to public engagement in the political process. Indeed, should the internet succumb to the legal limitations of broadcast media, we may see a return to the predominance of top-down provision of information in internet election websites.

References

ABC 2004 Federal Election Website (n.d.) Available online: abc.net.au/elections/federal/2004/weblog/default.htm (accessed 1 September 2004).

Abramson, J.B., Arterton, F.C., and Orren, G.R. (1988) *The Electronic Commonwealth: The Impact of New Media Technologies on Democratic Politics*. New York: Basic Books.

Australia First (n.d.) "The advent of Sydney 'anti-racism' and 'anti-fascism': the case of Matthew Henderson a.k.a. 'Darp'." Available online: ausfirst.alphalink.com.au/thestruggle/darpism.html (accessed 4 September 2006).

Balnaves, M., Walsh, L., and Shoesmith, B. (2004) "Participatory technologies: the use of the internet in civic participation and democratic processes," paper presented at the Australian Electronic Governance Conference, Melbourne, Australia, April. Available online: www.public-policy.unimelb.edu.au/egovernance/papers/03_Balnaves.pdf (accessed 1 April 2006).

Broadcasting Services Amendment (Online Services) Act (1999). Available online: scaleplus.law.gov.au/html/comact/10/6005/top.htm (accessed 9 October 2004).

Clarke, R. (2004) "The internet and democracy, future challenges for E-government – community collaboration." Available online: www.agimo.gov.au/publications/2004/05/egovt_challenges/community/democracy (accessed 4 September 2006).

Department of Communications (2005) "The current state of play." Commonwealth of Australia, Department of Communications, Information Technology and the Arts. Available online: www.unpan1.un.org/groups/public/documents/APCITY/UNPANO23005.pdf.

Diamond, W.J. and Freeman, R.B. (2002) "Will unionism prosper in cyberspace: the promise of the internet for employee organization," *British Journal of Industrial Relations*, 40, 3: 569–596.

Ferguson, I. (2005) "Australian government flags internet election campaign laws." Available online: www.zdnet.com.au/news/0,39023165,39184224,00.htm (accessed 1 December 2005).

Gibson, R.K. and Ward, S. (2003) "Letting the daylight in? Australian parties' use of the World Wide Web at state and territory level," in R. Gibson, P. Nixon, and S. Ward (eds), *Political Parties and the Internet: Net gain*, pp. 139–234. London: Routledge.

Gilder, G. (1992) "Telecomputing: the antidote to phantom public opinion," *New Perspectives Quarterly*, 9, 4: 25–27.

Gray, C.H. (2002) *Cyborg Citizen: Politics in the Posthuman Age*, New York: Routledge.

Kluver, R. (2005) "Political culture in online politics," in M. Consalvo and M. Allen (eds), *Internet Research Annual*, pp. 75–84. Newbury Park, CA: Sage Publications.

Putnam, R. (2000) *Bowling Alone*. New York: Simon & Schuster.

Stromer-Galley, J. and Foot, K. (2002) "Citizen perceptions of online interactivity and implications for political campaign communication" [Electronic version], *Journal of Computer-Mediated Communication*, 8, 1. Available online: jcmc.indiana.edu/vol8/issue1/stromerandfoot.html (accessed 4 June 2005).

Virtual Tally Rroom: The 2004 election results (2004). Available online: results.aec.gov.au/12246/default.htm (accessed 4 June 2005).

13 Hungary

Political strategies and citizen tactics in the 2004 European Parliament elections

Endre Dányi and Anna Galácz

Introduction

The socio-political transformation induced by the political changes of 1989–1990 in Central and Eastern Europe coincided with a communication revolution characterized by the appearance and increasing use of new information and communications technologies (ICTs), such as personal computers, interactive television, mobile phones, and the internet (Haddon 2004; Dutton 1996). Most political sociologists would agree that political change and changing communication practices cannot be analyzed independently of each other (Benhabib 1996). Hence, if one wants to understand how democracy works in practice in Central and Eastern Europe, the political uses of new communication technologies are certainly among the most salient objects of scientific inquiry. Election campaigns are particularly good opportunities for examining the political roles of new media – partly because on these occasions both politicians and campaign advisers get to experiment with a set of campaign techniques. However, it is also important to note that this relationship is reciprocal: the reception of subsequent campaign techniques shapes the way political players will think about campaigning itself in the future.

From a political perspective, the most often analyzed forms of new media are websites. However, attention has for the most part focused on the design and content of these websites. That is to say, online representations of political figures and organizations have been mostly examined as manifestations of strategic thinking, while users who actively shape these "technical objects" usually remain neglected (Bakardjieva 2005). The research described in this chapter intends to break with this tradition and show that certain interpretations of political situations can endow websites with various modes of use. We argue that analyses focusing on the political significance of communication technologies can be complete only if they pay equal attention to the design and related *everyday practices*.

There are many possible ways to conceptualize "everyday practices" related to the political uses of communication technologies. Michel de Certeau (1984) provides a particularly useful approach. He calls a *strategy* the action plan of those actors (both individuals and institutions) who are in a relatively strong power position. They are able to determine their own situation and thus can develop ideas about how to deal with external factors (competitors, environmental characteristics) that cannot always be kept under control. Conversely, a *tactic* is the calculated action of those actors who are not in the position of identifying their own territories; therefore, internal and external factors remain inseparable for them. The relationship between strategies and tactics is a crucial element of de Certeau's theory. As Andrew Feenberg formulated it,

> The tension between strategies and tactics is due to the multiplicity of codes that coexist in any society. Hegemonic codes lay down the framework within which the marginal ones play a tactical role. What de Certeau calls "exorbitant" practices are the equivalent of a dominant language. Everyone must speak it, but marginal practices, like local slang, can give it a special twist. Tactics thus belong to strategies the way speech belongs to the language.
>
> (Feenberg 1999: 113)

The distinction between strategies and tactics seems to be a useful concept to analyze the political uses of communication technologies (Garcia and Lovink 1997). Most theories on digital democracy suggest that conventional political players, such as parties, governments, supranational institutions, media companies, and civil organizations adjust to the logic of new media and develop strategies in order to preserve their positions in the field (Graber *et al.* 2003; Norris 2001). These strategies can be easily analyzed on institutional (and sometimes personal) websites. However, to comprehend the actual political significance of ICTs, tactical uses also have to be examined. This chapter tests this conceptual framework by examining the roles and characteristics of the most relevant political websites in the 2004 European Parliament (EP) elections campaign in Hungary.

Political uses of ICTs in Hungarian election campaigns

Before examining the characteristics of political websites in the 2004 EP elections, it is worth mentioning an earlier example where new media technologies had significant political roles in Hungary. ICTs were first used for political purposes on a mass scale during the 2002 Hungarian general election campaign (Dányi and Sükösd 2003). Although internet penetration was below the European average at the time (approximately 20 percent – see Dessewffy 2004), politicians were optimistic regarding the persuasive potential of new media technologies. Official party websites were heralded as forerunners of an era when boundaries between formal political organizations and groups of citizens would fade away and new patterns of interaction could foster political participation. Contrary to such expectations, however, party and candidate websites eventually played a rather marginal role in the 2002 parliamentary election campaign. The online appearance of political parties was the equivalent of simple electronic versions of official leaflets and posters (Dányi 2002). In contrast to earlier expectations, smaller parties did not express themselves online as efficiently as their bigger competitors, while the interactive elements on political websites were outnumbered by top-down, static information elements.

However, it would be a mistake to conclude that in Hungary ICTs had no political importance in the 2002 elections. Between the two rounds (7 and 21 April, respectively), thousands of campaign text messages and e-mails flooded the public sphere, giving new political meaning to mobile phones and the internet (Sükösd and Dányi 2003). Both government and opposition parties used mobile communication technologies to organize mass demonstrations, and circulate campaign messages and political jokes among their supporters. As hundreds of text messages (short message service, SMS) and more than 2000 e-mail messages collected by the Open Society Archives during the campaign demonstrate (Open Society Archives 2002), it was these electronic messages – rather than political websites – that made some observers realize the changing characteristics of election campaigns.

The 2004 European parliamentary elections provide a good observation point to assess the evolution of electronic campaigns. The elections took place in Hungary on 13 June 2004, approximately halfway between two national parliamentary elections. Both significant political actors and the electorate considered the EP voting to be a "dress rehearsal" for the 2006 parliamentary elections. Although two years may be little time in political perspective, the electronic communication environment can change significantly in such a short period. The number of internet users has been growing by 4–5 percent a year during the past couple of years; in 2004 almost one-third of the Hungarian population connected to the internet on a regular basis (Dessewffy 2004). Therefore, one important question during the 2004 EP election campaign was whether the main political players were able to keep pace with and employ technological changes to their advantage.

The rest of this chapter examines the ways various political actors used the web during the EP election campaign in Hungary. This research was conducted as part of the Internet and Election Project, which aimed to comparatively examine the political role of the internet in election campaigns in different countries. The results represent an attempt to go beyond the static content analysis of political websites and demonstrate the complexity of the political potential of new communication technologies.

Strategic use of the internet: the Hungarian web sphere

Researchers involved in the Internet and Election Project were primarily interested in examining the online structure of political action (Schneider and Foot 2002). Strategic uses of the internet in each country were scruti-nized based on the concept of the "web sphere," for which the unit of analy-sis is not merely a collection of websites, but a "hyperlinked set of dynamically defined set of digital resources that span multiple websites and are deemed relevant, or related, to a central theme or 'object'" (Schneider and Foot 2004: 118).

In our case, this central theme was the 2004 EP elections in Hungary. The first step was therefore to identify those websites dedicated to the EP elections as well as those that had the potential for covering this event anytime during the campaign. Websites were identified through the use of two search engines, *Google* and *Index Kereső*, a popular Hungarian search engine, using the search string "Európai" + "Parlamenti" + "választás" + "2004" ("European" + "parliamentary" + "election" + "2004"). In addition, we included those websites that appeared as active links on popular, politic-ally oriented portals. The authors' personal knowledge also played an important role, as we also included a number of relevant websites that were neither returned by these search engines nor featured in political website directories.

Website identification terminated on 16 May 2004, about a month before the EP elections. The next step was to categorize all election-related web-sites according to previously defined producer types: "party," "press," "can-didate," "citizen," "portal," "business," "educational," "NGO," "religious," "labor union," and "political professional." The sleuthing process was far more complicated than was initially expected, as we could hardly find any business, citizen, or educational websites (listed as "other" in figures and tables). The next step was to extract a sample of 100 websites, weighted by producer type. Finally, during the week prior to the election, we conducted content and function analyses of the websites in the sample according to a standard coding frame.

Broadly, website functional features were labeled as either "information" or "engagement." The former category refers to functions that support one-way communication, specifically the presence or absence of "election-related content" in general, of "about us/bio" information, "endorsements," the presence of "issue positions," "speeches," "calendars," instances of "issue comparisons," "information about the campaign process," "information about the voting process," "images," "audio/video files," "privacy policy statement," and "terms of use statement." The second category denotes func-tions that enable user interactivity: e-mail and offline "contact information," "join us" function, the capacity to "register to vote," "e-news" function, "donate money" function, the possibility to contribute to a "forum/communication place," the "offline distribution of election related material" function, "send links" function, "public support statement," "e-paraphernalia," and "volunteer" function. While we were unable to include other func-tions in the coding frame, such as online polls or blogs, the coding system enabled us to add personal notes about the sites' functionality.

The structure of election-related content

Overall, only 60 percent of our sample contained election-related content at the time of coding, which implies that more than one-third of the sites identified as potential elements of the 2004 Hungarian EP elections' web sphere did not deal with the election. In other words, 40 percent of the sites we expected to publish election-related material during the campaign remained passive. The final sample of 92 sites (eight were not accessible during the coding period) contained nine candidate websites, which makes this category seem to be of greater importance than, for example, press sites. According to the Hungarian Elections Office, however, 323 institutionally-listed candidates had been involved in the 2004 Hungarian EP elections, so having only nine websites in this category is quite surprising. One possible explanation for the small number of active candidate websites in the 2004 EP elections campaign is that candidates were institutionally attached to political parties. Candidate lists and information on politicians (biographies, contact information) were typically published on party websites. This clearly shows that in the mind of politicians, the EP campaigning period was less intense than the 2002 general elections campaign. The utter lack of citizen websites is also particularly interesting. Apparently, the use of the internet for political purposes by citizens is not yet a general practice in Hungary. Although "blog culture" is now on the rise, existing weblogs mainly dealt with "mundane" topics, while thematic blogs aiming to interpret and discuss political or public issues were missing.

Statistics about election-related content show a more precise picture. Information relevant to the election was mostly provided by parties and the press (see Figure 13.1), as almost all of the websites within these categories published content related to the EP elections (12 sites from 14 in the case of party sites and six from the seven press sites). The largest official party websites experienced surprising developments in the past few years – both in functional and aesthetic terms. In 2002, parties regarded their websites as electronic brochures, offering few or no interactive functions. In 2004, they seemed to be more professional, including downloadable campaign spots, detailed and frequently updated information on a number of issues, and online political games.

Besides party websites, the press played a major role in the electoral web sphere. Although the websites of newspapers and television channels were active, according to *Median WebAudit* (www.webaudit.hu) the two most popular Hungarian news websites were *{origo}* (www.origo.hu) and *Index* (www.index.hu). Both online-only portals provided original news, reports, and online interviews with politicians where registered users could ask questions in real time, discussion forums, and had a special section dedicated to the EP elections. The significance and characteristics of *{origo}* and *Index* will be discussed in more detail in the next section of this chapter.

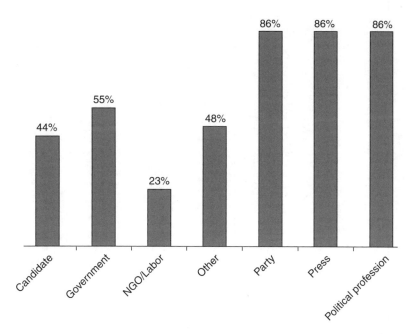

Figure 13.1 Percentage of websites in Hungary with election-related content by producer types.

Functional analysis of websites

In general, Hungarian political websites were quite poor in terms of information and engagement functions during the 2004 EP elections. Table 13.1 and Table 13.2 show the frequency of "information" and "engagement" items by site producers. The most frequent information items were images and biographies/"about us" sections, which were present on most websites. Typically, parties publicized their positions on various issues online (this item was present in nearly all of the analyzed party websites). At the same time, however, issue comparison was almost completely lacking on these sites (see Table 13.1); this function appeared only once on a press site.

The lack of any information about the voting process and about the campaign process in the Hungarian web sphere was also surprising. Internet users could rely only on a limited number of government, party, and online media sources. While government and party websites were relatively active on this front, the passive attitude of NGOs towards informing voters is striking.

Concerning "engagement" items, it is evident that the websites analyzed almost completely lacked interactive features. In general, Hungarian websites mostly follow a top-down model of information flow, as information

Table 13.1 Frequency of information items by producer types

Producer	Number of websites	Econ*	Bio	End	Ispos	Speech	Calen	Comp	Infoc	Infov	Image	Aud/vid	Privp	Term
Candidate	9	0.44 (4)	0.89 (8)	0	0.44 (4)	0.56 (5)	0.33 (3)	0	0	0	1 (9)	0.11 (1)	0	0
Government	29	0.55 (16)	0.86 (25)	0	0	0.03 (1)	0.10 (3)	0	0.7 (8)	0.28 (8)	1 (29)	0.10 (3)	0.14 (4)	0.24 (7)
NGO/labor	13	0.23 (3)	0.92 (11)	0	0.23 (3)	0	0.08 (1)	0	0	0.08 (1)	0.85 (11)	0	0.08 (1)	0.8 (1)
Other	14	0.48 (7)	0.59 (9)	0.12 (3)	0.24 (3)	0	0	0	0	0.06 (1)	0.76 (11)	0.06 (1)	0	0
Party	14	0.86 (12)	0.93 (13)	0.36 (5)	0.93 (13)	0.43 (6)	0.36 (5)	0	0.07 (2)	0.14 (2)	1 (14)	0.43 (6)	0.07 (1)	0.7 (1)
Press	7	0.86 (6)	0.43 (3)	0	0	0	0.29 (2)	0.14 (1)	0.14 (2)	0.29 (2)	0.86 (6)	0.14 (1)	0.29 (2)	0.14 (1)
Political professional	6	0.86 (5)	0.83 (5)	0	0.17 (1)	0	0	0	0	0.17 (1)	1 (6)	0	0.17 (1)	0.33 (2)

Notes
* Number of sites per political actor noted in parentheses.

Abbreviations:
Econ   Electoral contents.
Bio   About us/biographical information.
End   Endorsements.
Ispos   Issue positions.
Speech   Speeches.
Calen   Calendars of events.
Comp   Comparison of issues.
Infoc   Information about the campaign process.
Infov   Information about the voting process.
Image   Images.
Aud/vid Audio/video files.
Privp   Privacy policy statement.
Term   Terms of use statement.

Table 13.2 Frequency of engagement items by producer types

Producer	Number of web sites	Contact*	Join	Regist	Getmail	Donate	Forum	Offd	Send	Psst	Epara	Volu
Candidate	9	0.67 (6)	0	0	0	0	0.44 (4)	0	0	0.11 (1)	0	0
Government	29	0.97 (28)	0	0	0.14 (4)	0	0.48 (14)	0	0.14 (4)	0	0	0
NGO/labor	13	1 (13)	0.08 (1)	0	0.31 (4)	0.08 (1)	0.23 (3)	0	0	0	0	0
Other	14	0.94 (13)	0.18 (2)	0	0.18 (2)	0	0.24 (3)	0	0.06 (1)	0.06 (1)	0	0
Party	14	1 (14)	0.36 (5)	0	0.36 (5)	0.07 (1)	0.43 (6)	0.07 (1)	0.29 (4)	0	0.29 (4)	0
Press	7	1 (7)	0	0	0	0	0.57 (4)	0	0.14 (1)	0	0	0
Political professional	6	0.83 ()	0	0	0.17 (1)	0	0	0	0	0	0	0

* Number of sites per political actor noted in parentheses

Abbreviations:
Contact   Email and offline contact information.
Join   Joining function.
Regist   Capacity to register to vote.
Getmail   E-news function.
Donate   Donate money function.
Forum   Possibility to contribute to a forum/communication place.
Offd   Offline distribution of election-related material function.
Send   Send links function.
Psst   Public support statement.
Epara   E-paraphernalia.
Volu   Volunteer.

provision functions were far more common than engagement functions. As Table 13.2 shows, contact information was the only engagement item provided on almost all websites. The lack of "registration" features is likely due to the structure of the Hungarian voting system. Local authorities draw up a voter list based on residence registration, so normally registration of citizens is not required, as only those who wish to vote from abroad need to contact their local authority. As for the "donate" feature, Hungarian parties polling more than 1 percent at national elections secure public funding for the coming four years. Parties mainly rely on public funding, even though private donations are legal (anonymous up to HUF 500,000 – approximately U.S.$2500). However, it is not a common practice to donate money over the internet, which explains the few instances of this feature.

The most frequent engagement function present in the Hungarian EP web sphere, besides contact information, was online discussion forums; these were especially prevalent on press websites. Another feature (especially common on party websites) was the ability for visitors to sign up for newsletters and other e-mails. Somewhat surprisingly, neither the recruitment of volunteers nor the offline distribution of campaign material was facilitated online, although they are of great importance in Hungarian campaigns. On the other hand, however, some engagement features did not apply to all site producer types. For example, volunteer recruiting, joining online, and financial donations are irrelevant for governmental institutions and for the press. That is why, for instance, donation features were only present on party and NGO websites (although not widespread even in those cases, as only one site in each of these categories offered this possibility).

Further examination reveals that the overall online involvement of the NGOs was limited in the 2004 web sphere, as their sites were short of most interactive features. They did not exploit the opportunity to attract volunteers, make joining easier, or encourage opinion sharing. Surprisingly, government websites were also dormant. Online activity was limited to the websites of the few institutions that were officially bound to supply information about voting and campaign regulations (for example, the National Election Office). Even so, information and engagement features rarely appeared on local authorities' websites, even although electoral management of registration, polling cards, and the like, is mostly administered at local level.

User tactics within the electoral web sphere

In order to gauge the extent and nature of user behaviors in the Hungarian electoral web sphere, we decided to take our sample of websites as a starting point and analyze its most significant elements in detail. Feature analysis reveals the main characteristics of the sites in the sample, but it does not account for the popularity nor use of a site. This generates a broad but undefined picture, as a marginal blog and a major party website are weighted equally during the sampling, coding, and analysis. However, if we take the reach and potential influence of websites into consideration, the network gets a more realistic shape. According to usage statistics at *WebAudit.hu*, the most trusted web-monitoring institution in Hungary, the EP elections web sphere had two particularly significant centers: {*origo*} and *Index.hu*, both of which were coded as "press" in the strategic analysis discussed above. By examining these two nodes closely, we can get a clearer, fine-grained picture of the electoral web sphere.

For this study, two semi-structured interviews were conducted – one with the editor of the EU subsection at {*origo*}, and one with a person from the top management responsible for online content at *Index.hu*. We also interviewed two leading journalists working for these two press sites during March and April 2005, nearly one year after the EP elections. All interviews were conducted in Hungarian, and quotations in this section are our own translation. The main questions concerned EU enlargement, the EP elections campaign in Hungary, and other topics related to online tactics and user habits across these events. Our aim was to highlight, in Feenberg's (1999) terms, the relationship between "exorbitant practices" in the Hungarian web sphere and "local slangs" – the actual, everyday uses of the leading websites during the campaign. While the views of our informants cannot be regarded as unquestionable truths, they shed valuable light on how the intentions of strategic players in an online environment are being constantly interpreted, misinterpreted, and subverted by citizens.

Index.hu *and* [origo]

Index.hu and {*origo*} are the best-known and most popular news sites in Hungary (Kiss 2004a). Both are online-only newspapers that have played a crucial role in the formation of Hungarian online culture. Unlike traditional news portals, they have their own journalists and editorial boards who produce articles and usually do not publish reports or news from other agencies. Both {*origo*} and *Index.hu* were launched in the second half of the 1990s, the early years of the Hungarian internet. Interestingly, the two providers have radically different mission statements: as noted below, {*origo*} attempts to provide neutral, "objective" information, and *Index.hu* became and is popular for its blunt style and for the opinionated contents and controversial style of its journalists.

> We have never voiced any opinion whatsoever. [. . .] Therefore, if you take a close look, {*origo*} is neutral in style. It is not a coincidence that Index has a very distinct style, which is – in my own view – fine, but we are particularly neutral. *Index* addresses a sub-group within the online population, while {*origo*} targets a much broader public.
>
> ({*origo*})

> While {*origo*} wants to maintain neutrality, *Index* is simply independent. [. . .] *Index* has had its own unique voice and its own opinion from the

very beginning. We have never tried to be merely a mechanical information provider. Journalists at *Index* express their opinions, and they consider it important to do so.

(*Index.hu*)

Both sites have increased their traffic by more than 300 percent since 2001. Today, *{origo}* has more than 600,000 individual visitors a day, while *Index* has slightly more than 300,000. In the week of the 2004 EP elections, the aggregated number of visits increased to 818,000 and 450,000, respectively. These are very high figures, as the proportion of regular internet users during the first half of 2004 was about 30 percent among Hungarian citizens aged 14 or older (Dessewffy 2004). Statistics from *WebAudit.hu* show that these sites are clearly the two largest information poles of the Hungarian web in general, and of the EP elections web sphere in particular.

Interviewees from both websites emphasized that *{origo}* and *Index* play three important roles during elections. First, they produce news and background information about political issues and processes. Second, they host frequently visited and long-lasting online forum communities, comprised of hundreds of ongoing threads and tens of millions of comments, which have accumulated over the years. During elections, registered users – among them politicians and well-known journalists – participate in heated debates. Third, both have an advertising function; in the EP elections, campaign political ads from governing and opposition parties appeared on the front pages of *{origo}* and *Index*.

By concentrating on these three functions – news, forums, and political advertisements – we will be able to examine the strategies of users from various perspectives. What citizens do on the two major websites in Hungary not only influence the editors (who seek to maximize the number of visits), but also has an effect on political actors. Politicians appear as advertisers, interviewees, or simply subjects of news; *Index* and *{origo}* represent the only significant place of the Hungarian web sphere where strategic political uses of the web meet citizens, and where citizens respond to the strategies.

EU sections: news and public service

During the identification phase in the web sphere analysis, we noticed that both *{origo}* and *Index* had special, EU-related sections. On these sub-sites, there was detailed and updated information concerning not only the European Parliamentary elections, but also the process of EU enlargement and the organizational structure of various EU institutions. The sections also provided information on voting and campaign-related issues. According to our interviewees, both sites created these thematic sub-pages because they wanted their readers to be able to find all relevant information and news about the EP elections in one place. As the respondent from *Index.hu* put it,

"In an event like the EP elections, the creation of a separate section is not an option, but a must. The main goal was to make navigation easier for our visitors." In addition, these EU sub-sites functioned partly as "public service" pages in the sense that they published articles with the aim of "enlightening" or "educating" their readers about how the EU accession and the EP elections would affect their lives.

> We are really influenced by observing what is read by the users. We know that public service-like material, for instance, "how to vote?" "how to ask for the option to vote from home?" was very popular. [. . .] One can see that when we help the consumers or the voters – depending on the topic – with such information they are very-very enthusiastic to click on it, even if it's not newsworthy at all.
>
> (*Index.hu*)

However, the overall experience of content providers reflects the results of the web sphere analysis – compared to the last general elections, the first European parliamentary elections in Hungary only generated moderate attention. According to the informant from *Index.hu*, "The number of visitors was not as high as during the last parliamentary election campaigns. The apathy indicated by the low turnout appeared here, as well." Editors seemed to respond to reduced demand by lessening election coverage, although more in terms of breadth of coverage rather than quality, as the EU sections of both sites were very well designed. As the respondent from {*origo*} noted, "We did the same as what we did during a normal general elections campaign, but with smaller effort and less interest. Our interest was precisely as much smaller as that of the public."

Forums, chat, and political advertisements

We noted above the absence from the Hungarian electoral web sphere of "citizen" websites (for instance, political blogs and other personal sites concerned with the election). This, however, does not mean that Hungarian citizens did not engage in any online political discussions. The forums and chat rooms on {*origo*} and *Index.hu* are among the oldest and most popular electronic agoras on the Hungarian web. Usually, these forums become busier and emotionally agitated during election campaigns as an informant from *Index* noted: "[Forums] are very emotional even on an average day, and, of course, they usually become heated in politically active periods" (*Index.hu*). However, the European parliamentary elections constituted an exception, as the online forums remained relatively quiet. There was, as could be expected, a small increase in the number of comments, but this hardly compares with the sharp peaks recorded during periods of political scandals or previous election campaigns. In 2002, the number of political topics on *Index*, for example, grew by 50 percent (Kiss 2004b).

Besides online information provision and the forums, *Index* and {*origo*} function as a surface for advertisements. Since they potentially reach a larger audience than printed newspapers do, they are an important element of party and candidate campaign strategies. During the EP elections, both *Index* and {*origo*} published political ads, just as in the 2002 general elections campaign. According to our interviewees, in the past few years more and more political actors – especially parties – consider online campaigning important. Ads appearing on frequently visited websites slowly become standard elements in campaign strategies. As one informant noted, "[Online advertising] reaches a lot of people. [. . .] A party cannot say, after having looked at the high numbers of visitors of the two leading sites, that by simply putting an ad in the dailies they did their part" ({*origo*}).

The political influence of *Index* and {*origo*} is also apparent in the increasing number of politicians who participate in online interviews. Both sites conduct unconventional interviews with politicians, during which registered visitors can ask questions in "real time." According to our informants, politicians consider these interviews as important opportunities to express their views on certain topics. As the editor of {*origo*} put it, "I do not know any leading politician today who could afford to reject our invitation for an online interview." Since all registered users can ask questions, politicians rarely get away with the usual sound bites, political slogans, or by skipping the point.

Summary

Our interviews with the editors of the EU sub-sites, and leading journalists of *Index.hu* and {*origo*}, seem to confirm the findings of the web sphere analysis presented earlier in this chapter. That is, the EP election campaign in 2004 generated relatively little attention in Hungary. At the same time, however, there are signs that the internet has become increasingly important in election campaigns. This is indicated by the increasing reliance of parties and politicians on online political advertisements on sites other than their own. Interestingly, political parties and politicians are paying more attention to what happens in the web sphere and conforming, to a certain extent, to the demands of the politically active online community. In addition, the internet is becoming an increasingly important source of information and debate for citizens. Politicians may decide to ignore the opportunities of having their own websites, but they cannot afford to turn their backs on hundreds of thousands of users and potential voters. As the growing number of political ads on *Index* and {*origo*} show, politicians are starting to realize that online politics implies more than constructing websites, placing their programs online, and making their speeches downloadable.

Discussion

The main purpose of this chapter was to analyze the political uses of the internet during the 2004 European parliamentary elections campaign in Hungary, concentrating mainly on those websites containing material related to these elections. Our aim was to map the dynamic network of all those sites that might play an important role in an election campaign in Hungary. As a point of departure, based on Michel de Certeau's concept of "modes of use," we distinguished two types of internet uses. We called "strategic use" the appropriation of the internet by those political actors that are in a strong power position, that is, those who have the resources to make use of new communication technologies in a pre-planned way. On the other hand, the use of the internet by those who have little political power and who integrate new media in their everyday practices was called "tactical." We believe that by making this distinction we were able to say something about not only the online appearance of traditionally dominant political actors (political parties, governmental institutions), but also the reception of those strategies by site visitors.

The research presented above is an initial attempt to combine the particularly useful method of web sphere analysis with more qualitative ways to explore various uses of relevant websites. We argue that this research design might be useful in overcoming the rather rigid separation between "technology," on the one hand, and "the user," on the other. Taking aggregations of communication technologies *and* political agents as separate units of analysis is misleading, as this would suggest that such technologies exist outside of society. This is clearly not the case. As the various political uses of the two most important press sites in the Hungarian EP web sphere show, technologies and users interact and mutually shape one another.

One could expand on the research presented here in many ways. One possible option would be to concentrate on subsequent election campaigns and other major events in Hungary, and see how the web sphere evolves over time. However, in order to get closer to the understanding of the political roles of new media in certain situations, it might be even more exciting to include additional (old and new) communication technologies in the analysis. Websites operate in a very rich media environment, where mobile phones, local newspapers, national radio stations, and international cable television networks are simultaneously present. Thus, they are rarely interesting in themselves, but may be useful for researchers in investigating alternative communication practices in a given political system.

Acknowledgments

An earlier version of this chapter appeared in the "The World Wide Web and the 2004 European Parliament Election" special issue of *Information Polity* (Number 3–4, 2005). Data supporting the research were collected as part of the Internet and Elections Project, using software and procedures developed by WebArchivist.org. We wish to thank the research coordinators – Kirsten A. Foot, Nicholas W. Jankowski, Randy Kluver, and Steve M. Schneider – and all researchers involved in the project for the stimulation and support they provided. We also thank two anonymous reviewers for their useful comments and suggestions to improve the manuscript.

References

Bakardjieva, M. (2005) *Internet Society: The Internet and Everyday Life*. London: Sage.

Benhabib, S. (1996) "Towards a deliberative model of democratic legitimacy," in S. Benhabib (ed.), *Democracy and Difference: Contesting the Boundaries of the Political*, pp. 67–94. Princeton, NJ: Princeton University Press.

Certeau, M. de (1984) *The Practice of Everyday Life*. Berkeley, CA: University of California Press.

Dányi, E. (2002) "A faliújság visszaszól – politikai kommunikáció és kampány az interneten," *Médiakutató*, summer.

Dányi, E. and Sükösd, M. (2003) "Who's in control? Viral politics and control crisis in mobile election campaigns," in K. Nyíri (ed.), *Mobile Democracy: Essays on Society, Self and Politics*, Vienna: Passagen Verlag.

Dessewffy, T. (2004) *Mapping the Digital Future: The Hungarian Society and the Internet in 2004*. Budapest, Hungary: ITHAKA-ITTK-TÁRKI.

Dutton, W.H. (1996) *Information and Communication Technologies: Visions and Realities*. Oxford and New York: Oxford University Press.

Feenberg, A. (1999) *Questioning Technology*. London: Routledge.

Garcia, D. and Lovink, G. (1997) "The ABC of tactical media: manifest written for the opening of the web site of the Tactical Media Network," hosted by the Waag, the Society for Old and New Media, first distributed via Nettime in 1997. Available online: amsterdam.nettime.org/Lists-Archives/nettime-l-9705/msg00096.html (accessed 12 September 2005).

Graber, D.A, Bimber, B., Bennett, W.L., Davis, R., and Norris, P. (2003) "The Internet and politics: Emerging perspectives," in E. Price and H.F. Nissenbaum (eds), *Academy and the Internet*, pp. 90–119. New York: Peter Lang.

Haddon, L. (2004) *Information and Communication Technologies in Everyday Life: A Concise Introduction and Research Guide*. Oxford and New York: Berg.

Kiss, B. (2004a). "The media in Hungary," in M. Kelly, G. Mazzoleni and D. McQuail (eds.), *The Media in Europe: The Euromedia Handbook*, 3rd edn. London: Sage.

Kiss, B. (2004b) "Campaign in the forum: the 2004 European Parliamentary election campaign in Hungary," paper presented at the E-Campaigning: Governments, Parties, Social Movements workshop, Institute of Political Science of the Hungarian Academy of Sciences, September.

Kluver, R. (2005) "National variation in web deployment: The role of political culture and media regulation in internet politics," in M. Consalvo and M. Allen (eds), *Internet Research Annual*, vol. 2, pp. 75–84. New York: Peter Lang.

Norris, P. (2001) *Digital Divide? Civic Engagement, Information Poverty and the Internet in Democratic Societies*. Cambridge: Cambridge University Press.

Open Society Archives (2002) "Election campaign archive 2002." Available online: www.osa.ceu.hu/kampanyarchiv/english.html (accessed 22 April 2005).

Schneider, S.M. and Foot, K.A. (2002) "Online structure for political action: exploring presidential campaign web sites from the 2000 American election," *Javnost – The Public*, 9, 2: 43–60.

Schneider, S.M. and Foot, K.A. (2004) "The web as an object of study," *New Media and Society*, 6, 1: 114–122.

Sükösd, M. and Dányi, E. (2003) "M-politics in the making: SMS and e-mail in the 2002 Hungarian election campaign," in K. Nyíri (ed.), *Mobile Communication: Essays on Cognition and Community*. Vienna: Passagen Verlag.

14 Internet deployment in the 2004 Indonesian presidential elections

Shahiraa Sahul Hameed

The beginning of the twenty-first century was a time of political change in the Southeast Asian region. In 2004, national elections were called in a number of Southeast Asian nations, including the Philippines, Malaysia, Thailand, and Indonesia. Most of these elections were fiercely contested and held both national and regional implications. In Indonesia, the presidential election was significant not only for the role of president, but the election was seen as an initial step towards establishing a "true" democracy, as it was the first time that Indonesians were allowed to vote directly for their president and vice-president.

This case study provides a comparison between internet deployment in developing nations and in more developed nations with much higher internet penetration rates. The aim of this chapter is to explore systematically the features of the 2004 Indonesian presidential web sphere and the types of political actors contributing to it. Finally, it aims to examine the opportunities for online and offline political action supported by the Indonesian presidential web sphere.

Indonesian democracy

Although the *Reformasi* movement of the 1990s brought some understanding of democracy to the modern, urban Indonesian society (Lanti 2001), the rural Indonesian is still fairly uncertain of the meaning of democracy and its implications for him and his country and was unaware and unconcerned with some of Indonesia's main political concerns (A.C. Nielsen Survey 2003). Thus, although Indonesia has long been classified as a democratic nation, the practice and understanding of democracy is still emerging.

The new parliamentary and presidential elections in 2004 helped to pave the way for further consolidation of democratic politics in Indonesia and can be seen as the first step towards development of a specifically Indonesian brand of democracy. However, their impact on the culture of political participation and accountability in Indonesian politics has yet to be determined, as electoral patterns have yet to be formed (Sherlock 2004).

Indonesia's political system is similar to that of the American presidential system, but in the Indonesian system a president, vice-president and parliamentary members are elected every five years. The main difference between these two systems is that until 2004, Indonesian citizens could vote directly only for members of parliament, who then, once elected, voted among themselves for president and vice-president. However, nominations for the presidential candidacy are still closely tied to the parliamentary elections, therefore not completely separating the race for the presidency from the dynamics between the different political parties contesting for parliamentary seats.

The Indonesian parliamentary elections were held on 5 April 2004. Only parties that won at least 3 percent of the seats (or 5 percent of votes) in the parliamentary elections were allowed to field candidates for the presidential election. As a result, power to elect a president was taken out of the hands of traditional political elites and placed in the hands of the people with the hope that the president would then govern with the legitimacy of popular mandate. This chapter will focus on the presidential elections web sphere from the first round of elections, but it will also incorporate additional comments from changes in the web sphere resulting from the second round of elections.

The internet in Indonesia

Internet penetration in Indonesia, at 3.6 percent, is low compared to many other countries in the region, although it has almost quadrupled since 2000 (Internet WorldStats 2005), mainly due to government initiatives promoting internet use; and it is expected to increase over the next few years. However, a wide digital divide still exists between the elite and the majority in Indonesia, with the elite having the greatest access to the internet. Ordinary citizens, on the other hand, do not often have regular access to the internet, mainly accessing it by frequenting the *warung internet* or internet cafés that are widely available even in the most rural areas of Indonesia. Currently, this is the main method of internet access in Indonesia because it is relatively affordable (approximately 20 cents per hour in U.S. dollars) for Indonesians from all walks of life (Lim 2003). Internet penetration, and therefore its political and social impact, is also unevenly distributed across rural and urban areas.

Despite its low penetration, especially in comparison to that of other countries in the region such as Singapore, Indonesian political actors were among the first to use the internet for political purposes in this region (Lanti 2004). The internet was first deployed in Indonesian politics in the 1990s, where it was used subversively against former President Suharto's regime at a time when media coverage was strongly censored.

During the 2004 elections, guidelines set up by the KPU to regulate online campaigning were generally similar to those that guided other campaigning methods. Candidates and their parties were advised to campaign in a manner that would not incite violence or otherwise negatively affect the peace and harmony of the country. Guidelines provided on KPU's websites also stated that campaigning should only start four days after nomination day and should stop four days prior to the election (Laws of the Republic of Indonesia on the Presidential and Vice Presidential Elections 2003). These guidelines proved to be quite open-ended and the lack of a clear legal frame-work governing cyber activities provided political actors with flexibility in working around the existing laws.

Moreover, the first cyber-crime trial in Indonesia was held in September 2004, with the accused being charged with hacking into the KPU's websites in April 2004 (during the parliamentary election campaigning period), and changing the names of the various political parties into the names of fruits. Legislators had to try and identify appropriate existing laws that could be adapted for the case at hand, as no laws were in place at that time to deal with cyber-crimes.

The 2004 election cycle in Indonesia was the first time the internet was explicitly used by political actors as a campaigning tool. Thus, the Indone-sian presidential election of 2004 makes a particularly interesting case study for several reasons. First, the parliamentary and presidential elections in 2004 were only the third genuinely democratic elections to be held since Indonesia first gained independence from the Dutch in 1949 (Lanti 2004). Second, it was the first time that Indonesians directly voted for the two most powerful positions in their country, that of president and vice-president of the Republic of Indonesia. This, along with the revamping of parliamentary elections, can be seen as a reflection of the steps taken by the Indonesian government to strengthen and build democracy in Indonesia.

Third, as the largest nation in Southeast Asia, the largest Muslim nation in the world (85 percent of 240 million Indonesians are Muslim), and the world's fourth most populous country, Indonesia represents a vastly different political culture than many of the other nations studied as part of the Inter-net and Elections Project. The following analysis will seek to uncover what impact this aspect had, if any, on the use of the internet during the election.

Method

A web sphere is described as a "set of dynamically defined digital resources spanning multiple websites deemed relevant or related to a central event, concept or theme, and often connected by hyperlinks' (Schneider and Foot, 2005: 158). In terms of the Indonesian presidential web sphere, all websites that listed information, advocated candidates, or otherwise provided materials relevant to the presidential elections, were included in the web sphere.

E-democracy can be defined as electronic means of communication that enable or empower citizens in their efforts to hold their leaders accountable for their actions in the public realm (Treschel *et al.* 2004). The techniques of implementing e-democracy that will be examined in the context of this study are how e-democracy is employed in increasing the transparency of the political process and the deployment of ICT to augment the direct involvement and participation of citizens.

The sites can provide engaged citizens with the opportunity to participate in the campaigning process through the affordances set out by its online structure. We define online structure as a particular electronic space, comprised of various HTML pages, features, links, and texts within which the individual is given the opportunity to act (Schneider and Foot 2002).

In order to study the Indonesian presidential web sphere, six trained researchers (five student assistants and the researcher) participated in the identification and coding of websites. The five student assistants recruited were Indonesian, and familiar with the political climate of the country, in order further to ensure the accuracy and comprehensiveness of the websites identified.

Of the 185 websites that were identified, 100 were randomly selected for coding through a sampling frame stratified by producer type, but only 88 were codable. The remaining 12 websites required registration (three sites) or were not functional at the time of coding (nine sites). Nine sites were categorized as not functional because a time-out occurred when trying to connect to them, which could be attributed to the fact that the sites were not well maintained or were no longer in use, implying they were not a significant part of the campaign process. For the remainder of the chapter, our discussion will be based on findings from the 88 coded websites only. Table 14.1 depicts the producer types for sites that were coded for analysis.

As the internet and elections coding template was designed to be used across all nations involved in the study, we found that there were several features not directly applicable to the Indonesian presidential web sphere. For example, labor groups play an important role in European elections but do not have a strong impact on the political process of Indonesian politics. Second, some features present within this particular web sphere were not accounted for in the coding template, such as the presence of animated flash programs or graphics. To ensure that they were included in the final analysis, annotations of such features were made during the coding process.

Findings and results

Overall, the findings of this study show that even though Indonesia has followed many other nations in attempting a roll-out of internet services, the web was poorly used, if at all, as a campaign medium. The sites that did exist were often poorly designed and maintained, and there seemed to be little expectation that the internet would be used to gain much political information. This is best illustrated by the fact that during the parliamentary election many of the coded sites were outdated and displayed content related to the parliamentary elections which were held four months earlier.

Table 14.1 Coded websites within Indonesian presidential web sphere

Political actor	Number of coded sites within web sphere
Candidate	9
Government	6
NGO/Labor	6
Party	13
Press	28
Citizen	10
Portal	9
Religion	2
Business	4
Education	1
Total	88

One prominent example was the website of incumbent president Megawati Sukarnoputri, one of the daughters of Indonesia's founder, Sukarno, and a candidate in both the first and the second round of presidential elections. Not only was the site not updated prior to the presidential election, it bore a number of indicators of amateurism, including the fact that one of the most prominent politicians in Indonesia would rely on a free web-hosting service, such as tripod.[1] Moreover, the number of non-functional links present on this particular site reflects the lack of importance given to the internet among actors involved in the presidential campaign.

Site producers within the Indonesian presidential web sphere

Our findings indicate that few of the potential political actors who might have generated web content chose to do so. Table 14.2 presents the distribution of sites identified for this study that were produced by different types of political actors involved in the Indonesian presidential elections. As shown in the table, press organizations tended to produce more politically relevant websites than did any other type of political actor. This is not surprising, because most major mass media today have extensive online presence and contribute to the majority of net activity (Dahlgren 2001). It is surprising, however, that in a nation of over 200 million people, there was so little attempt to use the internet for the election. Only a small number of other political actors developed a web presence for this election. Several factors could contribute to this phenomenon, including the relatively high cost associated with developing and maintaining websites, a lack of expertise, and a low perception of the overall usefulness of the internet for campaigning in Indonesia.

Given the increasing importance of Islam and religious organizations in Indonesian politics, it was surprising that we found very few websites

Table 14.2 Websites within Indonesian presidential web sphere

Political actor	Number of websites identified by producer type
Business	7
Candidate	12
Citizen	17
Educational	4
Government	11
NGO	15
Party	34
Portal	20
Press	62
Religious	2
Total	184

produced by religious organizations (see Table 14.2). Although 85 percent of Indonesians are Muslims, only one Muslim site appeared in our sample. In addition, one of the two religious sites that appeared was a Catholic site: Gloria Cyber Ministries – Connecting Believers.[2] This could be a reflection of the well-educated Christian minority in Indonesia whose political presence is considered to be stronger than their actual numbers (Liddle 1996) supported by the 50 percent increase in the representation of Catholic parties in the 2004 Indonesian parliamentary elections (Evans 2004). Finally, this could more simply be attributed to the fact that Chinese Christians, a minority whose heavy involvement in business and trade provides them greater access to economic resources, employs more technologically advanced outreach methods.

On the whole, 135 out of the 185 sites identified were published primarily in Bahasa Indonesia. The remainder of the sites were bilingual, published in both English and Bahasa Indonesia. This can be mainly attributed to the fact that although English is an official part of the Indonesian school curriculum, it is not widely spoken among ordinary Indonesians. Thus, the production of bilingual websites (specifically those that are predominantly in English) is an indicator that these sites are aimed mainly at the elite who speak fluent English (and are most actively involved in the Indonesian political arena) or, in some cases, at foreign investors who sustain the Indonesian economy. There were, however, other websites present within this web sphere, primarily press sites, whose use of different dialects indicates that that they may be targeted at minority groups.

Interestingly, two of the presidential candidates in the first round of elections first launched their websites at least a year before the official nomination date. Another candidate launched his website even earlier, in October 2001. These actions were in breach of KPU guidelines stating that all campaigning should only start four days after the nomination of candidates and should stop four days prior to the election (Komisi Pemilihan Umum 2003). To our knowledge, no action was taken against these candidates.

Informational features within the Indonesian presidential web sphere

Information seeking is viewed as the first step towards encouraging political action and participation among citizens, based on the proposition that citizens are more likely to be persuaded to support a cause or campaign once they have started to seek relevant information on their own (Schneider and Foot 2002). Within the context of this project, informational features are defined as features within a website that provide visitors with information on a wide variety of topics, ranging from issue positions to terms of use of the website; see Table 14.3. Based on this table, it appears that the features that were most consistently present across producer types were election content, followed by images, and then biographies. The features that were least likely to be present on websites within the Indonesian presidential election web sphere were terms of use and privacy policies.

Upon further examination, regional differences emerged among a number of websites. Some press sites such as *Harian Komentar*[3] focused on general national-level election content, while others such as *Acheh Kita*[4] had a more specific, regional focus; *Acheh Kita* content was, for example, relevant primarily to Aceh province. During the campaign period, different factions within this province were actively fighting for independence from Indonesia and, as part of this struggle, large numbers of civilians had been killed or kidnapped by members of the Indonesian Armed Forces under the command of General Wiranto, a presidential candidate in the first round of the presidential elections.

Prior to and during the first round of presidential elections, *AcehKita.com* was filled with anti-Wiranto content. After General Wiranto failed to garner the support needed to contest in the second round of the elections, election-related content within this site significantly decreased, and is an illustration of the fragmented state of Indonesian politics.

We also explored the extent to which election-related material was present on sites produced by different actors. We found that "brochure-ware" (Kamarck 1999) was the most common online structure used by candidates to aid information seeking and facilitate campaigning. Moreover, many candidate sites functioned primarily as a center for information dissemination, focusing on the candidates themselves and their position on different issues debated. Noticeably absent from candidate sites were information on campaigning and voting processes, audio-visuals, privacy statements, and terms of use, collectively implying that most candidates did not view their websites as a means of educating Indonesians on the voting and election process, but instead viewed their sites as a self-promotional tool. This could be a result of a number of factors, including the large gap

Table 14.3 Informational-related features on websites of political actors in Indonesia

Political actor*	ELEC	BIO	IP	SPC	CAL	COMP	INFOC	INFOV	IMG
Candidate (9)	7	8	7	4	2	3	0	0	9
Govt (6)	9	1	1	0	1	0	3	3	4
NGO (6)	6	6	4	1	1	0	0	1	2
Party (13)	12	6	7	7	1	1	2	2	11
Press (28)	17	8	13	2	5	11	16	2	15
Citizen (10)	7	5	2	3	1	2	1	1	6
Portal (9)	7	2	0	2	1	2	2	2	5
Religion (2)	2	2	0	1	1	1	0	0	1
Business (4)	4	3	0	0	0	1	0	0	3
Education (1)	1	1	0	0	0	0	0	0	1
Total (88)	72	42	34	18	13	21	24	11	57

Note
* Number of sites per political actor indicated in parentheses.

between the masses and the elite within Indonesia on issues related to democracy and the fact that the internet at this point is not seen as an important tool for political education.

Out of the 13 political party sites, 12 of the sites displayed some election-related content. Among the parties that were not eligible to field their own candidates (based on parliamentary election results), some chose to support presidential candidates who were not directly affiliated to their respective parties, while others chose not to support any of the contesting pairs. However, even among parties that did take an official stance to support the new candidates, websites were not updated to reflect these new-formed alliances.

Newly formed coalitions between various parties at the second stage of the presidential election were not noted on both party and candidate websites. For example, the Golkar Party, which won the largest proportion of seats during the parliamentary elections, made the controversial decision to support the Megawati team in the second round of the presidential elections. But this was not reflected on their site or on the site of Akbar Tandjung, Golkar Party chairman and the person responsible for forming the partnership.[5] This is surprising, especially since one of the perceived advantages of the internet as a campaign medium is that it is relatively easy to update. However, the fact that even the most sophisticated of the websites did not reflect the new political alliances and realities demonstrates how insignificant the internet is perceived to be as a source of political information in Indonesia.

Within the *pancasila* ideology of Indonesia,[6] non-governmental agencies (NGOs) are required to remain politically neutral but, in reality, their agendas are often political. Among the NGO websites that were coded, for example, biographical information and election-related content was present across all sites, and issue positions related to the election was present on four out of the six coded NGO sites.

An example of a popular Indonesian NGO with a web presence was the *Jaringan Islam Liberal*[7] website. Although the official aim of this organization is to promote liberal Islamic teachings, we have coded it as an NGO because the organization identifies itself as such on the site. In addition, the organization promoted the application of Islamic teachings in many areas, including politics, and did not limit its content specifically to religious teachings. Instead, it contained politically oriented editorials, clippings, and forums, while indirectly lending support to more fundamentally Islamic parties, opposing to the *pancasila* ideology.

Only one educational site was included in our sample, and that one site presented the least varied types of informational features; displaying only election-related information, biographies, and images. One explanation for this would be that educational institutions, which are expected to remain neutral, only play a peripheral role in Indonesian politics. In Indonesia, this largely stems from the direct and active involvement of students in the

Reformasi movement of the 1990s, where students banded together to over-throw the Suharto regime, triggering a governmental backlash banning student or faculty involvement in politics (Lanti 2001; Saunders 1998). This is an interesting example of how Indonesian political culture is evolving to prohibit student involvement in politics as a result of overt student involvement. In contrast, in many Western countries, students are a primary target of political mobilization efforts.

Websites did not frequently contain information about the campaigning and voting processes, suggesting that this was not the main way Indonesians were educated about these issues. Minimal information on these issues was, however, sometimes available on press sites. The main source of online information on campaigning and voting was the Indonesian Electoral Commission (KPU) official website,[8] which provided visitors with comprehensive and detailed information regarding both the election and voting processes.

Engagement features within the Indonesian presidential web sphere

In addition to supporting informational features, online structures that are categorized as engagement features, can facilitate citizens' participation by providing them with opportunities to volunteer, register to vote, make donations, and download election- or campaign-related information (Schneider and Foot 2002; Strommer-Galley and Foot 2002; Norris 2001), and also have the capability to facilitate the engagement of citizens in the democratic process (Treschel *et al.* 2004). Their presence on different sites by producer type is presented in Table 14.4. One of the most notable observations from this table is the small number of engagement features present within this web sphere, with contact producer being the most frequent. Most websites within the Indonesian presidential web sphere had at least a mailing or e-mail address for the producer, which constitutes the basic level of engagement, with six out of the ten coded citizen sites and 23 of the 28 press sites displaying this information. During the data collection phase of this study, three site producers were e-mailed (two parties and one candidate); however, none of them replied, suggesting that the e-mail addresses were probably not monitored. Thus, we cannot automatically infer a level of engagement just because the feature is present.

The second most prominent feature was online forums, present on seven of the nine coded candidate sites. Forums are perhaps a more interesting form of engagement to be studied in this context because, if used properly, they "connect" users with each other, providing citizens with an avenue to provide feedback to the party or candidate. For example, our annotations revealed that more than half the press sites also had a feature that encouraged visitors to state their candidate preference or positions on a few politically related issues. However, upon closer inspection it was found that very few of these forums were actively used, especially those hosted on candidate

Table 14.4 Engagement-related features on websites of political actors in Indonesia

Political actor*	CON	JOIN	REG	GM	DON	FOR	OD	SL	PUB	E-P	VOL
Candidate (9)	8	1	0	0	0	7	4	2	5	0	0
Govt (6)	5	0	0	0	0	2	1	0	0	0	0
NGO (6)	6	1	0	0	0	1	0	0	0	1	0
Party (13)	9	0	0	4	0	6	1	2	6	3	0
Press (28)	23	11	0	12	1	9	2	4	12	1	0
Citizen (10)	6	2	0	3	0	4	3	2	3	0	0
Portal (9)	7	7	0	4	0	5	0	2	2	2	0
Religion (2)	2	1	0	1	0	1	0	1	1	1	0
Business (4)	2	2	0	0	0	2	2	1	2	0	0
Education (1)	1	0	0	0	0	0	0	0	0	0	0
Total (88)	69	25	0	24	1	37	13	14	31	8	0

Note
* Number of sites per political actor indicated in parentheses.

sites. One plausible reason is (as posited within the context of European web spheres) that citizens did not feel that their contributions would make an impact on a larger scale and consequently did not actively contribute to these forums (Treschel *et al.* 2004). This view is very much applicable in the Indonesian context, because active involvement in politics, especially in terms of decision making and power, has traditionally been limited to the higher echelons of society.

The third most prominent feature deployed was an ability to register support for the party or candidate, which was present on five out of the nine candidate sites, but was completely absent from government, NGO, and educational sites. Within the Indonesian context, these types of organizations are forbidden from directly supporting any candidate, and consequently this finding was expected.

Because the necessary infrastructure was not yet available in Indonesia, we expected that two features, allowing surfers to volunteer and to vote online, would be absent, and in fact, this was the case. This stands in sharp contrast to the 2000 U.S. presidential web sphere, where all candidate sites enabled citizens to volunteer and to register to vote (Schneider and Foot 2002).

The "join" feature was present on seven out of the nine coded portals within the web sphere and were not present on any of the party sites. One reason for this could be that, traditionally, Indonesian politics has its roots in face-to-face campaigning in the form of rallies, speeches, and festivals. In some ways, Indonesian political campaigning rallies resemble a large outdoor party, with mascots, food, entertainment, and dancing. The candidates often sing and dance along with voters during these rallies. The current president of Indonesia, Susilo Bambang Yudyohono, for example, was known for his great singing and dancing abilities during the campaigning process and is still affectionately known as "The Singing President" by many Indonesians.

Although soliciting for donations online is not prohibited by the KPU, only one site, the Green Left Weekly, a weekly online edition for an NGO based in Australia, had this feature, while other press sites featured paid pop-up advertisements. One possible explanation for this is that within some Asian political cultures, such as Singapore, parties are not encouraged to use their websites to raise funds because this is seen as an invitation to corruption (Kluver 2004).

Conclusion

The analysis presented in this chapter demonstrates that in terms of the key areas noted above, transparency and participation, the Indonesian presidential web sphere falls short of the ideal. Political actors rarely provided enough information to create anything approximating a transparent political process, even omitting the goals and motivations of the actors themselves. Furthermore, participatory features on the web sphere were also noticeably absent, suggesting that Indonesian politics, even when mediated via the internet, is still largely elite-driven, with little opportunity for normal citizen engagement. Websites tended to be seen as places to disseminate political platforms but not as places that in any way could transform the political process itself by inviting greater citizen involvement in the process. The top-down nature of Indonesian political culture is largely replicated in the online environment.

In the Indonesian presidential web sphere, the use of the internet to change the nature and shape of political discourse and democracy did not materialize. There are two main reasons for this. First, the internet is still seen as a peripheral campaigning tool in Indonesia. We found little evidence that any political actor invested significant time, energy, or money in developing websites. The most common type of site, media sites, did create better web presences, but we are unsure whether the content was exclusive to the web or was simply an online form of offline content. Second, strict candidacy guidelines imposed by the KPU favored major political parties by only allowing parties with 5 percent of overall votes from the parliamentary election to nominate candidates. Thus, the internet seemed to have no effect in leveling the playing field or in increasing the chances of marginal actors in the political scene.

The internet did, however, allow for more non-candidates to get involved in the political scene, both directly and indirectly. For example, sites within the Indonesian presidential web sphere did provide users with a grasp of the main issues involved in the election. These sites were mainly press, NGO, and citizen sites, suggesting that the internet has the potential to become a useful resource for political information, supplementing more traditional channels such as television and newspapers, already widely used for political campaigning in Indonesia.

This chapter also explored the range of online and offline actions made possible by the online structures within the Indonesian presidential web sphere. Engagement features were scarce within this web sphere and internet deployment in Indonesian politics seems to be more focused on information dissemination than on mobilization. As a result, the proposition that political internet deployment could lead to more bottom-up communication did not materialize (Norris 2001, 2003). Even when present, engagement features were not widely used, suggested by the lack of participation in online forums and e-mails that were unanswered by site producers. These results are similar to that of Treschel and colleagues (Treschel *et al.* 2004) who posited (in the context of the EU election) that if ICTs are not widely used, even when present, then the impact that they would have on the democratization process would be minimal, if not non-existent.

The results of this study do support the postulation by Cornfield and Rainie (2003) that the internet is most useful for information dissemination, especially since this web sphere was dominated by press sites. What was interesting within the context of this web sphere was that internet deployment allowed users to have access to more varied sources of information, especially from geographically distant provinces, that held opposing views to that of the mainstream press. Although political blogs had not yet gained popularity in Indonesia during the 2004 presidential elections, they are currently becoming more popular. This brand of "citizen journalism" will likely play a more important role in future Indonesian elections, thereby providing a source of alternative information, separate from the mainstream government-controlled press, which often provides more coverage to candidates who are in the government or who have personal ties to the agency (Carter Center 2005).

Other forms of ICT are also likely to play a more important role in future election cycles, especially as the convergence of different forms of new media gains popularity in Indonesia. For example, approximately nine months after the elections, President Yudyohono gave out his mobile phone number to a group of farmers, telling them to contact him should they have trouble "solving their problems." A day later, his mobile service crashed as a result of over 3000 people trying to call the number (UPI 2005).

As a whole, this study constitutes a preliminary analysis of the role of the internet in Indonesian politics. A more comprehensive analysis of political content within the web sphere, both during and after the electoral time frame, needs to be conducted. This would make clearer the perceived importance of internet deployment within Indonesian political culture for campaigning purposes during, before, and after the actual campaigning period. Furthermore, an analysis of the frequency of usage of these features should be conducted to understand better the efficacy and impact of the different features present across websites.

Notes

1 www.members.tripod.com/~megawati.
2 www.glorianet.org.
3 www.hariankomentar.com.
4 www.acehkita.com.
5 www.akbartandjung.com.
6 The *pancasila* ideology is the philosophical basis of the Indonesian state, and comprises five principles related to a Buddhist code of ethics. The five principles are belief in one God, just and civilized humanity, the unity of Indonesia, democracy guided by the inner wisdom in the unanimity arising out of deliberation among representatives, and social justice for the whole of the people of Indonesia.
7 islamlib.com/id.
8 www.kpu.go.id.

References

A.C. Nielsen and Charney Research of New York (2003) "Indonesia: a report on public opinion and the 2004 elections," *Asia Foundation*. Available online: www.asiafoundation.org/pdf/elections_survey_indo_03.pdf (accessed 6 September 2006).

Carter Center (2005) *The Carter Center 2004 Indonesian Election Report.* Available online: www.cartercenter.org/documents/2161.pdf (accessed 31 March 2006).

Cornfield, M. and Rainie, L. (2003) "Untuned keyboards: online campaigners, citizens and portals in the 2002 election," *Pew Internet and American Life Project.* Available online: www.pewinternet.org/PPF/r/85/report_display.asp (accessed 6 September 2006).

Dahlgren, L. (2001) "Cyberspace and the public sphere: exploring the democratic potential of the Net," *Convergence*, 38: 70–84.

Evans, K. (2004) "Indonesian elections and their implications," paper presented at the Indonesian Presidential Elections 2004 Seminar, Jakarta, Indonesia, May. Available online: www.csis.or.id/events_file/26/kevans.pdf (accessed 16 February 2006).

Internet WorldStats (2005) Available online: www.internetworldstats.com/stats3.htm (accessed 29 March 2006).

Kamarck, E.C. (1999) "Campaigning on the Internet in the elections of 1998," in E.C. Kamarck and J.J.S. Nye (eds), *Democracy.com? Governance in the Network World*, pp. 99–123. Hollis, NH: Hollis Publishing.

Kluver, R. (2004) "Political culture and information technology in the 2001 Singapore general election," *Political Communication*, 21: 435–458.

Kluver, R. (2005) "Political culture in online politics," in M. Consalvo and M. Allen (eds), *Internet Research Annual*, 2, pp. 75–84. Newbury Park, CA: Sage Publications.

Komisi Pemilihan Umum [Indonesian Electoral Commission] (2003) Chapter 6, Section 1, 15:1. Available online: www.kpu.go.id/peraturan_uu/uu_pilpres.htm (accessed 24 May 2006).

Lanti, I.G. (2001) "Back to the (slightly different) future: continuity and change in Indonesian politics," *Visiting Researchers Series No. 2 (2001)*. Singapore: Institute of South East Asian Studies.

Lanti, I.G. (2004) *Outlook on the Indonesian Parliamentary Election 2004: The Working Paper Series*. Singapore: Institute of Defense and Strategic Studies.

Liddle, R.W. (1996) "Leadership and culture in Indonesian politics," *ASAA Southeast Asia Publications Series*. Sydney, Australia: Allen & Unwin.

Lim, M. (2003) "From real to virtual (and back again): civil society, public sphere, and the Internet in Indonesia," in K.C. Ho, R. Kluver and K. Yang (eds), *Asia.com: Asia Encounters the Internet*, pp 113–128. London and New York: Routledge.

Norris, P. (2001) *Digital Divide: Civic Engagement, Information Poverty and the Internet Worldwide*. Cambridge: University of Cambridge Press.

Norris, P. (2003) "Preaching to the converted? Pluralism, participation and party websites," *Party Politics*, 9, 1: 21–45.

Rancangan Undang-Undang Republik Indonesia tentang Pemilihan Presiden dan Wakil Presiden [Laws of the Republic of Indonesia on the Presidential and Vice Presidential Elections] (2003) Chapter VI: 15–25. Available online: www.kpu.go.id/peraturan_uu?RUU_Pilpres.htm (accessed 16 February 2006).

Saunders, J. (1998) "Academic freedom in Indonesia," *Human Rights Watch*. Available online: www.hrw.org/reports98/indonesia2/ (accessed 20 April 2006).

Schneider, S.M. and Foot, K. (2002) "Online structure for political action: exploring presidential campaign websites from the 2000 American election," *The Public*, 9: 2–18.

Schneider, S.M. and Foot, K. (2005) "Web sphere analysis: an approach to studying online action," in C. Hine (ed.), *Virtual Methods: Issues in Social Research on the Internet*, pp 157–170. Oxford: Berg Publishers.

Sherlock, S. (2004) "The 2004 Indonesian elections: how the system works and what the parties stand for," *A Report on Political Parties*. Canberra, Australia: Centre for Democratic Institutions. Available online: www.cdi.anu.edu.au/research/research_downloads/Sherlock_Indonesian_Election04.pdf (accessed 24 May 2006).

Stromer-Galley, J. and Foot, K.A. (2002) "Citizen perceptions of online interactivity and implications for political campaign communication" [Electronic version], *Journal of Computer-mediated Communication*, 8, 1. Available online: jcmc.indiana.edu/vol8/issue1/stromerandfoot.html (accessed 29 March 2005).

Treschel, A.H., Kies, R., Mendez, F., and Schmitter, P.G. (2004) "Evaluation of the use of new technologies in order to facilitate democracy in Europe: e-democratizing the parliaments and parties of Europe," unpublished manuscript.

UPI. (2005) "'Approachable' leader's cell phone crashes." Available online: web.lexisnexis.com.ezlibproxy1.ntu.edu.sg/universe/document?_m=4bb60a3724d2274f1c399021021b4d76&_docnum=1&wchp=dGLbVlz-zSkVb&_md5=ac4c9a473f1b6b9e2500ae7d17f7da3d (accessed 27 October 2005).

15 Roles and regulations

Boundaries on the Japanese web sphere in the 2004 Upper House election

Leslie M. Tkach-Kawasaki

Introduction

This chapter examines how traditional campaign roles and regulations – two mutually supporting aspects of a nation's political culture – contributed to shaping the Japanese political web sphere, and political actors' use of the web, during the 2004 Upper House election campaign period. Japan is distinctive because it is one of the few nations that regulates the use of the internet in political campaigns.

Numerous scholars and observers have commented on the ways in which information communication technologies (ICTs), including the internet, have changed how political campaigns are run (Davis 1999; Margolis and Resnick 2000; Bimber and Davis 2003; Gibson *et al.* 2003). During the past decade, various political actors involved in elections – political parties, candidates, the government, the mass media, and organizations – have taken advantage of the internet's speed, communications capabilities, and relatively low cost to get their political message out to the public. It has also introduced novel ways for the public to become informed about and participate in elections, particularly through online forums or discussion groups that offer the opportunity to interact with other voters. In addition, new forms of campaign materials (e.g. "e-paraphernalia") offer visitors the opportunity to download digital versions of the traditional lawn sign or campaign poster. These multiple functions of the internet have allowed political actors in the web sphere to move beyond traditional campaign roles in terms of both communications and information provision.

Is such fluidity in campaign information and communication flow apparent in all political cultures? In this chapter, we address this question first by examining the Japanese political context to discern if there are any dynamics that serve as boundaries to the web sphere in Japan. One reason that may explain differences in campaign information and communication flows in various political cultures is whether online campaigns are regulated. Although the use of the internet in other national contexts may allow for a certain expansion of roles by various political actors, a comparative assessment of information provision and engagement features on the websites in the Japanese web sphere suggests that traditional campaign roles appear to be maintained.

Political culture in Japan

Understanding how the internet has been used during campaigns requires understanding a bit more about Japan's political environment, including the one-party predominance of the Liberal Democratic Party (LDP), the complicated mixed electoral system, and the traditional roles played by political actors during election campaigns. In addition, the national legislative infrastructure that manages campaigns in the form of the POEL (Public Offices Election Law) delineates campaign activities that may be undertaken by political parties and candidates, particularly in terms of their timing. The POEL, along with the traditional roles played by the government during campaigns, has culminated in a clear separation of the roles played by political actors. Provisions in the POEL originally were aimed at other media formats; however, it has been applied to online media during the past decade. In this exploration of the Japanese web sphere during the 2004 Upper House election campaign period, we will see a clear delineation among the roles played by various political actors. This examination in turn allows us to reach a fuller understanding of the function of the internet as a campaign tool within the broader perspective of a nation's particular political context.

The potential for an "online" political web sphere has its fundamental roots in the prevailing "offline" political context in which it is located. To understand the development of the Japanese web sphere, it is first necessary to relate it to certain features of Japan's postwar political context, namely, the continuous one-party predominance of the Liberal Democratic Party, Japan's mixed electoral system, and the strict guidelines of the POEL.

The first distinguishing feature of Japan's political environment is the continuous one-party predominance of the LDP through much of the postwar period. Except for a brief 11-month period in 1993–1994, the LDP has occupied office either through a majority government or as the leader of coalition governments (mainly since 1994) during the past 50 years. Its longevity has been attributed to its ability to draw on key support bases, traditionally in the agricultural and industrial sectors, and its success in responding to the prevailing political climate in terms of policy initiatives. A further key factor to the LDP's success lies in its internal organization. Making up for a lack of inter-party competition in Japan's political environment, there is, however, a certain amount of intra-party competition among five factions within the LDP (Flanagan and Reed 1996: 354).

The second feature is Japan's mixed electoral system, which was revamped in 1993 (during the brief period when the LDP was out of office) by a coalition government of eight small political parties led by Hosokawa Morihito. The Japanese national assembly (the Diet) is composed of two chambers, the Lower House (House of Representatives), with 480 seats, and the Upper House (House of Councilors), with 242 seats, for a total of 722 seats. In Japan's mixed electoral system, elections in each house are contested in different ways. In the Lower House, there are 300 seats in single-member districts throughout the country and 180 seats in a proportional representation system distributed among 11 nationwide blocs, and elections are held at a maximum interval of four years. The system for Upper House elections is somewhat different. Ninety-six seats in the Upper House are contested through a proportional representation system whereby voters cast a ballot for a particular political party or candidate, and the seats are apportioned according to the ranking of the candidate in terms of party vote totals (Flanagan and Reed 1996: 347). The remaining 146 seats are distributed among Japan's 47 prefectures, with each prefecture fielding at least two seats. Thus, voters cast two write-in ballots in these elections: one for the candidate running in their particular prefecture and the other for a party-list candidate or specific political party. Upper House elections are held at set three-year intervals, and half of the members are elected to six-year terms in each election (Flanagan and Reed 1996: 349).

These twin features of Japan's "offline" political context describe a political environment in which electoral contests are waged mainly by political parties and candidates. Yet these two political actors are not the only generators of campaign-related information. The Japanese government also generates campaign-related information that is distributed by local election management boards. Yet, regardless of its source, dissemination of campaign-related information falls under the purview of the POEL, which details the range and quantity of election-related information that may be distributed to the public.

Owing to the wide scope and detailed provisions of the POEL, Japan's election system is one of the strictest among the world's leading democratic nations. The current POEL has its origins in the Lower House election laws that were in effect prior to World War II (Hayashida 1967: 2–7). Curtis (1971: 211–213) points out that although candidates and political parties were relatively free of restrictions between 1889 and 1919, "revisions of the Election Law after 1919 have imposed increasingly severe limitations on permissible campaign practices," aimed mainly at political parties and candidates for public office. The first set of notable revisions was enacted in 1925 and included restrictions concerning the distribution of campaign literature and established campaign spending limits. During the 1930s, the POEL was further modified to increase the government's role in managing elections, including setting guidelines for campaign speeches, the printing of campaign brochures, and other aspects of campaigning (Curtis 1971: 213–214).

Although candidates for Lower House elections enjoyed a brief respite from the POEL's limitations in the immediate postwar period, major revisions to the POEL in 1950 and 1952 reinstituted many of the prewar restrictions concerning campaigning and also reflected postwar changes in the electoral system. Under the pre-1994 multi-member electoral system introduced shortly after the war, multiple candidates from a single party vied for anywhere from three to five seats in each constituency in Lower House elections. As candidates of the same party competed with each other for seats, for many candidates party sponsorship was less important than building their own individual support organizations (*koenkai*). To ensure fairness and to prevent candidates from the same party outspending their rivals, the POEL set out strict guidelines for the creation and distribution of campaign-related materials such as brochures and postcards over a specific geographic area. In addition, the POEL restricted the timing and number of official campaign speeches.

The POEL's limitations on campaigning cover a wide range of activities. The time frame for campaign activities is closely regulated (Section 129), and candidates are not allowed to engage directly in official campaign activities during the 14-day period immediately preceding Upper or Lower House elections. Sections 142 and 143 limit the number of postcards (35,000 per constituency), as well as the content, size, quantity, and geographical distribution of campaign posters produced by either political parties or candidates. Section 178 also prevents candidates from making official greetings (*aisatsu*) or distributing campaign-related materials immediately following the day of the election. Campaign practices that are standard in other countries, such as door-to-door canvassing by the candidates themselves or members of their support organizations, are also prohibited (Iwanami Shoten 2003).

The growing popularity of television and newspaper advertising as campaign media has also not escaped the purview of the POEL. Reflecting the growing importance of television broadcasting as political advertising media, the POEL was revised in 1964. Although political parties may freely purchase advertising in newspapers or television commercials, Upper and Lower House candidates are banned from doing so, and instead are offered two five-minute television commercials that are broadcast on NHK (*Nippon hoso kyoku*), Japan's national broadcasting network. The POEL allows candidates five publicly funded newspaper advertisements restricted to a certain size and column width.

While there may be strict limitations on the forms of campaign media that are directly distributed by political parties and candidates, the government, through local election management boards, is also an active participant in distributing election-related information. These local election management boards are responsible for setting up "poster boards" displaying candidates' individual election posters and distributing official bulletins with lists of candidates (*senkyo koho*). Section 19 of the POEL also specifies the role of local election management boards in preparing voters' lists (Iwanami Shoten 2003).

In summary, Japan's "offline" political context demonstrates that while political parties and candidates are the most active participants in elections, the POEL, by placing limitations on campaigning, has also ensured a role for the government in the management and distribution of campaign-related media. As shown in the next section, although the POEL does not directly address internet-based campaigning, it has served as a crucial dynamic in the increasing use of ICTs for election campaign purposes.

Growth of the political internet in Japan

The growth of the political internet in Japan has been influenced by the ways in which the POEL has been applied, mainly to websites produced by political parties and candidates. Although a small number of candidates established websites for the regularly scheduled 1995 Upper House election, it was not until the October 1996 Lower House election that the use of the internet – specifically websites – became an issue. Influenced by the use of the web during the American presidential campaign that same year, almost all political parties and a number of candidates created campaign-oriented sites.

The increasing use of the web did not escape the attention of the former Ministry of Home Affairs (now the Ministry of Internal Affairs and Communications), which is responsible for election management. In October 1996, the ministry indicated that candidate-produced websites that included election platforms, and party-produced websites with candidate profiles, rosters, and lists of constituencies, contravened the POEL's strictures concerning the distribution of campaign-related information in a particular geographical area, especially during the official campaign activities period immediately before an election. The ministry also expressed concern that the medium could be used for defamation or slander of political candidates.

Most political parties and candidates responded to the government's ruling by voluntarily removing their listings of candidates and constituencies (in the case of political parties) or by shutting down their websites completely (candidates). However, the recently established New Party Sakigake requested further clarification of the government's interpretation of the POEL as it applied to the internet. They pointed out in an official inquiry document submitted to the government in mid-October that websites not only provided election-related information to Japanese voters residing overseas, but also supported the original intent of the POEL, by minimizing the costs of election campaigning. After the election, which was held on 25 October 1996, the government issued a statement again upholding its previous interpretation of the POEL (Miyoshi 1996).

As use of the internet spread among the Japanese public in the late 1990s, from close to five million users in 1996 to over 36 million by mid-2001 (Intanetto Hakusho 1998, 2001), the issue of its use by candidates and political parties continued to surface. Prior to the next scheduled Upper House election in 1998, the DPJ (Democratic Party of Japan), the main opposition party, submitted a bill to the Diet to reform the POEL to address campaigning through the internet, but the bill failed to pass in the Diet.

During the Lower House election campaign of 2000, the growing popularity of e-mail newsletters and cellular phone-based websites led to further calls for revamping the POEL to address the use of ICTs by political actors during election campaigns. This campaign also saw the first wave of expansion of the Japanese political web sphere, as a number of citizens' groups and individuals established websites that included information ranging from evaluations of candidate websites to posting "black lists" of candidates to avoid (*Mainichi Newspaper* 2000).

In the past, the issue of the campaign use of the internet tended to fade from public view immediately following national elections. However, in the spring of 2001, the overwhelming success of newly elected Prime Minister Koizumi Jun'ichiro's e-mail newsletter again focused attention on the political use of the web. During the 2001 Upper House election, political parties and a small number of candidates also started distributing e-mail newsletters with the goal of further engaging the public in election campaigning. This election campaign period also showed further expansion of the Japanese web sphere as the number of candidates with websites surpassed 50 percent for the first time (Table 15.1).[1]

Shortly after the 2001 Upper House election, the government responded to increased calls for reform of the POEL by establishing a special deliberative committee, led by University of Tokyo professor, Kabashima Ikuo, to re-examine the issue of internet-based campaigning. After one year of deliberation, the committee endorsed internet-based campaigning with certain restrictions. The committee separated the functions of websites and e-mail by recommending only the use of websites for election campaign purposes. To address the possibility of defamation or slander, the committee suggested that each website display the e-mail address of the person responsible for establishing it. Finally, the committee recommended that third-party participants, in addition to political parties and candidates, be allowed to undertake campaign-related activities through their websites. Although the committee's recommendations have not been acted upon to date, its establishment and subsequent recommendations clearly demonstrate recognition

Table 15.1 Growth of candidate websites

	2001 Upper House election	*2003 Lower House election*	*2004 Upper House election*
Number of candidates with websites	271 (55.6%)	666 (66.4%)	239 (74.2%)
Number of candidates without websites	216 (44.4%)	337 (33.6%)	83 (25.8%)
Total number of candidates	487 (100%)	1003 (100%)	322 (100%)

Source: Data compiled by author.

of the growth of the Japanese political web sphere and the possibility for both traditional and non-traditional political actors to step beyond campaign roles originally set out in the POEL. In the following examination of the political web sphere during the 2004 Upper House election campaign period, we see not only a clear demarcation of campaign roles but also a number of third-party actors utilizing the web to participate in the campaign.

Methods

The main purpose of this study is to assess the roles played by various political actors in the Japanese web sphere. Are political actors utilizing the web's potential to provide information and citizen engagement opportunities to disseminate election campaign information and promote public engagement? Two steps comprised the research design. First, we gathered the website addresses of a range of political actors that could potentially be involved in the campaign. Second, we analyzed the content of these websites.

A variety of sources was used to identify the political actors and gather website addresses. Press and third-party portal websites provided a preliminary list of candidates approximately one month prior to the election. As no official listing of candidate website addresses was available, we used links on political party websites to identify the addresses for those candidates sponsored by political parties. We found websites of independent candidates using political portal websites and two popular search engines, Yahoo! Japan[2] and Excite.[3] The resulting master list of approximately 239 candidates was cross-referenced with the official list of candidates that was distributed as a newspaper insert approximately two weeks prior to the election.

In addition to the websites established by the Lower and Upper houses of the Japanese Diet, the Prime Minister's Office, and the Ministry of Internal Affairs and Communications, government-related political actors were identified through links available on the Association of Promoting Fair Elections (*Akarui senkyo*) website.[4] This website included links to election management boards in almost all prefectures and municipal areas in Japan. In total, 60 government-related websites were identified.

Search engines were used to create a list of other political actors who may have been involved in the 2004 Upper House election campaign. A search for non-profit organizations (NPOs) and non-government organizations (NGOs) was conducted using the category listings available at Yahoo! Japan and Excite. Links under the heading "politics" (*seiji*) on the main page were followed to "groups" (*dantai*) to create the list of 71 websites of NPOs/NGOs that might contain election-related information during the campaign period. A similar procedure was followed to identify political parties (*seito*), which resulted in a list of 16 major and minor political parties. The list of 12 press-related websites was created by following the link to "newspapers" (*shimbun*) on the top pages of both search engines. Searches were also performed using Japanese-language terms for other producer types such as "election planner" (*erekushon purana*) for political professionals and "election research" (*senkyo kenkyu*).

The second step in the methodological process, conducting a content analysis of the websites produced by these political actors, followed the definitions for certain features described by the Internet and Elections Project.[5] From within the total of 419 websites identified within the Japanese web sphere, stratified samples (*n* = 95) were drawn for features comparison. Information-provision features included biographical information, endorsements, issue positions, speeches, events, issue comparisons, information regarding the electoral process, voting process, images, audio/visual offerings on the websites, as well as privacy and terms of use policies. Engagement features consisted of contact information, information concerning joining the organization, voting registration, getting e-mail from the website producers, donations, discussion forums, offline distribution of election-related materials, potential to send links, public support statements, e-paraphernalia (e.g. downloadable screensavers), and volunteer opportunities.

Results

During the 2004 election campaign period, websites created by individual candidates dominated the Japanese political web sphere (Table 15.2). Of these, 94 percent contained content that specifically targeted the upcoming election. Government-related websites, mostly those of official election management boards and sites created by NPOs, NGOs, and labor union groups, also made up a sizeable portion of the political web sphere. However, websites created by labor union groups tended not to include election-related

Table 15.2 Websites created by producer types

Producer type	Websites identified	Websites sampled	Websites featuring election content (%)
Candidate	239	51	94
Government	60	12	92
NPO/NGO/Labor union	71	18	33
Political party	16	4	100
Press	12	3	100
Other[1]	20	7	71
Total	419	95	82 (average)

Note
1 "Other" includes business, citizen, educational, political professional, portal, and religious producers.

content. While the number of press-related websites was low, their presence in the web sphere does mirror the centralized character of the Japanese newspaper and broadcasting industry, which is concentrated on five national daily newspapers and five national broadcasting stations. A further feature of the Japanese web sphere was the relatively low number of sites produced by business, citizen, educational, political profession, portal, and religious producers. Few citizens produced sites as a means of participating in the election, and portal websites tended to be concentrated on the Yahoo! Japan and Excite sites.

Japanese candidates and political parties, as the principal actors in the political campaign, created websites with the widest range of information- and engagement-related features. In general, the contents of the websites created by these political actors focused on campaigning, featuring background information, issue positions, images for recognition purposes, and campaign-related events. Among all website producers in the Japanese political web sphere, sites created by these actors also featured the highest number of engagement-related features, which mainly allowed the public to contact individual candidates or political parties through e-mail, traditional post, or facsimile.

As shown in Table 15.3, a high percentage of candidates included images or photographs of themselves, in addition to background information (often on "profile" pages of their websites) and issue positions. A significant number also included endorsements and event-related information such as dates and locations of their public speeches. As perhaps expected in a political culture in which direct confrontation is avoided, very few candidates included issue comparison features on their websites. Information regarding voting processes was also conspicuously absent.

Candidate-created websites also offered the widest variety of means for the public to participate in the election or engage in direct communication with the candidates and their organizations (Table 15.4). Almost all candidates invited contact with the public through their websites in the form of direct e-mail or by post or facsimile. Yet the prevalence of other forms of direct or ongoing communication was noticeably uneven. While almost a quarter of the candidate websites surveyed offered visitors some way to receive e-mail from the candidate, the percentage of those offering campaign materials through offline means (post, facsimile, etc.) was somewhat lower. Rather than offering opportunities for online participation in the election (as the number of candidates with discussion forums or e-paraphernalia on their websites was quite low), candidates tended to include engagement features on their websites that channeled citizen participation into traditional forms such as joining the candidate's campaign organization (22 percent) or volunteering to help out with the campaign (18 percent). Although legal restrictions preventing candidates from individually soliciting donations for their campaigns were eased in 2001, few candidates supplied information about donating on their websites.

Table 15.3 Electoral information features by producer type (2004 Upper House election, Japan)

Political actor/features*	Candidate (51)	Government (12)	NPO/NGO/ Labor union (18)	Other** (7)	Party (4)	Press (3)	Total (95)
Biographical information	1.00 (51)	0.42 (5)	0.94 (17)	0.86 (6)	0.75 (3)	0.00 (0)	0.86 (82)
Endorsements	0.29 (15)	0.00 (0)	0.17 (3)	0.00 (0)	0.25 (1)	0.00 (0)	0.20 (19)
Issue positions	0.96 (50)	0.00 (0)	0.61 (11)	0.14 (1)	1.00 (4)	0.00 (0))	0.69 (66)
Speeches	0.10 (5)	0.00 (0)	0.00 (0)	0.00 (0)	0.50 (2)	0.00 (0)	0.07 (7)
Events	0.33 (17)	0.33 (4)	0.28 (5)	0.14 (1)	0.75 (3)	0.00 (0)	0.32 (30)
Issue comparisons	0.02 (1)	0.00 (0)	0.11 (2)	0.14 (1)	0.00 (0)	0.33 (1)	0.05 (5)
Electoral process	0.00 (0)	0.50 (6)	0.06 (1)	0.00 (0)	0.00 (0)	0.33 (1)	0.02 (2)
Voting process	0.04 (2)	0.75 (9)	0.06 (1)	0.14 (1)	0.00 (0)	0.00 (0)	0.04 (4)
Images	1.00 (51)	1.00 (12)	0.78 (14)	0.57 (4)	0.75 (3)	0.67 (2)	0.24 (23)
Audio/visual	0.22 (11)	0.08 (1)	0.06 (1)	0.00 (0)	0.25 (1)	0.00 (0)	0.15 (14)
Privacy policy	0.02 (1)	0.00 (0)	0.06 (1)	0.14 (1)	0.50 (2)	1.00 (3)	0.05 (5)
Terms of use	0.00 (0)	0.00 (0)	0.11 (2)	0.00 (0)	0.50 (2)	0.33 (1)	0.05 (5)
Total							95

Notes
* Number of sites per political actor noted in parentheses.
** "Other" includes business, citizen, educational, political professional, portal, and religious producers.

Table 15.4 Engagement features by producer type (2004 Upper House election, Japan)

Political actor/features*	Candidate (51)	Government (12)	NPO/NGO/Labor union (18)	Other** (7)	Party (4)	Press (3)	Total (95)
Contact	0.94 (48)	1.00 (12)	1.00 (18)	0.86 (6)	1.00 (4)	0.67 (2)	0.95 (90)
Join	0.22 (11)	0.00 (0)	0.44 (8)	0.14 (1)	0.75 (3)	0.00 (0)	0.24 (23)
Register	0.00 (0)	0.00 (0)	0.00 (0)	0.00 (0)	0.00 (0)	0.00 (0)	0.00 (0)
Get mail	0.24 (12)	0.00 (0)	0.11 (2)	0.14 (1)	0.75 (3)	0.00 (0)	0.19 (18)
Donate	0.14 (7)	0.00 (0)	0.28 (5)	0.00 (0)	0.50 (2)	0.00 (0)	0.14 (15)
Forum	0.10 (5)	0.00 (0)	0.11 (2)	0.29 (2)	0.00 (0)	0.00 (0)	0.09 (9)
Offline distribution	0.14 (7)	0.50 (6)	0.60 (1)	0.14 (1)	0.75 (3)	0.00 (0)	0.19 (18)
Send links	0.02 (1)	0.00 (0)	0.00 (0)	0.00 (0)	0.00 (0)	0.00 (0)	0.01 (1)
Public support	0.16 (8)	0.00 (0)	0.00 (0)	0.00 (0)	0.25 (1)	0.00 (0)	0.09 (9)
E-paraphernalia	0.02 (1)	0.00 (0)	0.00 (0)	0.00 (0)	0.00 (0)	0.00 (0)	0.01 (1)
Volunteer	0.18 (9)	0.00 (0)	0.06 (1)	0.00 (0)	0.25 (1)	0.00 (0)	0.12 (11)
Total							95

Notes
* Number of sites per political actor noted in parentheses.
** "Other" includes business, citizen, educational, political professional, portal, and religious producers.

The contents of political party websites during this election period mirrored those of the candidates in a number of respects. Here again, as with candidate websites, the political parties included background information such as party history, issue positions, and event information, and avoided issue comparisons or any type of information concerning the electoral process or voting. Since most political party websites included some type of online form for viewers to subscribe to the party e-mail newsletter or send opinions to the party, at least half of the party websites surveyed also posted privacy or terms-of-use policies.

Political party websites also included a high number of features aimed at engaging the public in the election campaign. All party websites included some type of contact information, and the majority allowed viewers to join the party organization, subscribe to e-mail newsletters, and receive campaign materials offline. Yet party websites were noticeably lacking in more technologically advanced ways of using their sites for campaigning; none of the sites surveyed included any form of e-paraphernalia or allowed voters to send links to others. As has been the case since the 2000 election campaign period, none of the parties offered discussion forums or links to such forums on their sites.

Further evidence of a demarcation of campaign roles was found on the websites produced by government-related bodies and the press. Websites produced by governments, newspapers, and television stations avoided issue comparisons and instead focused on the electoral and voting process (government-related websites) and issue comparisons (press-related websites) to a limited extent. The aim of these websites was mainly to inform the voters with this type of information in a top-down manner, as sites created by these producers also featured the least number of engagement features.

The role of informing the public regarding electoral and voting processes rests with the national-level Ministry of Internal Affairs and Communications, which is affiliated with the Association for Promoting Fair Elections (*Akaruisenkyo*) – a quasi-governmental entity that promotes involvement in elections through voting in elections at all levels. In addition to basic procedural information, the website for this organization[6] also includes voting statistics and links to the sites of local election management boards throughout the country, mainly at the prefecture level. Sites for these local election management boards comprised the majority of government-related websites surveyed during this election. In contrast to the active campaigning engaged in by political parties and candidates through their websites, the contents of the majority of these websites focused on electoral and voting processes; many also included voting statistics for their respective prefectures or large metropolitan areas. While all of these government-related websites offered some means of contacting the organization directly (many in the form of a telephone or facsimile number that voters could use to get further information), only half allowed for means to distribute election-related information offline.

Clear demarcations in the role of informing the public regarding the election or allowing direct participation either in the organization itself or through its website were apparent in the websites produced by the Japanese press and media. Japan's national press and broadcasting media historically have been noticeably objective during election campaign periods, partly because of the strict guidelines contained in the POEL concerning the publication of advance polls and election projections, but also because of the centralized structure of the Japanese media itself. Since the 2000 election, all of Japan's major newspapers have offered election-specific sections on their websites, posting major news stories concerning the campaign, reporting on campaign activities undertaken in various constituencies throughout the country (mainly focusing on key races), and providing lists of candidates, their ages, former professions, and constituencies. Yet the media has maintained its traditionally impartial stance concerning endorsements, issue positions, and coverage of speeches, as these features were not present on press websites. Engagement-related features were also noticeably absent; none of the media websites offered discussion forums or opportunities for posting public support statements.

While candidate and political party websites featured contents directly relating to the campaign itself, and government and press-related websites focused on background and supplementary information, the contents of the websites produced by non-traditional political actors such as NPOs, NGOs, labor unions, and other producers were decidedly mixed. The websites identified for this survey that were created by NGOs/NPOs are the online equivalents of citizen-run organizations that have become more popular in Japan in the past decade. Perhaps the most successful of these is the website created by the Promote Committee of Online Election [*sic*] (*On-Line Election suishin iinkai*),[7] run by a citizens' group based in Fukuoka, Kyushu. This group's website featured results of all national-level elections since 2000, a discussion forum, e-mail newsletters, links to political parties and news organizations, lists of constituencies, and links to candidate websites. Visitors could participate in public opinion polls conducted at regular intervals, submit e-mail to the candidates, and link directly to their websites. During the 2004 election campaign period, this group recognized the growing popularity of blogging, establishing a sister website called "Ele-log" ("Election Log")[8] on 10 June 2004, which features a number of individual weblogs created by candidates.

In general, other politically active NPOs and NGOs offered a variety of information- and engagement-related features on their websites. Similar to candidate and political party websites, a high percentage of those created by NPO/NGO organizations featured an "About us" section listing profile information and issue positions. Almost a third also included information concerning campaign-related events. These organizations also encouraged engagement through contacting, joining, or donating. While labor unions in other countries may assume a political role, mainly by endorsing certain political parties or candidates, this is not the case in Japan, as labor unions are mainly enterprise-based. In another example of how the Japanese web sphere tends to mirror real-life politics, sites created by these organizations had markedly little politically oriented information about the election.

As noted earlier, there were few websites produced by "other" political actors in the Japanese web sphere during this election campaign period. The lack of sites produced by businesses, political professionals, and religious organizations mirrors these producers' low level of involvement in the "offline" political sphere. Politically oriented websites produced by individual citizens were also low in number, possibly because of the technical expertise required to produce them and uncertainty regarding their content in the light of the strict guidelines of the POEL. Yet, despite the small scale of this portion of the Japanese political web sphere, producers in this category offered a number of engagement features on their websites, most markedly in terms of providing discussion forums.

Conclusion: an expanding web sphere?

In this chapter, I examined how certain dynamics of the "offline" political context may affect "online" campaigning. One particularly influential aspect of Japan's political context has been the continued application of regulatory provisions concerning election campaigning to web-based political campaigns. These regulations have had a decided effect as to how Japanese political actors use their websites for campaign information provision and engagement with the electorate. The results of the content analysis of information and engagement features found on the websites produced by political parties and candidates suggests that while they were the most active in the Japanese political web sphere, their contents tended to reflect traditional forms of campaigning and conformed to current interpretations of the POEL with regard to online campaigning.

Through the identification and examination of sites created by other producers within the Japanese web sphere, it is clear that other political actors are also utilizing this new medium in ways that reflect their "offline" campaign roles. Government-produced websites tended to focus on providing general background information regarding the election, the electoral process, and voting procedures. Press-related websites appeared to follow traditional patterns of providing background information (such as lists of candidates and constituencies), but did not offer many opportunities for the electorate to become actively engaged.

However, although limited numbers of NPO, NGO, and labor union websites offered election-related information and engagement features, those that did also appeared to participate actively in informing the public – particularly in terms of issue comparisons. Although the sample size for other producers was rather small, their participation in the election through their websites in areas such as providing discussion forums and other engagement features suggests future expansion of the Japanese political web sphere among these non-traditional political actors.

While to date the POEL has provided a set of boundaries on the Japanese political web sphere in terms of campaigning on the web, this situation may change over time. As discussed above, through the special investigative committee concerning the role of information technology in elections, the government has recognized the potential – and the pitfalls – of online campaigns. Its growing acceptance and use among political actors may lead to future revisions. The speed of technological change with regard to ICTs and the rapid rate of adoption of related technologies such as mobile telephones and blogging are areas that may need to be addressed in the future, as the increasing importance of information technology spreads throughout Japanese society. With the appearance of these new technological tools, it is quite likely that the Japanese political web sphere will expand in subsequent election campaigns.

Notes

1 The author compiled the data concerning website utilization among candidates during each election cycle in 2001, 2003, and 2004. Given the lack of an official list of candidates' website addresses, the author used a combination of resources to obtain as accurate a list as possible for each election. Approximately one month prior to the election, the author consulted the listing of candidates posted on the *Mainichi Shimbun* (Mainichi Newspaper) website. This listing was used to generate a preliminary list of candidates. Their website addresses were added by consulting political party websites (for candidates who belonged to or were endorsed by political parties) and also searching for links to candidate websites available at on www.election.co.jp, a non-partisan political portal website. To resolve any missing or conflicting website addresses, the author also performed online searches for candidate sites using Google Japan (www.google.co.jp) and Yahoo! Japan (www.yahoo.co.jp) by inputting the candidate's surname, first name, and the phrase *senkyo* (election) in Japanese characters. The data gathered refer only to the candidate's official website and do not include sites produced by fans or sites hosted on government servers.
2 www.yahoo.co.jp.
3 www.excite.co.jp.
4 www.akaruisenkyo.or.jp.
5 www.webarchivist.org.
6 www.akaruisenkyo.or.jp.
7 www.election.co.jp.
8 www.election.ne.jp.

References

Bimber, B. and Davis, R. (2003) *Campaigning Online: The Internet in U.S. Elections.* New York: Oxford University Press.
Curtis, G. (1971) *Election Campaigning Japanese Style.* New York: Columbia University Press.
Davis, R. (1999) *The Web of Politics: The Internet's Impact on the American Political System.* New York: Oxford University Press.
Flanagan, S.C. and Reed, S.R. (1996) "Politics in Japan," in G.A. Almond and G.B.

Powell Jr (eds), *Comparative Politics Today: A World View*, pp. 327–379. New York: Harper Collins.

Gibson, R., Nixon, P., and Ward, S. (2003) *Political Parties and the Internet: Net Gain?* London: Routledge.

Hayashida, K. (1967) "Development of election law in Japan," *Hosei Kenkyu*, 34: 1–54.

Intanetto Hakusho (1998) *Internet White Paper*. Tokyo: Impress.

Intanetto Hakusho (2001) *Internet White Paper*. Tokyo: Impress.

Iwanami Shoten (2002) *Konpakuto Roppo Heisei 14 nen (2002)* [Compact Book of Six Laws, 2002 Edition]. Tokyo: Iwanami Shoten.

Mainichi Newspaper (2000) "'Senkyo' shugisen, netto johosen mo honban shimin dantai tsugitsugi to rakusen koho risuto nado kouhyou" [Citizen groups make black lists of candidates available on the Internet], 1 June.

Margolis, M. and Resnick, D. (2000) *Politics as Usual: The Cyberspace "Revolution."* Thousand Oaks, CA: Sage Publications.

Miyoshi, Y. (1996) "'Denno senkyo' ni jichisho ga 'no' – homupeji wa kosenho no kisei taisho" [Ministry of Home Affairs says "no" to cyberelections, aims POEL at homepages], *Mainichi Shimbun* [*Mainichi Newspaper*], 30 October

16 Web sphere analysis for political websites

The 2004 National Assembly election in South Korea

Hyo Kim and Han Woo Park

Introduction

As information technology has spread, politicians and political parties have used the internet to interact with their current and potential supporters (Abramson and Arterton 1988; Davis 1999).[1] The power of the internet to increase support has become so important that the internet is now actively used in producing, archiving, and disseminating political information for issues and agendas that had been traditionally alienated or even abandoned by previous campaigns (McCaughy and Ayers 2003). Especially during election periods, the internet takes on an important role as a means of managing public relations by campaign managers and politicians, and raising issues by NGOs and common citizens (Benoit and Benoit 2000; Foot *et al.* 2003; Schneider and Foot 2003).

This chapter is a part of efforts to compare political uses of the World Wide Web among the countries in Europe, North America, and Asia in order to understand how the political role of the internet differs across nations. More specifically, the following two research questions drive the results presented in this chapter.

1 What was the political use of the internet during the seventeenth national election in South Korea?
2 How does the existence of certain types of website features relate to Korean political culture?

The chapter is organized as follows. First, we discuss some of the pre-election politics in Korea as well as relevant aspects of Korean political culture. Next, we analyze a number of websites in order to demonstrate the role of communication technology during the election campaign. We will then discuss the information and engagement features in the sample sites. This section will focus on features and issues unique to the South Korean web sphere. Next, we discuss legal and regulatory issues affecting political websites. Finally, we offer some general conclusions concerning the South Korean political web sphere.

Pre-election politics and the 2004 election

Compared to previous elections, political campaigns for the 2004 parliamentary election in South Korea were mostly conducted at the party level. While presidential elections in the country are generally focused on the competition between parties, parliamentary elections are much more candidate driven, where individual candidates compete to win a seat at the National Assembly with relatively little emphasis on party affiliation. However, the presidential impeachment that preceded the 2004 National Assembly elections changed this pattern. The impeachment process effectively divided the country into two camps: pro-Roh and anti-Roh. This greatly influenced voters to choose candidates based upon their party affiliation rather than their personal qualifications as lawmakers. This also meant that party websites became more prominent than individual candidate sites, as had been the case previously (Kang 2004).

After the inauguration, President Roh embarked upon a campaign of reform, which would affect many politicians across political party lines. Only a fraction of young and reformist politicians supported the president's position. Conflict within his own party over reforms divided the *Saechun-nyun-Min-Ju* (SMJ, Millennium Democratic Party) into two factions. Roh resigned his membership of the SMJ and remained neutral in the subsequent electoral campaign. The majority of the politicians in SMJ, who were composed of many vested interests, remained within the SMJ. A number of young politicians who supported the president's position created a new political party, the *Yeollin-Uri* (YU, Open Party for Everybody). This split in effect turned the ruling party into a minority party. Even though President Rho did not join the YU party, he was considered its practical leader.

The unprecedented presidential impeachment on 12 March 2004, only one month before the 15 April national election, resulted in the suspension of President Roh and prevented completion of the rest of his term. As a result, the impeachment became the main issue during the campaign. A major opposition party, Han-Na-Ra (HNR, Grand National Party), along with SMJ, which had initiated and strongly pushed for the impeachment, emphasized that their action was unavoidable because of the president's arrogant violation of the Constitution. One of the most serious charges was that Roh had been involved in partisan politics. Unlike many Western democracies, Korean election law prohibits the president from being involved in political activities during election periods.

Other events after this political split did not help the president. His political aides were accused of raising illegal political funds. The president's brother was also accused of receiving "black money," or illegal contributions. Political opponents argued that the president was aware of all of these activities.

In addition, even though the president was not an actual member of the YU party and election law prohibited him and other administration personnel from being involved in any sort of election campaigning, the president made official speeches in support of the YU party. In March, the National Election Commission (NEC) ruled that Roh had violated the law prohibiting partisan activities while holding the presidency. As a result, the opposition camps, which united conservative newspapers such as *Chosun ilbo* and *Dong-a ilbo* and the political parties HNR and SMJ, urged the president to make an apology to the public for this infraction. While he addressed the issue in a speech, he did not apologize. Rather, he suggested that conservative media were placing unnecessary blame on him and urged the need for reform.

After his speech, two political opponents, the HNR and SMJ parties, combined forces in order to push for an impeachment. The sixteenth National Assembly passed the impeachment with 193 in favor and only two opposing votes on 12 March 2004, a month before the National Assembly election scheduled to be held on 15 April. The YU party and its supporters severely criticized the HNR, and argued that the impeachment process was actually a coup masquerading as majority democracy. Further, they argued that the impeachment was against the will of the people, and framed the upcoming April election as a national referendum on the impeachment itself. The YU party website argued the impeachment was unjust, with captions such as "Judge the impeachment" and "Preserve the democracy." Thus, the 2004 election became a place for the South Korean public to reveal their opinions regarding the impeachment, since the result of the election could influence whether or not the impeachment would be upheld.

As early as the presidential election of 2000, civilians and NGOs used the internet to organize political activities. One group, calling itself the "alliance of citizenships for the general election" used the internet specifically to expose politicians, many of whom had secret histories of criminal records, tax evasion, and other unlawful and unethical activities. The list was widely distributed throughout the country, although in 2001 the Supreme Court deemed that such distribution constituted unlawful activity. Nevertheless, the internet quickly became an effective channel for providing information on unsavory politicians. Since then, the NEC has investigated politicians' backgrounds, examining their military service, possible criminal activity, and financial records. This was also attempted during the 2004 election, to less effect, because many of the worst offending politicians had already been screened out by earlier investigations.

Producers of the South Korean electoral web sphere

The Internet and Elections Project was launched shortly before the Korean national election campaign started. A systematic procedure was employed to identify sites comprising the country's parliamentary election web sphere in an attempt to identify as many websites as possible produced by all types of political actors relevant to the election. We designed the following sleuthing strategy.

First, we identified 440 candidate websites.[2] These were websites run by those nominated by the ruling party, YU, and the major opposition party, the HNR. Second, we identified all party websites hyperlinked from the NEC website. Third, we recorded sites belonging to groups affiliated with the "Red Card 2004," a representative body of the civic and advocacy groups conducting a rejection campaign against unfit candidates. Fourth, government websites mentioned on the NEC site were added to the list of identified websites. Fifth, the NEC identified more than 100 websites as "internet press," and these were included in our identification procedure.

This sleuthing strategy uncovered a number of websites produced by parties, businesses, candidates, government, labor unions, non-governmental organizations, portals, press organizations, and religious groups. Finally, we searched South Korean-specific domains using the Korean word for "election" on two search engines (www.daum.net and kr.yahoo.com) to identify additional sites for the analysis.

A total of 959 websites were identified as potentially containing electoral content and information services. Almost 10 percent of the identified websites (90 out 959) were included in a coding sample using a combination method of stratified and expert judgment sampling techniques. More specifically, all party websites – except for those that were not functioning at the time of this study – were part of the sample. Nearly 10 percent of candidate websites (37 out of 440) were selected. We identified all sites between 24 March and 6 April, and coded them in the period 7–14 April. Table 16.1 and Figure 16.1 summarize the sites identified by producer type. Six categories emerged: candidate, government, NGO/labor, party, press, and others. Since non-governmental organizations and labor unions are politically active in South Korea, they were identified as one category. All other types such as portals, political professionals sites, educational sites, and citizens' sites were categorized as "other."

Table 16.1 Political sites identified and included in sample

Producer type	Identified	Sample
Candidate	440	37
Government	94	11
NGO/Labor	208	5
	4	0
	22	2
Other	16	5
	23	8
	8	1
	4	3
Party	10	9
Press	130	9
Total	959	90

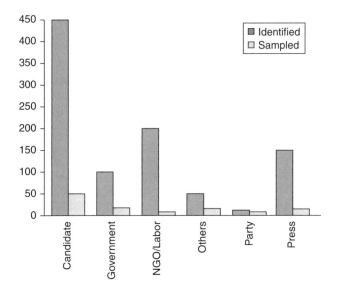

Figure 16.1 Political websites producers in South Korea, identified and sampled.

Information features in the political web sphere

Table 16.2 contains an overview of the different types of information provided by each type of website producer within the South Korean electoral
web sphere. It summarizes the information-related codes, organizing them
by producer type. The first column identifies the number of websites within
each category represented in the data set. All other cell entries represent the
proportion of websites within each category.

As shown in Table 16.2, political parties were the most active information content providers among all political actors in the sample. Party websites had the highest proportion: eight out of 13 categories. All of the party
websites examined included features from the following five categories: election content; biography/history/about us; endorsements for a candidate or
party; a list of issue positions held by a political actor; speeches by a candidate or party representatives; and images. Party sites had the highest percentage of five other types of features, although not all of these sites
contained the features or made them accessible. These included a calendar or
list with prospective election-related events (eight of the nine sites), issue
positions of parties or candidates (all nine sites), comparison of their positions to those espoused by their opponents (two of the nine sites), information about electoral campaign process (6 of the 9 sites), and information
about the voting process (six of the nine sites).

It is intriguing that only a small number of party websites provided a

Table 16.2 Information features in South Korean electoral web sphere

Pro type	ELC	BIO	END	ISPO	SPCH	CAL	COM	INFC	INFY	IMG	AV	PRV	TRM
Can (37)	1 (37)	1 (37)	0.54 (20)	0.97 (36)	0.86 (32)	0.65 (24)	0.14 (5)	0.32 (12)	0.24 (9)	1 (37)	0.92 (34)	0.05 (2)	0.41 (15)
Gov (11)	0.55 (6)	1 (11)	0 (0)	0 (0)	0 (0)	0.18 (2)	0.18 (2)	0.27 (3)	0.27 (3)	1 (11)	0.73 (8)	0.73 (8)	1 (11)
N/L (7)	0.71 (5)	1 (7)	0 (0)	0 (0)	0 (0)	0 (0)	0 (0)	0 (0)	0 (0)	0.86 (6)	0 (0)	0 (0)	0.57 (4)
Other (17)	0.88 (15)	0.82 (14)	0 (0)	0.24 (4)	0.12 (2)	0.24 (4)	0.06 (1)	0.24 (4)	0.29 (5)	0.94 (16)	0.47 (8)	0.47 (8)	0.82 (14)
Party (9)	1 (9)	1 (9)	1 (9)	1 (9)	1 (9)	0.89 (8)	0.22 (2)	0.67 (6)	0.67 (6)	1 (9)	0.89 (8)	0.33 (3)	0.89 (8)
Press (9)	0.56 (5)	0.67 (6)	0 (0)	0 (0)	0.11 (1)	0.22 (2)	0 (0)	0.22 (2)	0 (0)	1 (9)	0.11 (1)	0.22 (2)	0.44 (4)
Total (90)	0.86 (77)	0.93 (84)	0.32 (29)	0.54 (49)	0.49 (44)	0.44 (40)	0.11 (10)	0.3 (27)	0.26 (23)	0.98 (88)	0.66 (59)	0.26 (23)	0.62 (56)

Notes

1 Total number of each producer type is indicated in parentheses in the first column.
2 For each producer type, proportion score (the number of sites containing the column specific information/total number of a specific producer type) is listed.
3 The absolute number of each producer type is shown in the parentheses in each column (except the first column).

Abbreviations and descriptions of features:

Can	Candidates	ELC	Election
Gov	Government	BIO	Biography/History/About us
N/L	NGO/Labor	END	Endorsement
Other	Other	ISPO	Issue positions
Party	Parties	SPCH	Speech
Press	Press	CAL	Calendar
		COM	Comparison
		INFC	Information about electoral campaign process
		INFY	Information about voting process
		IMG	Images
		AV	Audio/Video
		PRV	Privacy policy
		TRM	Terms of use

comparison of their own issue stances to those of their opponents. Korean political parties tend to focus on discussion of specific issues rather than providing a comparison of their policies to those of other parties. The results suggest that the web has created a channel in which Korean parties provide site visitors with their own campaign information as much as possible, while omitting comparisons to competitors.

However, there are two other possible explanations. First, these findings may be an indication that parties in Korea do not differ from each other much in terms of ideological stance. That is, offering site visitors a comparison to other parties or other candidates might not be that effective inasmuch as their stances could be seen as relatively similar. This explanation is consistent with the findings of Park *et al.* (2005) who examined websites produced by Korean congressional members during 2003. They found that politicians mostly employed the internet as an informational tool that facilitated contact with constituents and supporters.

A second explanation for these findings might be that Korean politics is now focused more on image politics rather than issue politics. According to Table 16.2, both political parties and candidates provide a large amount of audio/video materials via their websites. These materials were usually songs, campaign dance steps, and the speeches of political leaders and candidates using streaming-video, content with more focus on promotion of politician/party images rather than issues.

Political leaders in South Korea have been traditionally depicted as patriarchal figures for the regions they represent and have tried to use their power to mold the population ideologically in their territories. Most South Korean parties are not based on the shared political beliefs or values among people, but on regional affiliation. Thus, aspiring candidates must seek the endorsement of a political party organized by a leader who is influential in that constituency. Getting a nomination from a territorially based party, therefore, is critical to winning a seat. This is unlike most Western countries, such as the U.K. and the U.S., where parties have long histories and maintain strong ideological boundaries.

This is likely to influence the political deployment of the internet in the Korean web space. Since the degree to which pairs of parties are different in terms of their political stances is relatively low, electoral websites do not readily expose comparisons between one party and another. Rather, a greater amount of content centers around features that embody and exemplify social and political stability, and the abilities of the governors to safeguard the welfare and the security of the citizenry in line with the expectations of a number of Asian polities (Kluver and Banerjee 2005). It is not just ruling parties who take this attitude, but also opposition actors. Within the Korean cultural framework (Confucianism), politics has always been oriented toward a certain social harmony and democratic order to provide a safe environment to pursue personal economic goals.

Governmental websites ranked first in terms of the presence of privacy policies, which contain legal information as to how a website producer will protect a user's information (government: eight of 11 sites), (other: eight of 17 sites), (party: three of nine sites), (press: two of nine sites), (candidate: two of 37 sites), (NGO/labor: zero sites). This is in stark contrast to candidate websites, which included far fewer privacy policies. This might be because candidates have privacy policies incorporated into their terms of use, and so they do not see a need for an explicit statement. Alternatively, some of them may regard their websites as only temporary sites for use during the electoral campaign, and thus have not invested the time in creating a clear privacy policy.

The types of information from parties and candidates included text, photos, graphics, and multimedia files. A wide variety of service types such as Video-on-Demand (VOD), flash animations, and music are possible because of the rapid adoption of internet technologies and the installation of a network infrastructure in South Korea. As mentioned earlier, these types of technological developments have encouraged the widespread use of candidates' image appeal during campaigns, especially in the hopes of gaining the attention of young people in their twenties and thirties. Parties competed to provide various animations and graphic images promoting their candidates. Further, attractive female party members were appointed as "cyber spokeswomen," and their photos were made available on these websites.

Other important features, such as promotions encouraging people to vote, and information about election-related events, issue positions, electoral campaigns, and the voting process were also prevalent on the websites produced by parties and candidates. While candidate websites tended to maintain election content for their own constituencies, party sites functioned mainly as portals for the general public as well as their members.

Portals, political professionals, educational, and citizen producers (classified as "other actors") provided the most varied types of information on their websites. Government agencies and the press followed. NGO and labor organizations provided the least varied kinds of content features. In the past, these actors were more likely to promote the election campaign via traditional media, such as newspaper advertisements and pamphlets. Now, however, an increasing number of people and organizations devote more energy and time to online campaigns. This may reflect a growing belief in South Korea that online services will stimulate a greater interest in the general election than traditional media will.

Engagement features in the political web sphere

Table 16.3 summarizes the engagement features of different types of web producers during the 2004 election and suggests that party sites were the most active in providing engagement features. Providing various channels of engagement, parties aimed to distribute information and issues both within

Table 16.3 Engagement features in South Korean electoral web sphere

Pro type	CON	JOIN	REG	EMS	DON	FOR	OFFD	SLNK	PUBS	EPA	VOL
Can (37)	0.86 (32)	0.59 (22)	0.19 (7)	0.46 (17)	0.76 (28)	1 (37)	0.38 (14)	0.14 (5)	0.38 (14)	0.14 (5)	0.51 (19)
Gov (11)	1 (11)	0.27 (3)	0.27 (3)	0.82 (9)	0 (0)	1 (11)	0 (0)	0 (0)	0 (0)	0 (0)	0 (0)
N/L (7)	1 (07)	0.43 (3)	0 (0)	0.14 (1)	0.29 (2)	1 (7)	0 (0)	0 (0)	0 (0)	0 (0)	0.43 (3)
Other (17)	0.88 (15)	0.65 (11)	0.06 (1)	0.41 (7)	0 (0)	0.88 (15)	0 (0)	0 (0)	0 (0)	0 (0)	0 (0)
Party (9)	1 (09)	1 (09)	0.56 (5)	0.78 (7)	0.89 (8)	1 (9)	0.89 (8)	0.11 (1)	0.22 (2)	0.56 (5)	0.33 (3)
Press (9)	0.78 (7)	0.44 (4)	0 (0)	0.33 (3)	0 (0)	0.78 (7)	0 (0)	0 (0)	0.11 (1)	0 (0)	0 (0)
Total (90)	0.90 (81)	0.58 (52)	0.18 (16)	0.49 (44)	0.42 (38)	0.96 (86)	0.24 (22)	0.07 (6)	0.19 (17)	0.11 (10)	0.28 (25)

Notes
1 Total number of each producer type is indicated in parentheses in the first column.
2 For each producer type, proportion score (the number of sites containing the column specific information/total number of a specific producer type) is listed.
3 The absolute number of each producer type is shown in the parentheses in each column (except the first column).

Abbreviations and descriptions of features:

Can	Candidates	CON	Contact information
Gov	Government	JOIN	Join
N/L	NGO/Labor	REG	Registration
Other	Other	EMS	E-mail subscription
Party	Parties	DON	Donation
Press	Press	FOR	Forum, BBS, chatting, poll
		OFFD	Offline distribution
		SLNK	Send links to others
		PUBS	Public support statement
		EPA	E-paraphernalia (e.g. RSS feed, screensaver, wallpaper)
		VOL	Volunteer

their sites (e.g. through forums) and externally through offline distribution (OFFD – offline distribution). Candidates provided three engagement features more than parties did: SLNK (send links), PUBS (public support statement), and VOL (volunteering). These kinds of engagement features, of course, were ones that the candidates needed to campaign successfully. Government sites provided more features, such as links to voting registration, and descriptive information about how to register.

The most common features across the producer types enabled communication between site visitors or between visitors and producers. These included forums, BBS (bulletin board system), chatting systems, and public poll services. Through these channels, political figures were able to converse about issues, debate with people, and listen to comments on their policies. As these sites fostered logical and intensive debates between people who supported different candidates and parties, they potentially could deliver much more valuable information to voters than the traditional media could.

Some practices appeared that were relatively new phenomena for the 2004 election. The first was the distribution of election or campaign materials for offline use. These materials often consisted of magazine-style collections of voting guides, election schedules, and posters. A second new practice was e-paraphernalia, or online campaign materials like webcasts, which enabled the users to engage in digital promotion of the electoral campaign.

One candidate created an opportunistic engagement feature that built upon the networked nature of campaigns. Duk-Hong Yoon's site provided a web page where visitors could sign up acquaintances that lived in his district, so that they, too, could receive e-mail newsletters about his campaign. However, privacy concerns meant that this feature was not present on the websites of most other candidates. Five of the 37 candidate sites and one of the nine party sites provided "send links" on their sites. Some candidates persuaded visitors to leave messages of endorsement on their websites.

Other issues: the press, legal and regulatory issues

A variety of other technological tools were utilized during this campaign, including CRM (customer relation management) software, UMS (unified messaging system) tools, CTI (computer telephone integration), and real-time public polls. The press and political parties highlighted companies specializing in integrating these kinds of services into the campaign. For example, e-win.com, which was mostly known as an offline campaign consultant during the 2004 election, emphasized the online services they offered. For these corporations, collecting e-mail addresses and securing them as a database for distributing campaign information became an important issue.[3]

Perhaps one of the most distinguishing features of the Korean online press is that they provide relatively flexible forums (e.g. discussion boards, bulletin board systems) for essentially every article and event. Each newspaper company tends to support a party and have a clear political inclination. Thus, regular readers for each newspaper are dominant in expressing their opinions in the article forums. However, visitors who support different parties often visit and leave contrary opinions. Since forum users can post anonymously, "flaming," especially around political and campaign issues, is common.

Right before the election, the EAC (Election Administration Commission) announced plans to require forum visitors to use their real names when posting. If the law had come into effect, the forum system administrators would have been required to create a device checking forum users' real identities whenever messages were posted; the law allowed for imposition of fines up to ten million won (approximately U.S.$10,000). These plans were made in an improvised manner and soon ran into severe opposition from the Korean Online Newspaper Association (KONS), many netizens, and press associations and NGOs, such as the National Human Right Commission of Korea (NHRC).[4] The argument by KONS against the proposed ruling included three points:

- The law should be universally applicable, and not enforced only for the election. KONS suggested that if the law went into effect, many unpredicted side effects would emerge.
- The proposal regulated, "anyone who practices internet journalism," a difficult entity to define. The term "internet journalism" was not clear; KONS wondered whether journals, broadcasts, or other technologies would be included. They worried that the law might be misused to regulate freedom of speech.
- The proposed law was unnecessary, as many newspapers already collected offline information about their users. Thus, the real identities of individuals could already be determined, even when pseudonyms were used or when postings to forums were placed anonymously.

One internet newspaper opposed to the law, *OhMyNews*, reviewed the issues regarding internet identity and voluntarily provided two versions of forums for each article – one for registered users and the other for anonymous users. *OhMyNews*, which provided only online news materials, found itself in an awkward situation. On one hand, according to the Periodicals Law, it was not considered a periodical (journalistic medium) since it did not produce any offline materials. This prevented it from running political interviews and political advertisements. However, when the EAC (Election Administration Commission) law was proposed, that law was designed to include *OhMyNews*. As a result, such laws regulate *OhMyNews* in a double manner – one regulates it as an offline periodical: the other regulates it as an online periodical. In February 2004, *OhMyNews* solved this problem by creating a weekly magazine called *Weekly OhMyNews*. It has been printed regularly, but a physical version has never been sold. Because of the stiff opposition to the proposed law, the EAC later abandoned it.

Sites running parodies of political candidates or events also became popular. Among others, one site originally designed to discuss new technologies in digital cameras, dcinside.com, provided a forum, "current affairs," in which the users could upload their pictures regarding current affairs. Visitors used this forum to upload original compositions, which often took the form of parodies. One particular composite picture showed two political criminals being questioned in front of a detective's typewriter. One character says, "I just did a political wrongdoing with this woman." Those two characters depicted are the politicians who played active roles in the impeachment. Another picture depicted another political figure who headed the impeachment for the SMJ party. It describes him as "The Lord of the Impeachment," a reference to the film *The Lord of the Rings*.

Conclusion

In summary, we found that the internet was a major means to organize and disseminate information by political parties in South Korea during the 2004 parliamentary election. Several activities were organized and executed by the parties rather than by individual candidates. The information available from these political websites ranged from text and graphics to multimedia, the latter made possible by Korea's high-speed communication network. The internet also emerged as a powerful political channel for participatory politics. Civic and advocacy groups maneuvered for better politics by publishing a "black list" on the internet, disclosing details of candidate backgrounds, such as criminal and tax evasion records, and by encouraging younger voters (20- to 30-year olds) participation in the election. Even though the Supreme Court ruled that the civic campaign against targeted candidates was illegal, the results of the campaign had remarkable consequences. Younger voters opposed the presidential impeachment that occurred immediately before the parliamentary election. This incident also initiated formation of civic movements that encouraged voting against the responsible parties. These movements urged young people to take part in the presidential polls via the internet and mobile phones. All of these efforts were made possible by the rise of the internet and new communication technologies. We believe that the internet played a major role in such movements and contributed to a better political and electoral system.

The election campaigns on the websites of South Korean parties were, in general, much more visible and popular than the electoral web spheres of many other countries. Some parties even created election websites that carried only electoral materials. The sites that political parties created were most significant in terms of the volume of information-related content, the types of services engaging visitors, and the availability of hyperlinks. The party sites provided a wide variety of information about candidates and policies. These offered various services encouraging visitors to take part in the election and vote for their candidates. Party sites were not only content- and service-rich but also better organized in terms of hyperlink structure. There was a very visible out-linking to political actors comprising the election web sphere. In addition, there were a number of hyperlinks flowing to the political parties rather than being exchanged directly among the candidates. This indicates that the party's role as the information provider hub was dominant. In other words, political parties positioned their websites as political portals for the general public as well as for politicians.

Although civic and advocacy groups in the sample were not active producers in terms of the different types of the information and engagement features they offered, their involvement in institutionalized politics was significant within the context of the competitive political culture between parties and candidates. The internet emerged as a powerful political channel in the diffusion of information through rather unorganized movements. The publication of the "black list" disclosing political candidate misconduct provided evidence that the internet can be a powerful weapon for "grassroots" democracy. Since the black listing movement in 2001, the NEC has offered detailed information about candidates on the electoral roll, including records about income, military service, and tax status. The emergence of internet journalism was also noticeable. By providing forum-like message boards, some internet journalism sites emerged as a form of online press and contributed to the creation of a "public sphere" for the citizens.

Notes

1 The authors acknowledge support from the Korea Research Foundation Grant (KRF-2004-042-H00004) for this work. Han Park is particularly grateful for the contribution from his assistants in the New Media and Society Laboratory.
2 The screenshots of the web pages described or cited in this chapter are available online: www.hanpark.net.
3 For example, companies such as EWin (www.ewincom.com/) and Polcom (www.polcom.co.kr/) were well-known political web agencies during the campaign.
4 As of this writing, YU, which later secured the majority of the National Assembly seats, is planning to discard this law. During the election, however, the law became one of the main issues.

References

Abramson, J.F. and Arterton, F.C. (eds) (1988) *The Electronic Commonwealth: The Impact of New Media Technologies on Democratic Politics*. New York: Basic Books.

Benoit, W.L. and Benoit, P.J. (2000) "The virtual campaign: presidential primary web sites in campaign 2000," *American Communication Journal*, 3, 3: 1–22.

Davis, R. (1999) *The Web of Politics: The Internet's Impact on the American Political System*. New York: Oxford University Press.

Foot, K., Schneider, S., Dougherty, M., Xenos, M., and Larsen, E. (2003) "Analyzing linking practices: candidate sites in the 2002 US electoral Web sphere," *Journal of Computer Mediated Communication*, 8. Available online: jcmc.indiana.edu/vol8/issue4/foot.html (accessed 24 February 2005).

Kang, M.S. (2004) "The political implication of the 17th general election and the plan of parliamentary politics reform." Available online: ebook.assembly.go.kr/ebooklnk/generalpub/pdf/general019102832.pdf (accessed 30 March 2006).

Kluver, R. and Banerjee, I. (2005) "Political culture, regulation, and democratization: the internet in nine Asian nations," *Information, Communication, and Society*, 8, 1: 1–17.

McCaughy, M. and Ayers, M.D. (eds) (2003) *Cyberactivism: Online Activism in Theory and Practice*. London: Routledge.

Park, H.W., Thelwall, M., and Kluver, R. (2005) "Political hyperlinking in South Korea: technical indicators of ideology and content," *Sociological Research Online*, 10. Available online: www.socresonline.org.uk/10/3/park.html (accessed 3 April 2006).

Schneider, S.M. and Foot, K.A. (2003) "Crisis communication and new media: the web after September 11," in P.N. Howard and S. Jones (eds), *Society Online: The Internet in Context*, pp. 137–154. London: Sage.

Part V

Comparisons and conclusions

17 Comparing web production practices across electoral web spheres

Kirsten A. Foot, Steven M. Schneider, Randolph Kluver, Michael Xenos, and Nicholas W. Jankowski

Each of the election-specific chapters in this volume provides a valuable lens on the use of the web by various political actors within a particular electoral web sphere. Considered together, they provide a mosaic of insights into a range of issues concerning the web in elections. The Internet and Elections Project was designed to facilitate the collection of comparable data on a few aspects of the web in elections, as well as to enable each nationally based group of investigators to pose questions of interest to them in dialogue with others internationally. This chapter draws on data from 19 of the national electoral web spheres that were studied in the context of the Internet and Elections Project to investigate questions regarding cross-national aspects of the web in elections.

Prior cross-national comparative studies on political uses of digital information and communication technologies (ICTs) have shown that levels of economic development and technological development, and national political structure, are significant predictors of the deployment of ICTs in politics (Norris 2000, 2001). A collection of case studies on the online activities of political parties in several countries shed light on some of the ways parties were experimenting with ICTs both in election and governance contexts (Gibson *et al.* 2003a), and a close comparison of online campaigning in the United Kingdom and the United States suggested interesting differences between candidate-centric and party-centric elections (Gibson *et al.* 2003b). These studies and others have contributed significantly to our understanding of the issues related to particular ICTs, political structures, and electoral, advocacy, and governance activities. However, in our view, insufficient attention has been paid to the role of political culture in the deployment of ICTs in politics, and to political actors other than parties and campaigns in the context of elections. Furthermore, extant research reveals a lack of large-scale cross-national studies of the web in elections conducted with a common methodological framework that enables strong comparisons across political, economic, and cultural contexts.

Addressing these gaps in the literature was one of the principal reasons we initiated the Internet and Elections Project. In this chapter, we aim to contribute to scholarship on the web and electoral politics through a large-scale, cross-national comparative analysis of the relationships between the web production practices of a wide range of political actors, and political culture as well as political, technological, and economic development. Our analysis was guided by three overarching research questions:

1   To what extent do the patterns in the production of election-related resources online observed in the present study compare with prior research in the field (notably Norris 2000, 2001)?
2   How do aspects of political development and political culture correspond with the production of election-related resources online?
3   To what extent do particular political actor types engage in the same web production practices across national contexts?

Variable conceptualization and model

To understand systematic variations in political web practices across a variety of web spheres, we began by creating four indices, which correspond to four types of communicative functions addressed in the study. The creation of the indices was primarily guided by theoretical concerns related to distinct differences in the types of features observed on all of the various sites in the study. Extending and modifying conceptualizations of web production practices developed in earlier research (Foot and Schneider 2006), and employed in Foot *et al.*'s chapter in this volume, we thus used functional differences to associate features with four practices, each representing a key dependent variable in the analyses that follow. The first practice, *informing*, concerns the most basic function of political communication online. Features that fall into the informing category convey basic information about the central figures in each electoral web sphere, the substance of their public discourse, and the election process itself. The second practice, *involving*, is evidenced in features that serve as a point of entry into a more interactive relationship between site visitors and site producers. The third practice, *connecting*, concerns the ways in which a site producer creates the means for site visitors to interact with other political actors and with websites produced by other political actors. Finally, *mobilizing* entails a set of features through which site producers enable visitors who are supporters of a candidate, party, or cause to become advocates for that candidate, party, or cause.

In our analysis of variations in each of these four practices across a variety of electoral web spheres, we employ several independent variables. Based on the results of prior comparative analyses of political websites (Norris 2000, 2001), we began with indicators of economic development, on the one hand, and technological development, on the other. By exploring the degree to which our observations of political actors' web practices in electoral web spheres are correlated with either or both of these variables, we may test and re-examine the notion of a global "digital divide" (Norris 2001; van Dijk 2005) with respect to political uses of internet technology in the context of elections. These variables enable us to compare our observations as directly as possible to prior international investigations of politics online.

To extend and develop understanding of international patterns of diffusion of online politics further, however, we added to our analyses two additional concepts. Moving beyond traditional material predictors of the online actions of political actors, this portion of the analysis was designed to test the notion that variations in national political contexts may provide substantive insight into international variations in political actors' web practices. Specifically, we look to two different aspects of the political contexts in the countries included in our study: political development, and political culture. The first of these, *political development*, relates to the variations in the political institutions and political structures within which the elections of 2004 took place. Although each country included in the study is, in some measure, democratic by virtue of having elections at all, there are still a number of vitally important variations between them in terms of constitutional, legal, and administrative characteristics associated with democratic governments. With the concept of *political culture*, we explore the extent to which online political practices may be driven by demand factors associated with the citizenry itself. Thus, our variables related to political culture are based on variations in the temperament, attitudes, and behavior of potential voters in each country, as evidenced through available secondary survey data.

A final set of variables included in the analyses that follow arises from previous research on web production in general, and candidate websites in particular (Crowston and Williams 2000; Foot and Schneider 2006; Xenos and Foot 2005; Yates and Orlikowski 1992). This research into the production of various kinds of websites, political and otherwise, revealed patterns of what Foot and Schneider (2006) called genre effects. That is, sites produced by the same type of actor and/or sharing a similar purpose often reflect certain regularities of form and function that become associated with the genre of the site by both producers and visitors alike. As Burnett and Marshall (2003) explain, genres develop as a constantly cycling interplay between audience expectation and producer delivery of audience expectation. In the case of personal web pages, for example, common or expected features include personal photos and contact information. In the case of campaign websites, the standard list of features begins with the candidate biography, and typically includes other informational features related to political or policy goals of the candidate. Foot and Schneider (2006) argue that recognizable and stable sets of site features carry elements of genre comparable to genre markers in other media. Site genres create pressure on would-be site producers to conform to others' expectations by employing the pertinent genre markers in their web production practices, and at the same time, provide tracks from which to improvise and diverge.

Since the sites analyzed in each web sphere studied in the Internet and Elections Project were produced by a variety of political actors, we included the producer types themselves as variables for two reasons. First, based on known relationships between various types of site producers and different kinds of communicative activities on the web, we anticipated that the inclusion of site producer type variables would improve the explanatory power of our models generally. More importantly, the inclusion of such genre variables also enables a further test of competing theoretical interpretations of the impact of the web as a communications medium on political activity. Specifically, such variables enable us to estimate the relative proportion of variation in political web production that is related to unique factors such as economic and political development or culture, or more universal forces such as a particular style of communication and presentation using the internet that transcends such geographical, economic, and political differences.

To summarize, our comparative analysis of variations in web practices across the international elections project centers on an explanatory model that compares four distinct kinds of web production strategies employed by political actors, along a number of dimensions. The practices we are concerned with are informing, involving, connecting, and mobilizing. The explanatory dimensions include economic, technical, political development, political culture, and genre effects.

Data collection and analysis

The data from which each of the four dependent variables was drawn were comprised of feature coding observations from 19 national election web spheres. After completing training exercises on five English-language sites, all participants were required to code the same set of ten archived English-language sites as a means of measuring agreement among coders. Four response options were provided for each item: (1) Yes, present on a page produced by this site producer; (2) Yes, but present on a page produced by a different site producer; (3) No; and (4) Not clear. Since our comparative analysis is based on the simple presence/absence of features, these response options were collapsed into three responses (Yes, No, and Not Clear) for the purpose of calculating inter-coder agreement. Because the display of archived websites can be problematic, participants had been instructed to use the Not Clear option when technical problems prevented them from viewing the archived page. Thus, coordinators assumed that a Not Clear response in the reliability test was due to technical archival display difficulties, and disagreements between coders that involved a Not Clear response were not counted as disagreements in the reliability assessment. Percent agreement was calculated between each individual coder in the Internet and Elections Project and a set of master codes agreed upon by the project coordinators. Percent agreement was also calculated between the coders within each sphere, relative only to the coders working within each sphere, to account for differences in interpretation of the measures due to language and political cultural differences across coding teams.

We chose to evaluate inter-rater reliability according to percent agreement among coders based on two important characteristics of the data. First, our primary concern in the systematic coding was with either the presence or absence of certain types of features and information, and did not incorporate continuous variables. Neuendorf (2002: 149) notes percent agreement is particularly appropriate in such instances, "wherein each pair of coded measures is either a hit or a miss." Second, the distribution of our measures was skewed in that fewer than half the sites sampled for reliability testing offered half of our 24 measures. Such distribution forces lower reliability calculations of agreement beyond chance even when coding is reasonably reliable (Potter and Levine-Donnerstein 1999). For these reasons, we established a threshold of 80 percent agreement both between each participant's codes and the master codes and between members of the research team for each electoral web sphere to create the cross-national data set for this comparative analysis. That is, there was at least 80 percent agreement between each of the coders and the master codes, and between the coders for the given web sphere, for each of the web sphere data sets employed in this analysis.

As described in prior chapters, for each web sphere, a variety of producer types were represented in the collections of websites for coding. Table 17.1 contains a list of the 19 countries included in this analysis, the proportion of sites from each producer category included, as well as the total number of functional sites coded in each web sphere. To operationalize each of the four practices of informing, involving, connecting, and mobilizing as dependent variables, indices of features were constructed representing these practices, consistent with the operationalization in Foot, Schneider, and Dougherty's chapter in this volume. As the number of features associated with each practice is not identical, the indices were created by calculating the proportion of the features for any given practice that were present on a site.

Informing

The informing index is comprised of five distinct and relatively straightforward features. The first is a biography or "About Us" text. On campaign sites, biographical information typically takes the form of pages where

Table 17.1 Descriptives of dependent variables used in comparative analysis model

	Mean	*Standard deviation*
Informing	0.40	0.23
Involving	0.25	0.26
Connecting	0.15	0.23
Mobilizing	0.13	0.20

Notes
Dependent variables are proportions ranging from 0 to 1.
$n = 1219$.

candidates provide their personal stories and backgrounds. On sites produced by other types of organizations, a description of the organization was treated comparably to a biography. The second feature is information about issue positions held by political actors within the web sphere, whether that actor was the site producer or some other actor in the political system, as when the site producer is press organization or political party. The third is information about voting, such as registration information and the location of polling sites. A fourth feature included in the informing index is general information about the campaign process. This would include information about the campaigning rules and possibly governmental regulations on campaigning in the country in which the elections are being held. Finally, the fifth feature used to construct the informing index is the presence of speeches, either in the form of audio files, video files, or simple transcripts.

Involving

The index for involving is also comprised of five features. First, the involving measure includes the presence or absence of features enabling the site visitor to join the organization or group sponsoring the site. Distinct from volunteering, which is also a part of the involving index, joining refers specifically to explicit membership of an organization or campaign. The second feature is the ability of the site visitor to sign up for an e-mail distribution list. A third involving feature involves the provision of forms or other materials that enable visitors to volunteer in the electoral process in some capacity. In the case of campaigns and parties, this typically takes the form of teams of canvassers and phone bank operators, while for less partisan non-governmental organizations, volunteering can take the form of more general efforts related to the election process. The fourth feature in the involving index is the provision of a calendar of events, typically sponsored by the site producer. Such calendars are a key line of communication between the organizers of political events, and those that may be drawn to participate in them through political communication online. Finally, the involving index also includes the presence of features used to allow site visitors to donate money either to the site producer, or to other political actors within the system that may be distinct from the site producer.

Connecting

The connecting index is based on three features by which a site producer creates bridges for visitors to other political actors. These bridges may be either cognitive, that is, invoking cognitive processes to make the connections between the actors, or transversal, incorporating and going beyond cognitive bridges by facilitating movement and a shift of attention from the connecting actor to the "connected to" actor (Foot and Schneider 2006). The first feature associated with the practice of connecting is the presence of an endorsement or endorsements of particular candidates or parties in the upcoming election by the site producer. The second is the presence of information that facilitates a direct comparison of parties or candidates on particular issues. Typically, this takes the form of an issue grid, which provides either a simple tabular entry or a link to information on the positions taken on various issues by a number of different candidates or parties. Finally, the third feature included in the connecting index is the presence of information or links that enable the site visitor to register to vote in the upcoming election.

Mobilizing

The mobilizing index is based on four features and, as indicated earlier, reflects the efforts of a site producer to enable supportive site visitors to become advocates. The first is the potential for, and encouragement of, users to access materials on the website for their reproduction and distribution offline. For example, this would include the ability to download images of posters or flyers to copy and distribute at meetings or rallies. A second feature placed in the mobilizing category is e-paraphernalia. E-paraphernalia serves a similar function to offline distribution, but as the name implies the communications that are encouraged and enabled by the site are electronic in nature. A common form of e-paraphernalia is the downloadable screen-saver, which communicates an affiliation or message to one's co-workers or others that share one's computer space. The third feature in the mobilizing index is the presence of features facilitating the making of public statements in support of a candidate or other political actor by site visitors. For example, site producers may encourage visitors to write letters to newspaper editors, or attach their name to a petition or endorsement in support of a policy agenda or political actor. In some cases, visitors may be able to enter their location and receive the contact information for all opinion page editors in their area. The fourth feature associated with mobilizing is a "web to e-mail" application for a site visitor to send a link to someone else's e-mail address.

Together, these four indices make up the principal dependent variables in our exploration of variations in political web practices across the web spheres included in our comparative analysis. Table 17.1 provides a summary view of the means and standard deviations for each of the four indices.

As described earlier, our independent variables consist of a number of factors and conditions that display noticeable differences across the cases in the study, and are believed to be related to variations in the ways that political actors use the internet. Specifically, we include as our primary independent variables measures of human, technical, and political development, as well as political culture.

Human development

To tap economic or human development, we rely on the Human Development Index (HDI) produced annually by the United Nations.[1] The HDI is a metric that provides a representation of general quality of life, that is comparable across the countries whose web spheres were examined in this analysis and thus sensitive to variations in general conditions. In addition to measuring economic development by including an index of gross domestic product within its general formula, the HDI also combines economic productivity data with measures of literacy and average life expectancy. In doing so, it produces a more comprehensive picture of development across various countries than a mere reliance on GDP figures alone.

Technological development

A second variable in the models presented below is the level of technological development present in the web spheres in which sites included in the study originate. Following Norris (2000, 2001) we use the average of three proportions to measure technological development, creating a new media index. The three proportions are the percentage of persons online within a given country, the proportion of personal computers per capita, and the proportion of hosts per capita. To calculate these proportions we used the CIA *World Factbook*'s 2003 figures to obtain data on the percent online in each country, and populations.[2] We obtained data on the number of PCs and hosts in each country from data sets made publicly available by the International Telecommunications Union for the same year.[3]

Political development

As mentioned earlier, in addition to measures of human, economic, and technical development, we also supplemented our analyses with variables designed to test for the possible influence of political conditions on the patterns we have reported concerning political campaigning online. To obtain measures of political development, we turned to a number of indicators. The first of these was the Freedom House ratings, which summarize assessments of civil rights and liberties into a simple index. However, since the present project is automatically limited to countries holding elections, Freedom House ratings displayed almost no variability across the countries included in our comparative analysis, making them unsuitable for use as independent variables in our regression analysis. Thus, we turned to another measure – the Index of Democratization developed by Tatu Van Hannen – to provide a slightly more detailed assessment of political development that captures the subtle variations in structural political conditions that may be related to variations in political web practices across the web spheres included in the study.[4] Van Hannen's index provides a detailed metric of what he defines as the preconditions to healthy democratic governance that is comparable across a wide variety of countries. The principal ingredients in this index are the level of electoral competition (calculated by subtracting the proportion of votes garnered in the last election by the largest party in the country by 100) and a measure of political participation (based on the proportion of the total population that voted in the last election). We obtained scores for all countries in the project that were available from the latest published figures, which are based on data collection from 2000, and then converted those scores to an index ranging from one to seven.

Political culture

A second dimension of overall political conditions is political culture, or the "ways in which values and attitudes influence political behavior, including political participation, mobilizations, and actions" (Kluver 2004). To capture variations in political culture across the different web spheres, we turned to data from the World Values Survey (WVS).[5] Although our measures here are certainly imperfect, they represent what we believe to be the most reliable – and most importantly – the most comparable set of indicators related to the general political temperaments and possible demand functions that may be working in various web spheres. In this area we explore two specific facets of countrywide political temperament, political participation (beyond mere voting, which is captured in the Van Hannen index), and another variable we term political engagement. *Political participation* is a simple additive index based on responses to items in the WVS querying respondents as to whether they have engaged in five types of political or civic engagement activities. The five activities were signing a petition, participating in a boycott, participating in a public demonstration, engaging in a "wildcat" strike, and taking part in a "sit down" strike. The sum of the activities was then aggregated by country to create a metric of the rate of non-voting political or civic participation in each of the web spheres under study.

A similar approach was taken with the *political engagement* index. The items used for this measure consisted of three questions from the WVS dealing with respondents' levels of objective and subjective involvement with politics as a matter of daily concern. The first is a simple measure of the rate of political discussion. ("When you get together with your friends, would you say you discuss political matters frequently, occasionally or never?"). Responses to the discussion item ranged from one (never) to three (frequently). The second item simply asks, "How important is politics in your life?" Responses for the importance item range from one (not at all) to four (very important). Finally the third item is a classic measure of political interest ("How interested would you say you are in politics?") with responses ranging from one (not at all) to four (very important). As with the participation index, responses were summed, and then aggregated by country to provide means, by web sphere, of political engagement.

Table 17.2 Descriptives of independent variables used in comparative analysis model

	Minimum	Maximum	Mean	Standard Deviation	n
UN Human Development Scale	0.60	0.95	0.85	0.11	1219
New Media Index	0.02	1.85	0.75	0.56	1219
2000 Van Hannen Democracy Rating	1.00	7.00	4.19	1.73	1219
Index of Political Participation (WVS)	1.21	1.92	1.62	0.22	1000
Index of Political Engagement (WVS)	5.53	7.32	6.59	0.56	1018

Together, we believe the five measures explained here provide the best available indicators of the concepts implicated in the model introduced earlier. Table 17.2 provides basic descriptive information about the means and distributions of these independent variables throughout the sample. Note: the Ns for the political culture variables are smaller than those for the other variables since data were not available on these measures for Sri Lanka and Thailand.

Site producer types

As discussed earlier, our explanatory model also includes variables for site producer types as a way to capture the known relationship between political website genres and constellations of features. Information on producer types was originally gathered by those who compiled the original site populations for each web sphere. As an added precaution, the categorization of each site as belonging to a particular producer type (candidate, government, party, press, NGO/labor, or other) was also confirmed at the coding stage. Before proceeding with coding on a site, coders were provided with the category of site producer initially selected by whomever identified the site as having been produced by an entity with a role or voice in the election, and were asked either to confirm this, or correct it. In cases of conflict, we deferred to the assessments of the trained coders. For the purpose of increasing comparability across spheres, we excluded sites that were noted as lacking election-related content at the time of coding. Table 17.3 provides a basic breakdown of the proportions of functional sites determined to have election-oriented content at the time of coding, categorized by producer type and by electoral.web sphere, that were included in this comparative analysis.

Findings

As explained above, there were three central questions motivating our comparative analysis of the data. First, we wanted to see the extent to which the patterns in online political communication observed in the present study

Table 17.3 Distribution of sites with election content by producer types in electoral web spheres analyzed

	Candidate	Government	Party	Press	NGO/Labor	Other	Total n
Australia	15% (13)	1% (1)	27% (24)	8% (7)	14% (12)	36% (32)	89
Czech Republic	27% (19)	9% (6)	33% (23)	12% (9)	7% (5)	11% (8)	70
Finland	51% (37)	10% (7)	15% (11)	10% (7)	7% (5)	7% (5)	72
France	31% (15)	15% (7)	17% (8)	10% (5)	17% (8)	10% (5)	48
Hungary	7% (4)	30% (16)	22% (12)	11% (6)	6% (3)	24% (13)	54
India	5% (4)	36% (32)	26% (23)	14% (12)	3% (3)	16% (14)	88
Indonesia	11% (8)	7% (5)	15% (11)	33% (24)	7% (5)	28% (20)	77
Ireland	23% (7)	20% (6)	43% (13)	3% (1)	3% (1)	7% (2)	30
Italy	41% (26)	6% (4)	24% (15)	10% (6)	6% (4)	13% (8)	63
Japan	61% (47)	14% (11)	5% (4)	4% (3)	9% (7)	7% (5)	77
South Korea	44% (32)	8% (6)	12% (9)	7% (5)	7% (5)	21% (15)	72
Netherlands	48% (30)	8% (5)	24% (15)	5% (3)	6% (4)	10% (6)	63
Philippines	31% (26)	8% (7)	4% (3)	11% (9)	10% (8)	36% (30)	83
Portugal	3% (1)	3% (1)	41% (12)	35% (10)	7% (2)	10% (3)	29
Slovenia	3% (1)	45% (17)	24% (9)	10% (4)	8% (3)	10% (4)	38
Sri Lanka	0% (0)	14% (7)	25% (12)	49% (24)	2% (1)	10% (5)	49
Thailand	5% (5)	32% (31)	8% (8)	34% (33)	3% (3)	18% (18)	98
United Kingdom	50% (30)	8% (5)	15% (9)	10% (6)	5% (3)	12% (7)	60
United States	43% (27)	16% (10)	11% (7)	5% (3)	13% (8)	13% (8)	63

Note
Number of sites by producer type in parentheses.

compare with prior research in the field. Second, we wanted to extend this work further, by adding some additional considerations into the model related to aspects of political development and political culture. Third, we sought to understand the extent to which particular types of political actors engaged in the same web production practices across national contexts. Overall, a number of notable patterns emerged from our analyses, which took the form of hierarchical regression models that explored the relationships between our dependent variables and a series of explanatory variables introduced into the model in succession. The results of these analyses are displayed in Tables 17.4–17.7, in which Model 1 represents results based simply on the human, technological, and political development variables; Model 2 reveals the contribution made by incorporating measures of political culture into the analysis; and Model 3 represents the full model, taking into account all these factors, as well as site producer types to assess genre effects.

The first pattern, seen in the results reported in the first column of each of the regression tables, is that the results for the human and technological development variables, while often significant, do not neatly correspond to the findings of prior comparative research on online political communication. Although the relationships between the New Media Index scores and the web practices of informing, involving, connecting, and mobilizing are

Table 17.4 Assessing alternative models to explain informing web campaigning practice

	Model 1	*Model 2*	*Model 3*
Human development			
UN Human Development Scale	−0.13	0.17	0.08
Technological development			
New Media Index	0.08***	−0.06#	−0.04
Political development			
2000 Van Hannen Democracy Rating	0.01	−0.00	0.01
Political culture			
Participation Index		0.22**	0.13#
Engagement Index		0.00	0.00
Genre effects			
Candidate site			0.17***
Government site			0.14***
Party site			0.22***
Press site			0.03
NGO/Labor			0.11***
Adjusted R^2	0.03	0.02	0.13
N	1219	946	946

Notes
*** $p <= 0.001$, ** $p <= 0.01$, * $p <= 0.05$, # $p <= 0.10$.

all significant and in the expected direction, the results for human development are somewhat puzzling. That is, in nearly all cases, the observed relationship between human development and each of the web practices under study appears to be negative or non-significant.

The second pattern, seen in both the first and second columns of Tables 17.4–17.7, is that the addition of variables related to political development and political culture makes a distinct contribution to the model. Though small, the effect of political development on the practice of involving (seen in Table 17.5) is statistically significant, and remains marginally so even after the site producer variables are added to the analysis in Model 2. Further, as seen in Table 17.4, the participation index is found to be significantly related to the practice of informing, again remaining marginally so even after the genre effects are taken into account. Finally, we also see a significant relationship between the participation index and connecting practices (Table 17.6), although this relationship too, fades to marginal significance after the genre variables are controlled for in Model 3. Moreover, as comparisons between Models 1 and 2 show, controlling for political culture factors tends to depress or eliminate the significance of variables related to human and technological development. Thus, we see support for the idea that elements of political context, such as institutional characteristics and emergent demand functions appear to be related to variations in

Table 17.5 Assessing alternative models to explain involving web campaigning practice

	Model 1	*Model 2*	*Model 3*
Human development			
UN Human Development Scale	−0.34*	−0.05	−0.16
Technological development			
New Media Index	0.15***	0.04	0.05
Political development			
2000 Van Hannen Democracy Rating	0.03***	0.03***	0.02#
Political culture			
Participation Index (WVS)		0.03	0.02
Engagement Index (WVS)		0.01	0.00
Genre effects			
Candidate site			0.12***
Government site			−0.08**
Party site			0.23***
Press site			−0.03
NGO/Labor			0.09**
Adjusted R^2	0.10	0.07	0.22
N	1219	946	946

Notes
*** $p < = 0.001$, ** $p < = 0.01$, * $p < = 0.05$, # $p < = 0.10$.

Table 17.6 Assessing alternative models to explain connecting web campaigning practice

	Model 1	Model 2	Model 3
Human development			
UN Human Development Scale	−0.18	−0.26#	−0.31*
Technological development			
New Media Index	0.12***	0.11**	0.12***
Political development			
2000 Van Hannen Democracy Rating	−0.03***	−0.03***	−0.03***
Political culture			
Participation Index (WVS)		0.15*	0.13#
Engagement Index (WVS)		−0.02	−0.01
Genre effects			
Candidate site			0.07***
Government site			0.00
Party site			0.14***
Press site			0.04#
NGO/Labor			0.07*
Adjusted R^2	0.04	0.04	0.09
N	1219	946	946

Notes
*** $p < = 0.001$, ** $p < = 0.01$, * $p < = 0.05$, # $p < = 0.10$.

online political communication across different web spheres. This suggests that at least in the case of democracies, models of online politics that only take into account human and technological development may be incomplete.

The third and most striking pattern within these data concerns genre effects. As explained earlier, the addition of genre variables to the model was a perfunctory step taken on the basis of our earlier experiences with similar data and a desire to improve overall explanatory power. However, each set of results suggests that these producer categories explain a large share of variations in features observed across the web spheres subjected to systematic comparative analysis. Indeed, once the genre variables are entered into the analysis, not only does the magnitude of the coefficients typically dwarf that of the others in the model, but overall variance explained (as indicated by the adjusted R^2s) increases dramatically. This suggests that among democratic nations, the influence of a website's producer type (e.g. campaign, political party, press organization) tends to outstrip the influence of factors specific to the geographic and political web sphere from which it originates.

Discussion

There are a number of possible interpretations regarding the first pattern in our findings, that is, the non-significant or negative relationship between

Table 17.7 Assessing alternative models to explain mobilizing web campaigning practice

	Model 1	Model 2	Model 3
Human development			
UN Human Development Scale	−0.18	0.00	−0.06
Technological development			
New Media Index	0.05*	−0.01	−0.01
Political development			
2000 Van Hannen Democracy Rating	−0.00	−0.01	−0.01#
Political culture			
Participation Index (WVS)		0.04	0.05
Engagement Index (WVS)		−0.00	−0.01
Genre effects			
Candidate site			0.06**
Government site			−0.07*
Party site			0.12***
Press site			−0.01
NGO/Labor			0.01
Adjusted R^2	0.00	0.00	0.08
N	1219	946	946

Notes
*** $p < = 0.001$, ** $p < = 0.01$, * $p < = 0.05$, # $p < = 0.10$.

human development and each of the web practices under study. It could be that our exclusive focus on countries with elections during 2004 masks or distorts the relationship between the level of human development and the likelihood that site producers engage in the web practices examined. Another possible factor influencing the observed relationship is our focus on electoral web spheres; other web spheres, perhaps those produced by government agencies or for commercial purposes, might yield the expected relationship. Further research is required to examine these relationships more closely.

There is an interesting tension between the second and third patterns in our findings. On the one hand, the strong similarities we found between the web production practices of political actors of the same type cross-nationally support patterns of international diffusion of innovation in the realm of politics and internet technologies from the U.S. and the U.K. to other countries in Europe and Asia found by Howard (2006). On the other hand, the fact that political development and political culture factors had statistical significance in predicting web production practices across our sample of 20 election-holding countries merits further attention. Despite the fact that these relationships are not as strong as those found for producer types, and indeed for one practice (connecting) the relationship is negative, on the whole this is remarkable considering the relatively narrow range of political cultures represented in our sample. Most of the nations studied are parliamentary democracies; in addition to the U.K., the U.S., and Australia, the political cultures of several other countries included in the study have historically been shaped by Anglo-American influences, including the practice of hiring political consultants, who often bring their experiences in one nation to another. Taken together, these patterns in our findings suggest that political actors in various countries are more likely to model their sites on those produced by similar political actors from other countries rather than modeling them on sites produced by other types of political actors within their own country. There are a number of possible reasons for this, including the aforementioned role of cross-national consultants, the desire to establish international legitimacy, and the particular needs of the web producer, and the purposes for the sites they produce.

Political culture and political development are difficult to define operationally and assess quantitatively (Pye 1985; Verba *et al.* 1987). While we contend that the measures we employed – the Van Hannen development index and aggregate indicators of political participation and political engagement – are important indicators of some aspects of political culture, they are by no means comprehensive, and undoubtedly fail to capture some of the more nuanced differences between the different countries. Furthermore, survey data related to political culture that could enable comparison across all the countries included in this study were limited. In addition to displaying relatively little variation across the countries in this study, survey data were not available for a few of the countries included in the analysis, as indicated by the lower Ns for the Model 2 and Model 3 results.[6] More fine-grained studies of political culture are needed to develop additional measures, and cross-national surveys on political attitudes and actions need to be implemented more broadly across regions.

Conclusion

Systematic cross-national comparative research is challenging to design, fund, and conduct on a large scale – and it holds inestimable value for the pursuit of knowledge. Only this type of research allows for the exploration of questions affecting great numbers of people in many countries. In this study, we have focused on teasing out the complicated relationships that explain the tendencies of a wide variety of political actors to engage in different types of web practices, across Europe, Asia, and the U.S.

In summary, we found that for the countries included in our analysis the type of political actor producing a site was more potent than human development, technological development, and political culture variables in explaining web production practices. The production of a national electoral web sphere happens in a global context: the production practices of one type of actors in a national electoral web sphere are more likely to be like those of the same type of actors in other electoral web spheres than like those of other types of actors within the same national electoral web sphere. For example, websites produced by political parties in the Philippines are more likely to be similar to websites produced by political parties in the United States than they are to be similar to websites produced by advocacy groups in the Philippines.

At the same time, we found that political culture has significant influence on how web production practices are implemented within national contexts. Even within the relatively narrow range of democratic nations included in this study, differences in political participation and political engagement among the citizenry corresponded with differences in political actors' web production practices.

Aside from the findings on genre effects and political culture, the positive relationship between technological development and each of the web practices confirms the association between overall level of technical development within a country and the types of web practices in which producers engage. As expected, countries with more diffusion of media technology, greater access to the media technology, and greater use of media technology, included producers who engaged in more types of web practices. Additional research is necessary to examine the observed negative relationship between the level of human development and the level of web practices.

Further research would be useful to both confirm and shed further light on these findings. Such research efforts could include a finer-grained analysis of the specific types of web practices found in websites produced by specific types of political actors. For example, a cross-national study of political party websites, focused on the particular functions and needs of political parties, could highlight those aspects of party websites that were common across political cultures, as well as identify aspects of party websites that were distinctive across political cultures. In addition, a cross-national study of a particular practice across multiple types of political actors – for example, the ways in which information is solicited from site visitors – could explain the relative influence of actor type and political culture.

Notes

1 hdr.undp.org/reports/global/2004/?CFID=1548133&CFTOKEN=71996467.
2 www.cia.gov/cia/publications/factbook/docs/notesanddefs.html.
3 www.itu.int/ITU-D/ict/statistics/.
4 Polyarchy Dataset: www.fsd.uta.fi/english/data/catalogue/FSD1216/. Van Hannen's Codebook: www.fsd.uta.fi/english/data/catalogue/FSD1216/FSD1216_variablelist.txt. Background materials: www.fsd.uta.fi/english/data/catalogue/FSD1216/bgF1216e.pdf www.prio.no/files/file42501_introduction.pdf.
5 data.library.ubc.ca/datalib/survey/icpsr/3975/03975-0001-Codebook.pdf.
6 World Values Survey data on political culture were not available for Hungary, Thailand, and Sri Lanka.

References

Burnett, R. and Marshall, P.D. (2003) *Web Theory: An Introduction*. New York: Routledge.

Crowston, K. and Williams, M. (2000) "Reproduced and emergent genres of communication on the World Wide Web," *The Information Society*, 16, 3: 201–215.

Foot, K.A. and Schneider, S.M. (2006) *Web Campaigning*. Cambridge: MIT Press.

Gibson, R.K., Nixon, P., and Ward, S. (2003a) *Political Parties and the Internet: Net Gain?* New York: Routledge.

Gibson, R.K., Margolis, M., Resnick, D., and Ward, S. (2003b) "Election campaigning on the WWW in the US and UK: a comparative analysis," *Party Politics*, 9, 1: 47–75.

Howard, P.N. (2006) *New Media Campaigns and the Managed Citizen*. New York: Cambridge University Press.

Kluver, R. (2004) "Political culture and information technology in the 2001 Singapore general election," *Political Communication*, 21: 435–458.

Neuendorf, K.A. (2002) *The Content Analysis Guidebook*, Thousand Oaks, CA: Sage.

Norris, P. (2000) *A Virtuous Circle: Political Communications in Postindustrial Societies*. Cambridge and New York: Cambridge University Press.

Norris, P. (2001) *Digital Divide: Civic Engagement, Information Poverty, and the Internet Worldwide*. New York: Cambridge University Press.

Potter, W.J. and Levine-Donnerstein, D. (1999) "Rethinking validity and reliability in content analysis," *Journal of Applied Communication Research*, 27, 3: 258–284.

Pye, L.W. (1985) *Asian Power and Politics: The Cultural Dimensions of Authority*. Cambridge, MA: Harvard University Press.

van Dijk, J.A.G.M. (2005) *The Deepening Divide: Inequality in the Information Society*. Thousand Oaks, CA: Sage.

Verba, S., Nie, N.H., and Kim, J.-O. (1987) *Participation and Political Equality: A Seven-nation Comparison*. Chicago: University of Chicago Press.

Xenos, M. and Foot, K.A. (2005) "Politics as usual, or politics unusual: position-taking and dialogue on campaign Web sites in the 2002 U.S. elections," *Journal of Communication*, 55, 1: 165–189.

Yates, J. and Orlikowski, W.J. (1992) "Genres of organizational communication: a structurational approach to studying communication and media," *Academy of Management Review*, 17: 299–326.

18 Epilogue

Reflecting on elections and the web

Steven M. Schneider, Randolph Kluver,
Nicholas W. Jankowski, and Kirsten A. Foot

The confluence of two distinct forces contributed to initiation of the Internet and Elections Project. First, the emergence of the internet as a significant tool for electoral activities worldwide – derived, in part, from the proliferation of campaign websites in the United States during the 2000 and 2002 elections – stimulated questions concerning the relationship between political culture and internet activity. And second, the large number of national elections scheduled in 2004–2005 offered the social science equivalent of the "perfect storm." This last aspect allowed us to hold the time factor relatively constant and provided opportunity to conduct comparative research across distinct political cultures. Our overall objective was to understand the relation between the web and electoral politics during the 2004–2005 election cycle on a global scale. This meant, on the one hand, broadening the scope of study through inclusion of countries from around the world and, at the same time, narrowing the range of research questions in order to provide an intensive, systematic snapshot of the political web within a demarcated period in time.

We began our work with a few assumptions, all of which we wanted to test against systematically collected data about the actual behavior of political actors on the web. First, we assumed that as access to the internet grew in a nation, it would eventually be deployed in political action. Second, we assumed that the ways in which internet technology was taken up would, to some extent, depend on the unique or even idiosyncratic characteristics of the respective national contexts. Finally, we assumed that different types of producers of web content would employ the technology in ways that best suited their own purposes. We find considerable evidence in the case studies presented in this book that suggest an increase in political use of the web goes hand-in-hand with diffusion of the internet in a nation; we also find many examples of distinctive uses of the web in different political cultures. At the same time, our comparative analysis presented in Chapter 17 suggests that different types of political actors are more similar across than within political cultures. In summary, the work presented here provides only limited support for our initial assumption that political culture would play a determining role in the nature of the web's deployment during elections, at least in the relatively open democratic environments that were included in our study.

The chapters in this volume, although quite different from one another, tell a multi-faceted story about how the web was being used in 2004–2005 among nations holding elections in that time frame. This story is best told through an assessment of political actors as web producers, a review of these actors' attempts to reach diverse constituencies via the web, and an exploration of the role of political culture in the diffusion of web technologies.

The studies in this book suggest a remarkable conformity around the world in terms of how web producers of a similar type deploy the web in the electoral arena, what we have termed in Chapter 17 the "genre effect." More specifically, the studies that emphasized the behavior of political actors as web producers suggest a relatively low level of enthusiasm for online structures promoting civic engagement. Parties and candidates examined in Finland, the Netherlands, Slovenia, the Czech Republic, and the United States tended to use websites to provide information to potential voters, journalists, and other political actors, but did not seek to engage or involve or mobilize citizens. At the same time, there are clear indications that use of the web did not simply reify existing political structures. In Finland, for example, the web was used more heavily by fringe candidates, younger candidates, and women candidates than their establishment counterparts. In the Netherlands, mid-range rather than the largest parties tended to be the most active users of the web, and the uses of the web tended to be consistent with the transformation of parties from member-oriented to professionalized institutions. Newcomers to politics were more likely web producers in the Czech Republic, and a clear attempt to attract marginal voters, often ignored in traditional campaigning, was evident.

Web producers across the various nations examined clearly shared the goal of reaching other political actors in the electoral arena, of either creating a new audience or engaging an existing audience. These studies suggest that, contrary to early – and perhaps utopian – expectations that the internet would empower larger audiences and engage portions of the citizenry not typically included in the electoral arena, the internet is more likely to be used to fragment and isolate communities. Generally, we see, in the 2004–2005 electoral web spheres, a "recreation" of a political audience not significantly different than the political audience that existed prior to the deployment of the technology. In that sense, our research supports the normalization thesis referenced in Chapter 1, that the internet in a number of countries around the world merely reinforces, or even reifies, existing political divisions, realities, and animosities. In Sri Lanka, for example, the electoral web sphere ignored the voting population in favor of international public opinion. The more highly educated English speakers in the Philippines were favored by the web activities of political actors over the Tagalog-speaking portion of the population. Similarly in India, the web was aimed at the urban, educated, and elite portions of the electorate. At the same time, there is evidence that the web is being used to attract specific audiences on their own terms. For example, while websites produced by political actors in the United Kingdom that explicitly targeted youth voters were less likely to include issue positions than websites produced by political parties, the youth-oriented sites appear to view political engagement as meaning something other than merely voting, and thus are more likely to offer opportunities for political discussion and volunteering.

While we did not find political culture to be strongly associated with the general way in which the web was deployed within national electoral web spheres, the studies in this volume do point towards important findings concerning the intersection of these two variables. Each of the chapters delves more deeply into the ways in which the political contexts, assumptions, regulations, and values are worked out in an online environment. For example, it is clear that the regulatory environment of Japan constrained how the web was deployed; it is equally clear that the political lethargy surrounding the European Parliament election probably curtailed the role of the web in that event. The vibrant and contentious political clash in South Korea helped to energize the use of the web as a campaign tool, while the use of the web as a campaign device did little to resolve the ambiguity of Indonesia's political identity.

This extended analysis of the state of online politics in 2004–2005 helps us to answer these and other questions, but there remain many issues insufficiently explored. One of these involves the intended objectives of website producers and the experiences of the users of those sites. This is similar to the classic quest in traditional print media research to appraise the three main components of the communication process – news editors, newspaper content, and newspaper readers – in efforts to understand that process adequately. Some of the research reported in the book chapters does include additional data sets for this purpose, like the inclusion of survey research by the Finnish team and interviews with key actors by the Dutch research team. Such integration on a larger scale, however, would provide for a richer understanding of the relation between the internet and electoral politics.

Another area in which further research would be warranted is the extent to which there is a globalization effect in web campaign practices. The findings presented suggest that there is, indeed, some cross-national impact of websites online, what we have termed "genre effects," but we are unable to determine whether these effects are the result of imitation or campaign necessity. In other words, do political actors simply imitate one another in how they deploy the web or are they responding to a communicative need of the moment and their perception of the potential of the internet?

The Internet and Elections Project took place within a specific time frame. However, the nations whose electoral web spheres are examined in the studies in this volume were at different levels of penetration and user acceptance and some of the divergent findings across nations may be explained by this factor. Furthermore, each of the elections examined took place within specific political contexts. Some of these contexts will have changed by the time of the next elections: the frenzy, for example, in South Korea regarding the possible impeachment of the country's president will have diminished. Others may continue to shape the electoral web sphere: the reservations concerning expanding European Union membership and the general lethargy over the European Parliament are likely to be relatively constant. The research reported in many of the chapters of this book suggests that these contextual factors have a substantial impact on the role of the internet in any single election. This observation merits consideration in follow-up investigations.

Technological change has also dramatically influenced the nature of the electoral web sphere. During the time period of this research, 2004–2005, downloadable media files were the state-of-the-art in terms of political web design, but a year later that state-of-the-art has been eclipsed by the rise of weblogs (blogs), video blogs (vlogs), user-driven sites such as YouTube, podcasts, mobile phone campaign messaging and recruiting, and a host of other innovations. While a popular consensus seems to exist that newer technologies and web innovations are more engagement oriented than the traditional websites upon which much of our analysis was based, this conclusion may prove, upon closer and systematic investigation, to be as illusory as the initial utopian assumptions about the impact of the internet in the late 1980s.

Of one thing we can be certain: this volume is by no means the "last word" in understanding how the internet is interacting with and being incorporated into political practice. Although we have some level of confidence that we have accurately captured an understanding as of 2004–2005, we are fully aware that we have examined a moving target that is likely to have experienced significant change even in the period between our analysis and the publication of this book. While we found, in a number of countries, that the web presence of political actors was primarily information-oriented, top-down communication, we are fully aware, at an impressionistic level, that there is considerable ferment in the patterns of web campaigning.

Two factors are contributing to this evolution. First, a new generation of political actors who have come to power using the internet are replacing those who have spent the twilight of their political careers adapting to the internet. Second, a new generation of internet technologies that have been developed to enhance and replace the initial internet are replacing those technologies that were designed to replace or enhance print and television technologies. To the extent that the emerging styles of web campaigning, resulting from a new generation of political actors and a new generation of internet technologies, are more sensitive and responsive to the needs of the citizens than the technologies prevalent in 2004, it may mean that some of our conclusions require qualification. At the same time, we hope this book does contribute to our collective awareness regarding how political belief and reality interrelate with what the internet is and what it might become. Above all, we hope this book contributes to realization that new communication technologies are but one of many factors involved in social and political change.

Appendix

Website coding instructions and guidelines for country reports

Below is a list of questions researchers addressed during the coding of websites included in the samples for each of the project case studies. These questions were included in a web-based coding application developed by WebArchivist.org and made available to project participants. The coding of websites was completed using this online application, thus ensuring consistency in data collection and collation across cases. Participants were asked to limit their observations to the first and second level pages linked from the front page of each URL included in the sample of sites for the electoral web sphere they studied. Specific instructions and definitions corresponding with the underlined terms were provided to project participants, and are listed below each question. Following the list of questions are guidelines supplied to research teams for preparation of country reports that were used subsequently as a foundation for the case study chapters in this volume and for comparative analysis.

Coding template

1 Is this site *codeable?*
   Coders must be able to view the content of the site in order to code it. If the site is nonfunctional, choose "No, the site is nonfunctional," and move on to the next task. Some sites require visitor registration with the site to view the content. Coders are not required or expected to register with a site to view content. If the site requires registration and the coder is not willing, or does not have permission to register to view site content, choose "No, registration required; I will not register," and move on to the next task. If the site requires registration and the coder is willing and has permission to register with the site, choose "Yes, registration required; I will register," and continue coding the site.

2 Is the correct *site producer* type listed above?
   Confirm the site producer type listed for this site using the producer type definitions provided on the IE Tools web page. The site producer

type is listed at the top of the page with the link to the site. If the correct site producer type is listed, choose "Yes." Otherwise, select the correct producer type.

3 Does this site provide *election-related* content?
If a visitor can find election-related content anywhere on or through this site, choose the appropriate "Yes" response and paste in the URL on which you find election-related content.

4 Does this site provide a biography, history, or *"About Us"* section?
A biography, history or "About Us" should include biographical, historical, or organizational information about the political actor that is producing the site you are coding.

5 Does the site provide *endorsements* for a candidate or party in an upcoming election?
An endorsement is an explicit statement that one political actor supports another. Coders should not have to interpret text to determine the presence of an endorsement.

6 Does the site provide a list of *issues positions* held by a political actor?
Issues positions are statements of opinions on political topics held by a political actor (e.g. candidate, party, NGO). This also includes a list of the editorial positions of news organizations.

7 Does the site provide *speeches* by a candidate or party representatives?
Speeches can be found on a site in audio files, or as transcripts of speeches given by candidates or party representatives.

8 Does this site provide a calendar or list of prospective election-related events?

9 Does the site provide *comparison of issue positions* of parties or candidates?
Candidates and parties can provide a comparison of their own issue stances to those of their opponents. Look for clear mentions of the political actor's opponent(s), and discussion of the differences between issue positions.

10 Does the site provide information about the *electoral campaign process* in the country studied?
Information about the campaign process will include information about the campaigning rules and/or governmental regulations on campaigning for which elections are being held.

11 Does the site provide information about the *voting process* in the country studied?
Information about the voting process will include information about voter eligibility, or where and when to vote. If there is information on how to register to vote, code this item positively, and also code "Register to vote" item positively.

12 Are there *images* on the site?
Images include photographs and graphics, including their use as logos. Code "Yes" if there is any component on the site that would be considered an image from a user's perspective.

13 Does the site provide *audio or video files?*
If any audio or video files related to the election are present on, or accessible from the site, choose the appropriate "Yes" response and paste in the URL where the audio or video file is located.

14 Does the site provide a *privacy policy?*
A privacy policy for a website will contain information for the user about how the site will protect a user's information that may be entered into the site, such as an e-mail address, or an IP address.

15 Does the site provide a *terms of use* statement?
The terms of use of the site will define the site producer's rights to display and take responsibility for the information displayed on the site. Terms of use will also define guidelines for appropriate use of the site.

16 Does the site provide *contact information* for the site producer?
Look for a "Contact" page on the site. If the site lists the site producer's e-mail address, postal address, or telephone number, choose the appropriate "Yes" response and paste in the URL where the information is displayed.

17 Does the site provide opportunities for visitors to *join, or become members* of the organization?
A site can enable a visitor to join a party, campaign, or organization. Features that enable volunteering but not specifically joining should not be coded positively for this item.

18 Does the site enable visitors to *register* to participate in the election?
This feature may be a link to an outside site enabling voter registration, or may be a description of how to register to vote.

19 Does the site provide an opportunity for a visitor to sign up to *receive e-mail* from the site producer?
Campaigns, parties and organizations can offer an e-mail newsletter service that enables a visitor to enter an e-mail address and receive e-mails from the site producer.

20 Are *donations* encouraged or enabled on or through this site?
Does the site encourage or enable a visitor to give money to a campaign, party or organization involved in an election? A visitor can use the site to donate if there is a direct or indirect request for donations, a postal listing to send payment offline, or online payment options.

21 Can visitors to the site participate in an *online forum* or other communication space?
If the site offers access to message board, forum, chat or other type of communication space, choose the appropriate "Yes" response and paste in the URL where a visitor can participate.

22 Does the site encourage *offline distribution* of electoral campaign or election materials?
If the site provides printable documents containing campaign or election literature for distribution offline, choose the appropriate "Yes" response and paste in the URL where these documents are found.

Examples of election literature are voting guides, election schedules, brochures, bumper stickers, posters and flyers.

23 Is there a feature that specifically enables a site visitor to *send a link* from this site to a friend?

Sites can provide a link forwarding service that a visitor can use to e-mail a friend URLs from the site. These features may appear as e-postcards, or may be labeled "send links."

24 Is there a feature that encourages or enables a visitor to *make a public statement* supporting a political actor or issue?

Political actors can encourage visitors to write public statements in support of a campaign, party, or organization. Statements of support may be letters to newspaper editors, endorsement statements that will be publicly displayed on- or offline, or signing a petition that will be publicly displayed.

25 Does the site enable the user to engage in digital promotion (*e-paraphernalia*) of the electoral campaign, party, organization or voting in general?

Sites can offer downloads of web banners, desktop wallpaper, and screensavers that promote the campaign, party, organization or issue.

26 Does the site encourage visitors to *volunteer* for the electoral campaign?

Does the site encourage visitors to become involved in the campaign in any way other than the six previous questions have indicated? Look for a section of the site labeled "Volunteer" or a form that a visitor can send to the site indicating campaign activities in which the visitor might participate.

Note: The following seven questions were appended to the coding schema used by the research teams studying the 2004 European Parliament election.

27 Is there content on the front page of the site related to the EU and/or to the 2004 EP election?

28 Does the item contain *announcement of EP election* on front page?

29 Does the item reference *candidates for EP elections* on the front page?

30 Does the item reference *environmental policy* on the front page?

31 Is the content on the site related to EU/EP *content located elsewhere* on the site (within two links from front page)?

32 Are there *EU/EP-related news items* in the news section of this site?

33 Is there content on the front page of the site related to *youth*?

Country report guidelines

1 What were some of the most significant events during the campaign season leading up to this election? (e.g. the death of a candidate, a scandal involving a party)?

2 Which types of political actors were most significant in producing the election web sphere?

3 Based on the Information table, what is significant about the prevalence (high or low) of each information type within the sphere as a whole and by particular types of site producers/political actors?

4 Based on the Information table, note which types of site producers offered the most varied types of information and the most important types of information: What might be the reasons why particular political actors offered these types of information (or not) in view of the political culture and structure of this election?

5 Based on the Engagement table, what is significant about the prevalence (high or low) of each engagement feature within the sphere as a whole and by particular types of site producers/political actors?

6 Based on the Engagement table, note which types of site producers offered the greatest number and most important features for engagement: What might be the reasons why particular political actors employed these engagement features (or not) in view of the political culture and structure of this election?

7 Were there any legal or regulatory factors that constrained what kinds of information or engagement features any particular type of political actor could provide on the web, and when?

8 Overall, what do the coding data indicate about the characteristics and structure of this electoral web sphere and the kinds of political action it enabled on the part of citizens?

Index